A BRIDGE

LAILA SAID

THROUGH TIME

A Memoir

SUMMIT BOOKS
NEW YORK

10 9 8 7 6 5 4 3 2 1
First Edition

Library of Congress Cataloging in Publication Data

Said, Laila.
A bridge through time.

1. Said, Laila. 2. Egypt—Biography.
3. Women—Egypt—Social conditions. I. Title.
CT2718.S27A33 1985   962'.05'0924   85-8036
ISBN 0-671-45426-9

To my father, Nessim, who gave me his spirit
And to Gloria—and all the women who fight

ONE

*Men are in charge of women because
Allah hath made the one of them to
excel the other.*

—*The Koran*

HER NAME was Om Abdou, mother of Abdou, her eldest son. From him she derived her identity and her being in that small village in upper Egypt, too small even for the train to stop there. She had a name, my mother's mother. It was Asma. But everyone referred to her as Om Abdou. It is customary to acknowledge a woman thus in Egypt, to acknowledge her as one who has given birth to a son.

Om Abdou always wore black. Her hair was always tied beneath a black scarf. A respectable widow must never reveal any part of her body, and she had been widowed twice. Her first marriage was to Boutros, who was twenty-four years older than she. Her second was to Mikhail, thirty years older. Both of the marriages had been arranged.

Her marriage to Boutros was arranged by her father over a sweetened cup of Turkish coffee. The first time she set eyes on him was during their wedding ceremony. She had four babies by him, but they all died in infancy. Boutros died when she was twenty-three.

When she married Mikhail, he was a widower in his sixties, she was twenty-five. Her father arranged that marriage too, for "khawaja" Mikhail (as Copts were often referred to) owned a thousand acres, and was a powerful man in the *mudiriyeh*, the province. He was old, yes, but would a twenty-five-year-old widow find a better man?

Om Abdou never learned to love Mikhail. Boutros had been

9

more attentive, more demonstrative, more loving. Mikhail was distant, preoccupied only with farming his large estate, which he rose to supervise every dawn. Nonetheless, she bore Mikhail four children. She was not allowed to sit at meals with him, though she shared his bed, and in the false serenity of the rural night, she dutifully opened her thighs to receive his sperm; the sperm of a man who, in the daytime, acknowledged her presence only as part of a retinue of children and servants. If Om Abdou resented this life, she did not complain. But one day, when khawaja Mikhail ordered his morning coffee, she asked for one as well. Millennia of male supremacy grew red with indignation as the blood rose in khawaja Mikhail's face. His mustache twitched and he leaned forward in his chair to stare at his wife's audacious brown eyes. Om Abdou's gaze did not waver.

Many years later, as she told the story to Samira, my mother, she recalled her feeling of pride as the coffee was brought in for the two of them. It was the first of many victories to come.

When khawaja Mikhail died, my mother was eight months old, and Abdou was only three years old. As Mikhail's widow, Om Abdou would inherit but an eighth of the land. His sons, and he had many, would inherit twice as much land as his female children. That was the law, and is still the law. Om Abdou's two sons from Mikhail were almost babies when their father died, so their older half brothers (Mikhail's sons from a previous marriage) immediately proclaimed their "authority" over the family and decided that they would administer their father's estate.

Om Abdou protested. It was a protest which was to save her life and to ensure the future of her four children. But the family was outraged, the village was outraged, and when the rumor reached it, the nearby town of Assiut was outraged. Om Abdou, a woman, wanted to administer her estate? What audacity! The *majlis al-hasby*, a council of village elders and notables that existed solely to govern the affairs of widows, was convened. Om Abdou was asked to explain. Why was she unwilling to do what was proper and let her husband's sons, who were fully grown men, take over the reins and rule the family?

With her hair covered under a black-knotted scarf, and her heavy body shrouded in a full-length black tunic, she stood in front of the elders and spoke. She wanted to raise her babies on her own. For that she needed to have her own money. She also wanted to make her own decisions in the household. After all she was thirty years old. She had had two husbands and had borne many children. Now she wanted to be left in peace with the surviving ones. Was that too much to ask? The majlis of village elders looked at one another incredulously and then looked at her. Om Abdou looked right back at them. "All right, Om Abdou," said one of them gravely, "have it your own way. But, remember, you will have to give the majlis yearly accounts of every penny you spend until your children reach the age of twenty-one. That is the law." Om Abdou nodded but her eyes gleamed.

And so, until her children were fully grown, Om Abdou presented the majlis with a yearly day-by-day accounting of her children's living expenses. Khawaja Tadros, the ginger-haired, mustached Coptic bookkeeper, would come to inspect her books, and to make sure she was keeping straight records.

During the long nights of her life, Om Abdou, sitting cross-legged on a narrow bench, as was customary in the village, would sew clothes for the children of the peasants who cultivated her land. After her daughter Samira had been married, also by arrangement, and given birth to me, I would keep my grandmother company during some of those nights, seeking warmth in the wrinkled folds of her large black frame.

Like my grandmother's and my mother's, my marriage too was arranged. It was the late fifties, but things as far as women were concerned were no different from Om Abdou's time.

It was a Sunday afternoon, much like any other, or so I thought. The family, my father and mother, my younger brother Nabil, my sister Asma, and I, would go to a park, and then to our favorite kebab restaurant on Emad-al-Din Street, where two square tables with slightly soiled white tablecloths would be pushed together to accommodate us and all of our food. But this Sunday we were going to the Mena House Hotel, announced my mother. And she added, "Wear your red dress, the new one."

When we arrived at the large, sunny terrace of the hotel, overlooking the pyramids of Giza, there was a wide circle of formally dressed people waiting for us. The men were dressed in dark suits and silk ties, and the women wore cashmere sweaters, expensive sunglasses, and jewelry that glittered in the sun. The moment I took my place in this circle, I knew what was happening. Is this how they marry you off? I wondered. There was a soothing breeze which not even the circle which was tightening around me could dispel. Is this how they marry you off—so gently? A woman with carefully drawn, thick, penciled eyebrows turned to me and said, "Laila, how you've grown. And how slim you have become!" I did not answer. I was not slim. I have never been slim. The woman, who had not even pretended to wait for my response, turned away and started to chatter excitedly with my mother, who smiled all the time. I was seventeen and a virgin.

I had heard about such events. At school, my girlfriends and I often asked ourselves what we would do when the day came and we were "displayed," how we would behave. For that was obviously the point of this meeting. But who was I being displayed for? Who was the man sitting in that affluent circle who would decide that afternoon whether he would have me for his wife? The breeze caressed my face again, but I was in turmoil. Why was I sitting there, trapped like a helpless animal? Because my parents wanted it? Because the ancient laws of the land required it? Because I was a woman?

A second meeting was soon arranged. This time the circle of conspirators was smaller, just two young men and an older woman. I was accompanied by my mother. The woman was to be my mother-in-law. Her son was tall, in his twenties, with docile brown eyes and neatly combed wavy hair. All very proper, very "comme il faut," as the Cairene bourgeoisie would say. My future husband sat next to his mother in silence. Next to him was an extremely short friend with an ugly little face.

My future mother-in-law gesticulated with sapphired and emeralded fingers. As my mother listened in pretended fascination, she complained about her chauffeur, her butler, her maid. Now and then she would turn to her son and, gold-filled teeth flashing, give him a pat on the cheek.

"You are so lucky," said my mother as soon as the meeting had ended. "They are a very well-known landowning family and there are not many of those left." I did not reply. I was not asked to respond. The deal had been concluded.

The third visit took place in my father's house. The young man was alone this time but he held the *shabka* or engagement gift—a diamond-studded watch handed to me in a handsome case, which he opened sheepishly. I murmured thanks, and barely glancing at it, placed it on the table before me. We chatted aimlessly for about half an hour at the end of which he announced that he would be calling me regularly on the phone. Afterward, I handed my mother the shabka. She exclaimed with delight as she examined it and then locked it up in the jewelry closet along with all her other valuables. But with this shabka, my future husband had bought the rights to me.

He was now free to visit me as frequently as he wished. He was free to do anything he wanted except take my virginity. That was forbidden by our traditions. A girl must remain a virgin until her wedding night.

At the fourth meeting, which took place at the elegant Semiramis Hotel, overlooking the Nile, my future husband was accompanied by his short friend. We sat around the table waiting for the meal to be served, the two men murmuring to one another. Finally, I was addressed: "Do you like horses?" asked the short friend. Then he added, "Amin loves horses." Suddenly I realized that the comme il faut answer expected of me was that I too loved horses. And so I stammered something about loving horses. My future husband lifted his head and looked at me with sudden interest. "Aha!" exclaimed the friend, with his mouth full of bread, "the two of you have so much in common. It couldn't be a better match!"

One day my husband-to-be and I were left alone in my father's study. It was the first time we had been without chaperones. Sitting next to me on the couch, he took me in his arms and began to kiss me again and again. In spite of myself, I began to respond to the touch of this stranger; I had never been touched by a man before.

A few weeks later, my future father-in-law came to pay us a visit. Taking me gently by the arm, he said he wanted to tell me something very important: "Amin tells me that you wish to go on studying for a university degree. I want you to know that neither of us has any objections," he added patronizingly. "Thank you," I said with all the deference expected of me. But a ray of hope stirred within. This was my chance to postpone the wedding.

A girl seeking an education was not unusual in those days. The revolution, Nasser's revolution, had taken place in 1952, and Egypt was changing at an accelerating pace. With the deposition of King Farouk, the country was transformed from a decadent monarchy to a republic which at last belonged to the twentieth century. Socialism, science, and above all education, even for women, was in the air. Cairo University, the major national university, canceled tuition and opened its doors to the growing urban proletariat.

The power of the feudal, landowning class which had dominated Egyptian society for centuries had finally been broken. Up until the revolution, less than one percent of the landowners of Egypt, of which Amin's family was one, owned over a third of the cultivable land. Now, land reforms introduced by Nasser made it illegal for anyone to own more than two hundred acres. The confiscated land was distributed among the peasants in five-acre lots.

These realities were probably behind Amin's family's willingness to allow me to go on with my education. They also explained why they encouraged their son to become an officer in Nasser's army. For it was evident that Egypt was becoming a military society with a military elite. Besides, to Amin and to the majority of Egyptians, Nasser was a hero. Had he not rid

Egypt of a decadent and corrupt monarch? Had he not nationalized the Suez Canal in 1956, expropriating it from the European company which had devoured its profits? That canal which had taken 120,000 Egyptian lives to build? Had not Nasser put an end to the aggression of Israel, France, and Britain when they invaded Egypt in 1956? That Nasser had become a great national figure was beyond dispute.

Amin continued to be a supporter of Nasser even after his family was put under "sequestration," their lands and private property confiscated. Nasser's charisma, his promises of social justice, and the nationalistic image he projected made patriots even of his enemies.

A year went by. I was enrolled at the American University in Cairo as a literature major. I became increasingly engrossed in my studies and more determined than ever to postpone the marriage. The political events of the moment only made things easier for me. The two-hundred-acre quota was cut in half. And as a further step in the direction of socialism, Nasser nationalized industrial trading companies and all other property of the capitalist class. Amin's family home, which had been divided into apartments to increase the family revenue, was nationalized by the government, and Amin's family even had to pay rent for their share. They let the chauffeur go, and the English maid, and the butler's salary was cut in half. My future mother-in-law rarely left her rooms and stopped wearing her jewelry. They had become impoverished.

I wondered if I would be released from this liaison now that Amin was no longer wealthy. But my mother was adamant: "What will people say if we break the engagement now that they have lost their money and land?" she asked, not really expecting me to answer. "Besides, they still have a good family name and we don't need their money." My father spoke quietly on my behalf: "Let her finish her university education before rushing into this marriage. After all, Laila may need to work one day." My fiancé, with his newly acquired poverty, could not object.

I would remain free for a while at least. I worked like a fiend to make good grades. There were student scholarships available for graduate studies in the United States. I saw my chance. I would try to get one of those much sought after scholarships. It was my only hope of escape.

Another year passed and I was still free. The Cairene bourgeoisie grew more shocked by the day at this flagrant disregard of our customs. Marriage usually followed soon after the making of the deal between the families. To be engaged for two years was unthinkable.

"Laila will have to become officially engaged," said my mother one day, pacing up and down in her boudoir. "The whole thing has become a scandal," she said. "You must have a *gabanyot,*" she added. "A what?" I stammered. "You must have a religious ceremony and wear your fiancé's ring. He will have to go and buy you a diamond ring which will make the whole thing proper, at least for appearance' sake." "You mean it will be like a marriage?" I said, aghast. "No, a gabanyot can be broken, though I hope you have no intention of breaking your vows to your fiancé after all this," she snapped. "But I don't love him," I said. "You'll learn to love him," she replied quietly.

A few weeks later, I was officially engaged to Amin in a religious ceremony of the Coptic faith—the Orthodox Christian faith of over eight million Egyptians who pride themselves on being the true descendants of the ancient Egyptians. The Coptic Church was founded in A.D. 36 when Saint Mark introduced Christianity to Egypt. The black-robed Coptic priest murmured words from the Bible over our bowed heads. Then, placing his cross first on Amin's forehead and then on mine, he declared us betrothed to one another. Two hand-scrawled documents were presented us to sign as our families and friends stood in a circle around us, the sweet smell of flowers and chocolate petit fours filling the air. As we put our names next to each other's on the two documents, the circle tightened. When I looked up, everyone was smiling. Everything had become final, religious.

I worked harder than ever at the university, still hoping for a scholarship, while at the same time reassuring Amin that I would marry him as soon as I finished my college degree. But, one day, no longer able to keep my plan to myself, I decided to confide in my father. I asked him point-blank if he would allow me to travel to America if I obtained a scholarship. He was silent for a moment, but then he said in his most forthright way, "Education is your best friend, Laila. After all, where would I be without mine?"

My father belonged to a generation of Egyptians for whom education was the highest achievement. As a child in Luxor, he had known dreadful poverty. There were nine children when his mother died and my grandfather had to struggle to support the family on his meager salary as a civil servant. But somehow, he managed to send my father to Cairo for a high-school education. In Luxor in those days you could only get a primary education. My father stayed with rich relatives in Cairo, landowners who looked down on their impoverished cousin. And he would never forget the sting of humiliation from that time, even though he excelled in his studies and obtained a scholarship for study at the Faculty of Medicine in Cairo, which is what he set out to do. At the faculty he graduated in the forefront of his class, which resulted in another scholarship, this time to study radiology at Cambridge University in England.

Having obtained his fellowship—accreditation by the Royal College of Radiologists in England—"with honors," as he loved to tell us, he returned to Cairo penniless but confident of his mission. He was a pioneer in radiology—a new field of medicine in the Arab world—and his degree was the first of its kind in Egypt. But the powerful medical establishment refused at first to recognize the merits of his work. "It was up to me," said my father, "to prove to them that X rays were more effective in diagnosis than the naked eye. They resisted, but eventually I won. In case after case, my X rays indicated to them, better than anything they had known, what was wrong with their patients." With his hard-fought recognition came the beginnings of prosperity—an American automobile, a wardrobe of custom-made suits of imported English cloth, and an elegant private practice in the best part of town. And yet he never forgot the poverty of the old days. Even after he became a wealthy doctor, he still guarded himself from it. That is why he decided to marry me off to Amin's family: to protect me.

One day, a couple of months away from my graduation, my father brought home an American guest for dinner. "This is Mr. Sheldon," he announced. Then, tapping the foreign guest on the back, he said, "Mr. Sheldon is an important man. He is the vice-president of a famous university in America." Mr. Sheldon beamed at me and I gave him a big smile. "My daughter here," continued my father, "has plans to study in your country." "Great!" came the answer. My mother said nothing, but offered our American guest an hors d'oeuvre.

A few months later we received a letter of congratulations from Mr. Sheldon's office. My application for a tuition scholarship at the University of Chicago had been granted, and I had been accepted for the master's program in English literature. I was beside myself with excitement.

My secret plan was secret no more. Amin visited me with reproach written all over his face. "It will only be for a year," I mumbled apologetically. He did not reply. But my mother was inconsolable. "What will people say," she moaned, pacing up and down in her bedroom. Then, realizing that my father was no longer an ally, she called her youngest brother, who came right away. He stormed up the stairway of our villa, shouting, "What is this I have been hearing? Everybody is talking about this latest scandal of Laila's!" Reaching the top of the stairs, he glared at me, saying, "Laila, you must get married immediately." My father stood by silently, listening to his brother-in-law deferentially. But when he glanced in my direction, his eyes twinkled.

The weeks before I left were spent busily filling out forms, mailing transcripts, taking medical exams, visiting and revisiting the American embassy for a visa. I also had to apply for an exit visa, take the Toeffel test to prove that I could speak English, correspond with the university to arrange for a dorm, and obtain all sorts of security clearances. Finally, with a dossier piled high with approvals and acceptances, I was ready to be admitted to the United States.

Meanwhile, the pressures to "change" my mind were intense, coming from all directions: Amin, my mother, friends, cousins, uncles, and even my girlfriends. "Laila, how can you leave your fiancé?" was a question asked by all. "Suppose he finds someone else?" they said.

A week before my departure, I visited one of my instructors, a woman in her thirties who had obtained a Ph.D. in the United States. It was said that she had gone on studying because she was too unattractive to find a husband in Cairo. But for me she was the epitome of everything I wanted to be—a successful professional woman.

She received me with warmth and concern. She, too, had heard the Cairo gossip. "What should I do?" I asked in desperation. "Should I give up my scholarship and stay here with Amin?" She lit a cigarette and hesitated before answering. Then she said, "I don't know."

The road to freedom is long and hazardous. As I boarded the plane that was to take me to America, I knew it was the beginning of a new life for me. But I was also leaving all that was familiar and beloved. My father kept wiping his eyes with his white linen handkerchief. "You may never see your father again, if you leave," my mother told me over and over again. "With his heart condition, he may die any minute." And yet I was leaving. I couldn't say no to the promise of freedom. But how hard it is to take that road. How painful freedom can be.

I cried all the way to America, but the transparent cord had been ripped.

I WAS ASSIGNED a cell-like room at the International House on campus. It had a sink but to get to the bathroom one had to walk through a long, dark corridor. There was a fire escape with the word EXIT flashing above it, an elevator, and a stairway: there were many ways out. Terror seized me as I entered that room with its narrow window overlooking the strange Gothic buildings. Later, as I stood in line in the cafeteria with a plastic tray and a dollar in my hand, my terror was magnified by the sight of the mucky meat stew which had been lumped onto my plate. I sat alone with the tasteless food. Outside, the weather was gray.

As I stood in long lines for my ID card and other registration papers, my euphoric vision of America dissolved in the regimentation I saw around me. "You will have to keep up a B average in order to retain your scholarship," warned my adviser, a middle-aged woman with steel-framed glasses and a gray suit. I nodded, but I was filled with panic, and in the ensuing weeks the pleasure of reading literature was replaced by the discipline of writing scholarly papers with long bibliographies.

One day an American girl who rode the elevator with me smiled in my direction. "Hiya," she said, "I'm Sally. Where are you from?" When I told her she replied, "Gawd, that's so far away. I bet you're homesick." I nodded. "You should get to meet some of the boys around here." "I've never had a boyfriend," I replied. "Oh, don't worry. They'll love you. You have big boobs."

I was too inhibited to take Sally's advice, and instead befriended the candy machine in the basement. Besides, I was too busy making good grades to find time for anything else. After classes, I sought refuge in my room, and curling up on the narrow bed, I spent all my waking hours reading and writing papers. Sometimes, in the evenings, I would go to the library to do some research. One day I stayed on until the library closed. It was cold as I stepped outside, the streets were empty, and snow was beginning to fall. Suddenly a police car stopped next to me and an officer stepped out. "What you doing out so late, miss?" he asked. I mumbled that I was on my way home to the dorm. "You shouldn't be walking the streets at this hour. This is the South Side!" he grumbled. "We'll see you home," he added, and getting back into the police car, he followed slowly behind as I hurried to my dorm.

Next morning I told the black maid who cleaned my room what had happened. Grinning, with her gold teeth glinting, she said, "Oh, honey, those white folks are so.scared of us. But you have nothin' to worry about . . ." she added with a gesture of her hand, as if to say, You are one of us. I smiled gratefully. "Do they put you down as Caucasian when they ask about your race?" I asked her naively. "No, hon," she replied, "just Negro."

In spite of my feverish pursuit of B's, I was slowly becoming cognizant of the racial tensions that were tearing at America. But soon the warmth and tenderness shown me by Alice, the maid, riveted my attention to the civil rights movement.

Gradually, I began to make friends with other foreign students, especially an Egyptian girl who was studying for a Ph.D. in art history. She was a divorcée who had vowed never to return to Egypt. We had long discussions about this; I would always try to persuade her to change her mind. I admired her very much because she was an A student, and to be such a student at the University of Chicago was a great achievement. She had even less money than I had, and she often had to subsist on a diet of corn flakes.

Three months after my arrival in Chicago I received a letter from Amin: he missed me so much, he had managed to obtain a leave of absence from his job and he had been accepted by the University of Illinois at Urbana. I received this news with mixed emotions. I bitterly regretted the loss of freedom just as it was beginning to flower. On the other hand, I looked forward to seeing him, to the reassurance and supportiveness that his presence would provide.

A few weeks later, I was summoned to the student lounge where he waited for me, his eyes full of longing. As I surrendered to his embrace, I felt the walls of the jail I thought I had escaped close around me. My freedom never seemed more precious than in that moment when I exchanged it for the security of Amin's embrace.

As of the time of Amin's arrival, I plunged even more intensively into my work—the only aspect of my life over which I still had some control. And I loved the work. There was an excitement in taking courses from great teachers: Morton Zabel, the Victorian scholar; R. C. Bald, the Shakespearean scholar; Gwin Kolb, the Samuel Johnson scholar; Elder Olsen, the literary critic; and Walter Blair, the American literature scholar. But no matter how fascinating my studies I could never for a minute forget the academic tightrope which stretched ahead of me. Grades were *everything*. A few months in America and I had become a competitive demon.

Two months before I was to take the final comprehensive examination—a much dreaded event by English students—I received a telephone call from my mother. My father had been very ill, she said, and required surgery. "He insists on having it in the United States so as to have a chance to be with you," she added. Then my father's voice was on the line: "Don't believe her, I'm as fit as a fiddle," he said lightly. "We all miss you very much, that's all." "I miss you too," I shouted over the bad connection. "Asma wants to say hello to you," he said now. But his voice sounded feeble. My baby sister was speaking but I hardly heard her. I was filled with anxiety over my father's health; would my mother's predictions come true? When I put the receiver down I wondered how I would survive the weeks until my father arrived. What if he died before his voyage was completed? I asked myself over and over. For a few days my concentration was disrupted, but I managed to pull myself together, knowing that my success meant as much to my father as it did to me.

Finally, the day of his arrival came. As I caught sight of him stepping off the ocean liner in New York Harbor, I experienced a sense of relief and joy which was almost paralyzing. He had grown much thinner, though, and his thick mane of hair seemed whiter than when I last saw him. Supporting him by the arm was Asma, who immediately spotted me and waved enthusiastically in my direction. My mother walked behind them. I ran up the ramp and hugged my father. I could see tears in his eyes. The whole family wept, but Middle Eastern tears dry as fast as they spring up, and in the car my father turned to me and said, "And how are your studies?" I was pleased that this was foremost on his mind. I told him that I had completed the course work and was studying for the final exam. "You'll make it, Laila, you are your father's daughter," he said with laughter and confidence in his voice.

In the car, a used Chevy which Amin had bought and was now driving us to Washington in, I asked my father how things were back home. "Egypt has become a police state," he said. "Nasser is terrorizing everyone with his secret police. Even we are watched." "You mustn't speak like that, it's dangerous," interrupted my mother. "No one is going to stop me from speaking my mind," he snapped, and then lowering his voice as if he had forgotten for a minute that he was not in Cairo, he added, "Do you know that all the telephones are tapped? Do you know that they even open your letters from America? You must be very careful what you write." "But why has all this happened?" I asked. "The man went crazy after his attempt at unity with Syria failed. He blames it on the capitalist class, who did not wish to have socialism there. So what does he do? He takes it

23

out on us. The sequestrations are at their height and anyone who criticizes Nasser is thrown in jail." "Your father is angry," my mother remarked, "because he can't get X-ray films on the market anymore." "That's only part of it," he muttered. "Imagine not a single box of X rays in the whole damn town, not even from the Eastern bloc countries!" I tried to suppress a smile. "Instead, Nasser is spending all our foreign currency on the war in Yemen." I shook my head. "In Yemen, of all places! His people are starving and he sends our poor Egyptian boys to fight for the Yemenites. Seventy thousand of them! There are rumors that we are losing one million pounds sterling a day in that war. But no one dares to criticize him."

When we reached Washington, the family settled down in a comfortable hotel near the hospital. I had made arrangements to take my final exam at Georgetown University in a month's time. It was agreed that the wedding would take place after my father's surgery and after I had taken my exam.

It was not easy reading Keats and Jane Austen, knowing that my father would be operated on in a week. Sensing this, he insisted that I isolate myself from the family and study. Locked up in my hotel room, I studied continuously for almost three weeks, leaving the hotel only an hour each day to visit my father. Sometimes we would pass the hour discussing politics. Other times, I would take my books with me and study beside his bed. No matter how we spent the time my father was always in good spirits, joking with his doctors and flirting with his nurses. He had friends on the medical staff who assured him he was in good hands. But the day of the surgery was traumatic. My father insisted I remain at the hotel to study. I obeyed. But the words before me were nothing but black smudges. Finally, after many hours, a telephone call came from one of my cousins, a nephew of my father's who was interning at Walter Reed Hospital. "Don't worry, Laila, he's fine, but he's in pain. When he came out of the recovery room, he swore at his American doctors with every conceivable Arabic obscenity—if he can swear like that, he's fine!"

●

One week later, I sat in an oak-paneled study at Georgetown University, a sealed brown envelope waiting to be opened by a faculty member there. I looked at the envelope as if it contained a reprieve from a life sentence. . . .

The questions took two days to answer, and I wrote as if my whole life depended on my performance, even though it had been decided by Amin and the family that the wedding would take place the very next day. I would not even have time to try on the wedding dress my mother brought from Cairo.

The morning of the wedding I put on the dress. It was too tight. I had put on weight from all the candy I had eaten while I was studying. Sitting on the hotel bed, my mother frantically let out the seams, saying, "I've never heard of anyone not having time to try on their wedding dress. How am I going to finish this half an hour before the ceremony!"

Asma hovered around me excitedly, in a white muslin dress. She was to be my maid of honor, and watching her arrange flowers in her hair, I noticed how beautiful she had grown. "Hurry, hurry," she kept telling my mother, who grumbled and mumbled as she furiously sewed the dress. Finally it was ready. A hastily bought satin hat was banged down on my head, and some white flowers which Amin had bought were thrust at me. I was pushed into the elevator and into the car driven now by my cousin.

As I entered the Greek Orthodox church where we were to be married because it was the closest thing to a Coptic church, the tune of "Here comes the bride" faltered from a piano. "It's our cousin Nadia playing," whispered Asma excitedly. I looked at my sister dubiously. "She's only trying to give a touch of America to the ceremony." She shrugged. Amin looked very solemn through all this.

Waiting for us at the red and gold altar was Bishop Samuel, a leading clergyman of the Coptic Church who happened to be in America at the time. He greeted us with the plaintive, nasal chants of our ancient liturgy: "Kyrie eleison, kyrie eleison." Two choirboys accompanied and echoed his refrain. We were seated on two chairs that had been placed on the altar with Asma standing by us. I looked at Amin who looked mesmerized by the words being uttered by the bishop: "Wives submit yourselves unto your husbands as unto the Lord. For the husband is the head of the wife, even as Christ is the head of the Church. Therefore, as the Church is subject unto Christ, so let the wives be to their own husbands in everything." Then, holding a small urn in his hand, the bishop tipped it with his finger and smeared the oil within first on Amin's forehead and then on mine. "May this oil keep Satan away, this is the oil of the Holy Spirit," he murmured. I looked at Asma who began to giggle. Suddenly, I began to giggle too. Amin nudged me with his arm. But neither of us could stop. Tears came to the corners of my eyes. I looked helplessly at the bishop, but he continued his libations unperturbed: "Bless together, O Lord, the joining of Amin and Laila. Save them from all evil. Let them lead a gentle and calm life lighting the eyes of the heart so that they may do thy will, because thou art merciful, most merciful." The giggling was over.

In the meantime, two paper crowns, hastily made from gold paper, were placed on our heads—in Egypt they would have been real. "Bless these crowns that we prepared to put on your servants, O Lord. They are the crowns of joy and happiness, of rejoicing and steadfastness. O Lord, let them take joy in the children that they shall give birth to, and let them remain faithful and staunch in our Orthodox faith, forever and ever." Asma was gazing dreamily into the distance; Amin's head was bowed. The bishop continued in high tones: "Let them be fruitful, granting them a live seed, so that they may be surrounded by children and live happily and peacefully for the sake of the Lord Jesus Christ."

I could tell by the cadence in his voice that the ceremony was finally ending. "You are now her master. Be kind to her, treat her with tenderness. He is your husband now, forget your people, obey him, for he is your master. God has willed that you obey him, as you have obeyed your parents." My gaze traveled along the rows of benches to where my father was seated. I smiled at him. Feebly, he smiled back.

•

"Mr. and Mrs. Wanis, yes, here is the reservation." The hotel clerk beamed. "You have the bridal suite on the twelfth floor," he said knowingly. I felt embarrassed in my wedding dress and was anxious to get out of it as soon as possible. I looked at Amin who seemed more relieved than happy. In the elevator, he kept his eyes on the floor. Champagne and flowers were awaiting us in the suite. Amin poured some champagne while I changed into a negligee provided by my mother. He then changed into his pajamas. I quickly became drowsy from the champagne which I sipped slowly. It had been a long day. Amin took me gently in his arms. I was still a virgin.

The turquoise-blue ocean, the whitewashed bungalows, the long, cool pineapple drinks of our Caribbean honeymoon could not dispel the inward gloom I felt. There was nothing to look forward to now that I was married. There was a finality about that. But then my father called from Washington. "Guess what we got in the mail today," he said, his voice vibrating with joy. "What?" I asked. "You passed the exams! Congratulations! I am so proud of you." An unfathomable peace kept me from responding. "Laila, are you there?" came my father's voice. "Yes, yes, it's wonderful," I replied. Then he asked very quickly, "How is Amin and the honeymoon?"

"Perfect, everything is perfect," I replied.

That night over a candlelit dinner, I told Amin the news: "I passed my examination. The master's," I added. "Well done, I knew you would," he replied. "Now that I have an M.A. I can go on for the Ph.D. It will give me something to do while you finish your master's," I said. He looked at me blankly. "After all, you still have another year to go," I said in faltering tones. "I heard they have a good theater department at Urbana and I have made up my mind today to apply there." He did not comment. We finished our meal and our honeymoon in silence.

It was the sixties and you couldn't miss it even on the sprawling, provincial campus of the University of Illinois. There was constant talk of the Vietnam War and the civil rights movement in the air; students dressed in jeans, even the academic life-style was relaxed. I started to attend my theater classes and immediately realized that *this* was my real passion. I devoured every lecture, brought home as many books and plays as I could read, attended rehearsals, performances, and auditions.

Meanwhile, Amin and I settled down in a married-student housing complex. We were surrounded by other married couples, foreign and American. But it was Amin who selected our friends. Like the couple from Kansas City. They had two children, and through them I was able to get an insight into the married life of a middle-class couple; they'd rented a wood-frame house, and they had a station wagon. Their living room was strewn with toys and their kitchen had shiny gadgets. Amin admired their life-style and their values. This was domestic bliss, he thought. But I was merely *bored* by it all. And during our frequent get-togethers with the Kansas City couple, I would be more and more preoccupied with the theater.

I would have preferred to get to know the students who were organizing the political debates in the student union, or some of the theater students. But Amin preferred his Kansas friends. Eventually, I learned to like them, at least until they began pressing me to tell them when I was going to have a baby. As if I didn't have anything better to do—as if I wasn't studying for a Ph.D.

For me, the mention of babies did not have the mystique it had for my American friends. In Egypt most babies are born in mud huts or in the cotton fields. Small children can be seen running through the streets half naked, or working eight-hour days in the fields. Motherhood means to sit abjectly next to your young, selling your eggs or your vegetables from a grimy basket in the midday heat. In my country, life is cheap and death is covered with yesterday's newspaper. To be born means to be poor.

As I settled down in Urbana, the good life, devoid of hunger and misery, was continuously juxtaposed with the shadows of my own people. The realities of my country loomed large in this clean, tree-shaded, idyllic community. I began to dread that moment when I would have to come face-to-face with reality again, especially because I would be seeing it with new eyes: eyes made more susceptible by this double image. I began to feel that my life in America was unreal, a Disneyland, a joyride which would soon come to a screeching halt.

I plunged into my work with desperate relish, as if every play I read would be the last, every rehearsal and lecture the final one. My work had become my lover, the only lover I had ever had. But soon I was to leave it.

Less than one year later, Amin had finished his degree. By that time, I had managed to complete all the course work required for the Ph.D., but there was still a very extensive written examination, "the prelims," which had to be passed. My academic adviser looked at me skeptically when I told him I would take it in six weeks. "We have students here who have spent two years studying for it, even more," he informed me. "If I don't take it now, I never will. I have to leave the country with my husband," I replied.

Amin was extremely cooperative. He wanted to tour Europe before returning to Cairo and, therefore, was eager for me to pass my exam as soon as possible. I was awakened at seven every morning and allowed to go to bed at midnight. For six weeks, I locked myself in with my books, without even an occasional movie or TV show. Amin prepared our meals. The pressure was overwhelming, but I was never more motivated. If I passed the prelims, my adviser would see to it that I would be allowed to write a dissertation in Cairo. I would eventually earn my Ph.D. simply by returning for a short visit for the defense of my thesis. Everything, therefore, depended on that exam.

The day of the examination I was so exhausted I did not know how I would find the strength to write. The questions involved theater history, dramatic literature, criticism, directing, acting, costuming, and scene design. The exams lasted two days. At the end of each day, Amin would be waiting for me in his used car, anxiety written all over his face; he knew how much it meant to me.

The exams had to be read and approved by all the professors in the department. It would be at least a week before I would know the result. To distract myself, I began to pack our belongings and do some last-minute shopping.

"I'll kill myself if I don't pass," I told Amin jokingly one day in the midst of packing. "You'll pass," he replied. Five days later, the chairman of the department called me at home: "I have some good news for you. You've passed the prelims. Frankly, I didn't think you'd make it. You had so little time to study—anyway, we've all been pleasantly surprised by this." I thought I would burst with happiness as I put the receiver down. I began to dance around the room, jumping about like a demented woman. "Thank heavens," Amin said soberly as he observed me, "now we can go home."

We drove to New York where we boarded the *Queen Elizabeth,* which was to take us to Southampton. As the anchor was lifted, everyone rushed on deck to observe the famous skyline receding in the distance. It was getting dark as the ship circled slowly around the Statue of Liberty and made its way out to the open sea. The harbor was beginning to glitter with the lights of New York. The ship moved farther and farther away, the darkness enveloping the deck. Gradually the lights of the city faded and the distant skyline disappeared like a mirage.

W HEN WE ARRIVED at the airport in Cairo one month later, we found it covered with posters of a beaming Nasser and the slogans of the new socialist state: Unity—Discipline—Work. "Tafteesh, inspection," ordered the customs official as our bags were opened, our clothing flung around, and our records and gadgets carefully scrutinized. Policemen stood everywhere, and here and there, army officers and military police glared at passengers. We had heard rumors that the great leader was bitter at everyone. Even the Russians. That year there had been a crackdown on all Egyptian communists of public stature. Rumor had it that anyone with foreign friends or contacts was under suspicion, and that people were arrested on the spur of the moment.

Amin's short friend was waiting along with Amin's family. Their faces looked gaunt and tense. "Welcome home, hamdellah ala al-salama," they all repeated as they embraced us. Then we were huddled into a car and to my in-laws' apartment. I felt almost panic-stricken as I watched the familiar, badly lit streets rush by. Cairo had become a dark, somber, emaciated city. "I think we made a mistake coming back," I whispered to Amin in the car. "You'll get used to it again," he answered curtly.

Amin and I were obliged to move in with his family. Amin could not afford an apartment and I was too proud to ask my father for money. There were apartments to be had in Cairo,

31

but only if you could afford the key money, a bribe to greedy landlords who took advantage of the housing situation.

Our luggage was taken to Amin's room—a cold, gray room with a narrow bed and schoolboy's furniture. "The city looks as if it is in a blackout," I commented as I looked out of the only window of the room. "Electricity costs money. This is Egypt," said Amin.

Amin returned to his old job, where he spent long hours. I had grown accustomed to his companionship, and now I found myself alone for entire days. I would wake up in the morning to an apartment empty but for my mother-in-law shuffling about in the corridors, or arranging and rearranging the linens or shirts in one of her many closets. At home, she wore a thin cotton housecoat and no makeup, which made her deep-set eyes look sad. She was trapped in that apartment, in those corridors she spent so much time meandering in. And so was I.

There was nowhere to go, nothing to do. My parents, who were infuriated that we lived with my in-laws and not with them, expected me to visit them every day. It was an obligation I was happy to fulfill, for I had become a stranger in Cairo. I had even lost touch with my girlfriends, who had all married and were up to their second and third babies.

Every afternoon, after Amin had left for his evening job, I took a taxi to my parents' home in Heliopolis. The streets were grimy, the pavements broken, and bedraggled children ran in front of the cars. Open carts, pulled by heaving horses and donkeys, carrying garbage or stones, filled the streets. People hanging on to the fenders of buses peered into my empty taxi and made me feel guilty. The poverty of my people deepened my gloom.

By contrast, our villa in Heliopolis was a bourgeois paradise. Once the iron gates were closed behind me, the reality outside vanished. My father, in his bathrobe, amid his bookshelves and fireplace, would embrace me warmly. We would sit next to one another on a velvet couch. Opposite us was an elaborate Chinese table with French porcelain objects. "I can't stand the sight of poverty," I told my father. "It's because you've lived in

America. America has spoiled you," he said lightly. "I don't think so. It just seems worse than I ever remember," I said. "If only we had a leader who loved this country," said my father.

Later Amin would pick me up or I would return in a taxi. At night, as I made my way through the long corridor which led to Amin's room, I would be reminded of that little cell in the dorm at Chicago where I had been so free. Amin's room at the end of the long corridor, a dark corridor like the tunnels inside the pyramids which you must walk through with bent back so as not to offend the pharaohs lying there, was also a cold space—just like the pharaohs' tomb. A space where only death can imprison and contain the silent God. And so, with my life, my freedom. It too seemed to have come to an end, to have been imprisoned in that room at the end of the long corridor.

Tensions began to erupt in my marriage. My in-laws and my parents began to quarrel. My in-laws didn't mind if we lived with them forever, while my parents wanted us to have a place of our own. My mother, in particular, still cherished hopes that I would live in the comme il faut fashion befitting my "social standing." At my parents' home, my mother would say, "Laila, you look so poor, why don't you wear some jewelry?" And, at my in-laws', my mother-in-law would say, "This is no time for wearing jewelry. We've had enough confiscations." Another time my mother would say, "Your husband and his parents should find a decent place for you to live," while my in-laws would lament, "We have no money. What can we do?"

During my visits to Heliopolis, I often complained to my father about having nothing to do. Things would change when I had a place of my own, he would say.

A year went by and we were still living in Amin's room. Then one day my mother called me with an announcement: "I've found an apartment in Zamalek for you. If your husband can't afford the key money, then I will pay it. But enough is enough. You can move in in a couple of weeks."

It was a delightful place: two rooms on the roof of a building in the residential district of Zamalek, with a large terrace overlooking a tributary of the Nile. It had a small living room and a bedroom with blue walls and a double bed. It would have been the perfect love nest if there had been any passion in my marriage, but I was overjoyed to have it anyway. Most of all, I loved the terrace with the view of the river. From the very first moment I set eyes on the glistening water below, I knew I had come home. I was born in Zamalek, and although we moved from there when I was a child, it continued to draw me, in spite of myself.

Zamalek is an island right in the middle of the Nile, connected by bridges to the city. Zamalek wants to be alone, to be isolated from the realities of Cairo and to be faithful only to the affluent Egyptians and foreigners who inhabit its plush villas, its gardens, its tree-shaded apartment blocks, ornamented by acacia trees and white-turbaned Nubian *bowabs*, doormen. There, isolated by the river on both sides, that river which glistens and shimmers at every twist and turn, you can forget that just on the other side of the bank, human beings exist one on top of the other in stagnant, muddy tenements where running water is scarce and where it is so dark at noon that you have to light a match to find your way through the debris of garbage and rats.

Zamalek makes you forget. It intoxicates you with its sunshine, its palm trees rising haughtily above the polo grounds, tennis courts, and golf course of its private country club. Here, wealthy Egyptians drive a Mercedes or Jaguar and forget that they are not in Paris or Rome. In Zamalek, there is no Egypt, only river cafés and houseboats, where Scotch is sipped and white suits will not be sullied by the grime and dust of the city.

As soon as Amin and I moved in, we took on the routine of a typical married couple in Cairo. I shopped for the food, prepared meals, and waited patiently for him to come home. After lunch, which was usually silent since Amin would come home hot and morose, we would have a siesta. Then Amin would go back to his office, returning in the evening, usually accompanied by his trusted friend. The three of us would spend the evening in, or we would have a snack at a restaurant or the

Hilton or Sheraton coffee shop. On Friday, we had lunch with Amin's parents. On Sunday, with mine. On Thursday nights we went to the movies.

"Your life will become full when you have a baby. This is what gives a woman's life purpose," said my mother one day when I was visiting our villa in Heliopolis. My father had made a fire in the living-room fireplace and Asma was preparing hot cinnamon for us to drink. As he threw another log on the fire, my father nodded his head in approval at my mother's words. I remained silent. Asma came into the room with the hot cinnamon. We exchanged looks. She knew that I was afraid to confess that I didn't want to have a baby.

On another day, Amin's short friend came in and said, "People are talking about you two. They are wondering which one of you is the one who can't have children." I was stunned but managed to tell him that was ridiculous and that we just didn't want any children yet. Then I looked at Amin, thinking he would back me up. But he simply lowered his eyes and changed the topic of conversation.

It was Amin's virility that was at stake. In Arab society, a man's sexual prowess is measured by the number of children he has. One child, one little child, would prove that he was a man; it would be befitting to his position in society and it would honor his clan. I ridiculed these attitudes, but I felt the pressure: "A child will keep you company," said my mother's sister. "How about a good book?" I retorted. She stared at me as if I were mad. I felt like Om Abdou confronting the majlis-al-hasby. "You can never be sure a man is yours until you have his child," said my mother's cousin. And my mother added, "Laila, if you wait too long, it will be too late." "Besides, a child will make you forget everything," said another cousin of my mother.

Exactly what I feared.

Finally one day I broke down in front of my father. I explained that I didn't have the urge to have a child, that I felt it would interfere with my plans and my studies. My father's wide forehead wrinkled with concentration as he absorbed my words.

35

I waited for his reaction as if it were a verdict. "You're right. No need to rush into it." My mouth fell open in astonishment. He was on my side. I went over to him and hugged him tightly. "Thank you for being so understanding, papi." "I do want you to finish your Ph.D.," he said, giving me one of his winks. Then with eyes full of mischief he scratched his head and added, "I have a friend in the Ministry of Culture. I will talk to him about giving you a job. What you need is work."

I heaved a sigh of relief.

> *Theatre investigates the conditions
> which influence the committing of
> actions, the process of action itself, and
> therefore is continually involved with
> questions of existence, since action is the
> means whereby existence becomes
> self-defining.*
>
> —*Robert Benedetti*

PROFESSOR RAMSIS gave me a glance without lifting his head from his papers. We were sitting in his austere, gray office in one of the major state-subsidized theaters in Cairo. The walls were patched with theatrical posters. Professor Ramsis was an important man in the Ministry of Culture and Social Guidance, which had been established by Nasser ostensibly to spread culture to the people, but actually to indoctrinate them with Nasser's political ideology. I glanced once more at the posters while Professor Ramsis continued to leaf through his papers. They were posters of Professor Ramsis' plays, all written since the 1952 revolution. "Your father told me that you have studied theater in America," he said suddenly. I was so happy to be addressed, I was almost speechless. "Yes, yes, sir," I managed to say. He did not look up at me. "We are about to produce three one-act plays by prominent playwrights," he said without looking at me. "Wonderful," I stammered. "We will hire you as an assistant director," he added with a tone which implied that the meeting had come to an end. "Thank you, thank you very much," I said as I backed out of the room. But I felt as if I were walking on clouds. He had given me my first job in the theater.

The auditorium where the cast met for the first rehearsal was a converted movie house which had been confiscated and converted by the state. The actors were young and talented, but the director, an English professor at Cairo University, didn't know what he was doing. The play was Professor Ramsis'. I saw my chance.

"Yes, what is it?" said Professor Ramsis, again barely acknowledging my presence. I had been kept waiting in his anteroom for an hour. "Excuse me, sir," I said, trying to sound confident. "Well?" he asked impatiently. "That first reading of your play . . ." I stopped when I realized he was looking straight at me, and then with all the force I could muster, I said, "The English professor doesn't understand it. He's going to ruin it." Professor Ramsis sat back in his chair, put his pen down, and scrutinized me. "How?" he asked. I then explained, giving my own interpretation of the script. Then he nodded his head in my direction and returned to his papers. My audience had come to an end. I've spoiled everything, I thought as I left the theater. The next day when I went to rehearsal, I was informed that the director had been fired. I was to replace him.

"First Egyptian woman stage director," read the newspaper caption after the bill of three one-act plays opened. The reviews were good, but the critics attacked Professor Ramsis' play for being too "subjective." It was a satirical anatomy of a Don Juan, but it was devoid of social content and in the Nasser days all plays had to have "relevance." But the second play was praised because it was written by a famous leftist writer and had a political theme. It took place in a police station in one of the worst sections of the city, where a police sergeant dreams out loud of an Egypt where social justice and equality will prevail. The third play on the program was also praised because it ridiculed a member of the feudal, landowning class which Nasser was in the process of abolishing.

In spite of our success, we did not have a very long run because it was a theater-club production and another program was waiting to succeed us. As is customary in the theater on the final night, we had a cast party. I danced with an actor whom I had grown very fond of during the rehearsals. He held me close. Maybe too close. The next thing I knew, Amin was on the dance floor, slapping the actor in the face.

We drove home in silence. The party, even my success, had been ruined, cheapened by Amin's behavior. But I felt guilty. Dancing with the actor had aroused me. I looked at Amin's silhouette in the dark. He had never aroused me like that. Being aroused was a good feeling, though—it had connected me with myself. Could it be that my work in the theater was somehow responsible? I wondered.

In the next couple of weeks, I tried to forget the magic of the theater and settle down to real life once more. But one evening, when Amin was away at the office, I phoned the actor. He said he missed me and missed our work together. We chatted for a long time. I felt alive again. At the end of the conversation I asked him to visit me the following evening, at home in Zamalek. He accepted at once.

As I waited for him the following evening, the cry of the *qarawan*, the nightingale, filtered through the dense and perfumed acacia trees: a cry of sorrow, of anguish. A cry of hunger and need. I allowed all these sounds and smells to play on my senses as I waited for the actor. I dared not think what the outcome of the evening might be. I just sat there, as if I were about to watch a play.

He arrived all polished and perfumed, reeking of seduction. We made silly conversation and he seemed nervous and ill at ease. I knew it was my fault, because I felt guilty. As the evening progressed, I began to feel weary. Was this going to be my life? Escape from my marriage through a maze of infidelities? I looked at the actor, whom I had succeeded in keeping at bay until this moment. He looked back at me, gazing into my eyes. I lowered my head. He stood up. "I had better go," he said. "Do stay," I said politely. He took my hand and kissed it. It was a gesture of respect, an indication that he approved my decision to be faithful. He couldn't possibly have known that I was being honorable for myself and not for my absent husband.

Meanwhile my involvement in the theater was raising eyebrows. One day, at a luncheon at my in-laws', a guest of theirs asked me, "How can the daughter of a famous doctor, a man of science, choose such a profession?" I laughed in order to dismiss the question, but Amin's parents looked embarrassed.

The English display pictures of their greatest actors in their museums—in veneration of them. But in Egypt there is no such tradition. Rather, the state of the histrionic arts resembles what it was in Europe in the Middle Ages, when actors were not even allowed a Christian burial. Moreover, there was no theater in Egypt until the nineteenth century. Islamic culture did not encourage live theater. There were puppet shows and shadow theater, but no live theater. Eventually, in the footsteps of a nineteenth-century wave of nationalism and Western influence, theater made its entry in Lebanon with adaptations of plays of Molière, Corneille, and Racine. But it was not until the 1870s that Cairene audiences were able to see a real theatrical performance.

But theater, an unabashedly Western art, was tolerated only as long as it behaved itself. In 1878, *The Tyrant* opened at the Cairo Opera House. It became the first of countless plays to come which were to use history and the Arabian Nights tales as a camouflage for criticizing contemporary events. The "tyrant" in question, Khedive Ismail, responded by banishing the actors from Egypt.

Once the theater was launched, however, even censorship could not stop it. And yet, even after the revolution and the adoption of the theater by the state, the position of Egyptian actors and actresses remained very low. They were considered, as they had been in medieval Europe, just a little above circus performers and prostitutes. But I was not an actress and so I thought I was above it all.

A few weeks after the plays had closed, a leading intellectual who had seen them asked me to his office to discuss future projects. A secretary ushered me in. He sat behind a very large desk in a small room lined with bookshelves. The room was dark and cool with the only light coming from a desk lamp. "Please sit down," he said, gesturing to a narrow sofa. He fixed me for a while with his light brown eyes, as if he were trying to hypnotize me. I began to fidget. "I've been waiting to have this meeting for a long time," he said finally. "Before I saw you in your theater," he continued, "I thought I would be meeting a woman in her forties, square, nearsighted, fat." I tried to smile. "We really must get to know each other better. An artist like you and a writer like me . . ." I decided to interrupt: "Have you written any plays recently?" He moved from behind his desk and said, "Before we talk about that we should get to know each other better." I got up abruptly and announced that I was leaving. "Allah, Allah, don't lose patience. You need to feed your talent." I rushed out of the office without even looking in the direction of the secretary and ran down the stairs. I never got to direct any of his plays.

I had thought that my foray into the theater would somehow release me from my marriage, but once again I found myself pacing the dainty, tropical hothouse which had become my new prison. A prison more insidious than my in-laws' home, because I could come and go as I pleased. But I couldn't leave. I had nowhere to go. I had become the jailer of my own existence.

Meanwhile, Amin was becoming increasingly distant and sullen over my refusal to become pregnant. But my body was my last stronghold and only I had a right to control its destiny, I thought.

In order to get out of the house as frequently as possible, I decided to begin my dissertation. I was to write on the actor-manager Najib al-Rihani, the creator of Egyptian social comedy in the thirties and forties. Rihani's name was a household word. He became almost instantly famous in 1916 with his impersonations of Kish Kish Bey, the naive village mayor who comes to Cairo, where he is robbed and mocked. Later, he created a Chaplinesque character, a poignant, pathetic, impoverished member of the urban proletariat, who wins a lottery or by some such chance finds himself in the world of the rich, where his values have lost all meaning; values which were representative of all that is authentic and good in Egyptian life. Thus, in this fashion, Rihani ridiculed the growing middle class, as well as the Egyptian aristocracy of those days. He even made fun of the monarchy.

Om Abdou, I was told, never missed a play of his. My father, who identified with Rihani's personage, could recite entire speeches from his plays, and as a child, I was taken to see all the films he had made in the forties, which were still being shown.

That Rihani was immensely important to the development of Egyptian theater no one could deny, except the ideologues of the sixties, who refused to acknowledge him because he portrayed the middle classes. Therefore he did not receive any scholarly attention. It was now up to me to reconstruct his theatrical history—from old newspapers, periodicals, and records —and to collect his unpublished plays.

Every day, as soon as I had finished the housework, I would take a bus or a taxi to one of the numerous libraries which contained my research material. A little before two I would return home, set the table, heat the food, and wait for Amin. In the evening, when he returned to his office, I would read and document the research. The next day I would return to one of the libraries for additional information or for the verification of the title of a play or the date of a production.

The plays were not easy to find or document. There were many plagiarized versions. But gradually I was able to tell the difference between a real Rihani and a false text. Finally, a nephew of the comedian, Badie Rihani, took pity on me and let me have access to his private collection of the plays. There were about forty of them, all waiting to be read, dated, analyzed, and evaluated critically.

One day as I was leafing through some periodicals in the library of the American University in Cairo, a foreigner approached me. He spoke with a European accent. "I've been wanting to meet you. I've heard about your productions," he said, smiling with deep blue eyes. He told me that he was an Arabist who taught in the United States, and that his name was Paul. Then he invited me to attend a seminar at the Oriental Hall the following day. I promised to be there.

When I entered the Oriental Hall, a small meeting hall with

wooden arabesque windows and screens decorated with Koranic calligraphy, I found an esoteric group of Arab and Western scholars of modern Arabic literature engrossed in learned talk. Their world of aesthetic abstractions seemed remote from my world and the realities of Egypt, yet I found myself enjoying this academic gathering. All of a sudden the European Arabist turned and addressed a question about the Egyptian theater to me. I was surprised and embarrassed but also pleased that he should treat me as an authority. I fumbled and stammered my answer and he backed me up by elaborating on it. At that moment we both knew that there was something between us.

After the session was over, he mentioned something about going to the bazaar and I offered to take him and a colleague of his. As we made our way through the crowded streets in the intense August heat, it became clear that he was a lover of Cairo. He knew the names and locations of the tiniest alleys in the Khan Khalili bazaar; we would stop to admire a hidden medieval mosque or a sixth-century wall, with its arabesque ornaments, its history fresh in his mind. As I walked by his side in this ancient part of Cairo, where medieval Islam still lived in arched ornamental doorways decorated with stalactites, open courtyards with fountains in the center, and covered arcades all around, I began to see the city through his eyes. The heaving donkeys with their heavy loads, the traffic noises, the shrill cries of the street vendors, all dissolved as together we stood admiring a gleaming mother-of-pearl arch, or the lattice window of a famous mosque.

We made an appointment to see each other the following day as if it was the most natural thing in the world. But as we shook hands, I knew that my life had changed.

The next day we walked through the ancient palaces and houses of Cairo—flat-topped structures built around open courtyards with secluded living quarters for women. We walked through metal-studded wooden doors, and looked at windows inlaid with geometric designs, slender columns supporting arches and walls, molded in stucco and painted and gilded. In-

43

side one of the houses was a garden and a trickling tiled fountain, where time stood still. For me, time stood still.

He was to leave for America the following day. Back to his job, his wife, and his sons. That night we took a stroll in the dimly lit streets of Zamalek. The smell of jasmine mingled with the Nile-scented breeze. We walked in silence, the silence of sadness and separation, broken only by the cry of the qarawan. We stopped in a spot concealed by trees, away from the eyes of the inquisitive bowabs. We stood in the dark, afraid to touch. Finally, he said quietly, "I will write," and then he was gone in the shadows, exactly like in a forties movie.

In addition to my research in the libraries, I was now embarking on a search for the surviving *muchakhasakiya,* impersonators, as actors used to be called. One of them, a contemporary of Rihani's, lived in the servants' quarters of an apartment building in downtown Cairo. It was not easy locating Amin Attallah, who had been a well-known comic in the twenties and thirties, but I was able to track him down through a reporter who had interviewed him a couple of years back.

I climbed a dark staircase leading to a roof where I found a number of women and children scurrying about, washing their clothes in aluminum basins, or peeling vegetables, while others were cooking on kerosene burners. The smell of fried onions permeated the air. All seemed happily busy in this community of poverty. A woman with a pregnant belly under her *galabiya* smiled at me. When I inquired after the actor, she left her washing and beckoned me down a long passageway flanked by barren rooms. She pushed me into one of these and there he was, a pioneering actor-manager, sitting cross-legged on an iron bed, his scrawny, toothless face shrouded in a scarf of dirty cotton. His wife, who had been his leading lady, was also there. Though she must have been seventy, she had flaming, henna-dyed hair. They welcomed me effusively.

Once he got started on his reminiscences, Attallah couldn't be stopped—the hours flew and we forgot the poverty around us as the theater transported us to other places and happier days. In spite of his hardships, Attallah had no regrets, no bitterness.

The theater, he told me, was a *resala,* a mission. That was the only way to approach it—as a mission.

One day, over a typically silent lunch, Amin suddenly blurted out that he wanted me to get off the pill. I promised to stop taking the pill in order to reassure him, but told myself that if I did get pregnant I would get an abortion at once. Even though abortions were illegal, many doctors performed them for a fee.

Our life together continued along the same unimpassioned curve, though I did get pregnant before long. "But Amin is a good man, a kind man; he will make a good father if you let him," said my father. "It's not that. It's that I want to complete my degree first," I said in despair. "If I have a child now I will never get back to my thesis. It will never get completed." "But you're pregnant," said my father. "I hadn't thought I was going to get pregnant so easily," I replied. "Don't you love your husband?" he asked now, looking at me searchingly. "Of course. I'm very grateful to him. He's never stood in my way," I replied. "Then the least you can do is have his baby," said my father.

After three months in which my own efforts to terminate my pregnancy—hot baths and other such remedies—had failed, I announced that I was going to have an abortion. Amin called my father in desperation, and my father asked me to come and see him. "It's almost too late for an abortion now," he said cajolingly. "You're young. Now is the time to have children and then you can go on with your degree." "But I have a deadline. If I don't return before a year, I will no longer be considered eligible for my doctorate. Besides, how could I have a baby and then go off to America and leave it for months?" I pleaded. My father's forehead creased with worry. "I can't force you," he said. "I can only advise you."

It was my father who made the appointment with an abortionist. Even when an abortion was performed illegally, a woman still needed a husband's or a father's consent.

I went to the office alone and found it full of middle-class women, for this was an expensive abortionist. The women sat listlessly in their chairs, waiting to be called. Suddenly one woman began to sob quietly while another wept and cursed as she convalesced in a nearby room. A third woman emerging from the same room started to vomit right in front of the rest of us. I wanted to run but it was too late.

Finally, I was ushered in. The doctor had a kind, fatherly face. Then I saw that contraption they strap you into for an examination. It was the first time that I had ever seen one. I was asked to remove my clothes. A blue gown was thrown over me and fastened from behind by the nurse. I stood rooted to the floor. "Get onto the chair," said the nurse impatiently. I felt humiliated at having to spread my legs like that. Putting on rubber gloves, the doctor delved professionally into my vagina. I screamed with pain. He removed his hand and said with a note of disgust, "It's a three-month-old fetus. Almost too late. Come back tomorrow at seven and don't eat or drink until then. My regards to your father." I dressed hurriedly and made my way past the hysterical women. I ran down the steps of the dark, downtown building, through the tiled hallway to the street, to a taxi, to my apartment, to my unrelieved grief.

The next day, I returned to the clinic accompanied by Amin and my parents. Like so many other things, it was a family affair. As we waited in the antechamber, I yearned for this feminine nightmare to end. I loathed this biological self which men invaded with their penises and their surgical instruments.

After a short silence, my father began to joke with Amin, obviously trying to cheer him up. Amin smiled weakly. My mother sat silently, disapprovingly. I was summoned by the nurse.

"Open your legs wide and put them in the straps," she ordered. The doctor was busy with his instruments. Even in that moment I realized how lucky I was to have a proper doctor and anesthesia. I had heard many stories of women who were forced to stay awake while a scalpel scraped their wombs, their "babies" chunks of flesh and blood scooped into a surgical dish. I was lucky I could sleep through it all. The doctor was fumbling with my arm. The syringe missed the vein. I screamed with pain and he looked at me in annoyance.

Suddenly I was cold with fear. I kept my eyes fixed on the

cream-colored walls. Soon an echo enveloped me and I began to feel as if there were nothing inside me, as if I had been emptied of my entrails, my heart, my brain. Sleep, I begged myself, go to sleep.

The echo resounded in my ears and I seemed to be walking in a cavity of my own body, hiding behind my bare skeletal ribs, hiding from the flashing steel which was being brandished toward me. "Get up, it's over, it's over," the nurse was saying. I felt as if my abdomen were a watermelon that had been sliced in two. I began to weep from the pain. "Stop that," ordered the nurse. But she gave me a painkiller and helped me dress. "What's that?" I asked, noticing a jar beside me on the surgical table. "Your fetus. Would you like to have it for a souvenir?" she inquired ironically. I took the jar—and walked numbly out.

That night, Amin suddenly began to sob uncontrollably. I looked at him in silence. How could I tell him that I would have died as a person, as myself, with that baby's birth? How could I explain that it had to be me or that baby? But even if I could have produced the words, he would not have understood.

For weeks, Amin's eyes, dark, round pools of suppressed tears, would follow me everywhere, uncomprehendingly. One night, hearing him cry softly next to me and unable to contain my feelings of guilt and rage anymore, I ran to the bathroom and took the jar down from the shelf where I had kept it concealed, and I smashed it across the wall. Like slime, the fetus with its entrails, eyes, heart, smeared silently across the wall, leaving behind it an indelible trace of sorrow.

Pain and suffering have a way of drawing people together or pulling them apart. After the abortion, the gap between Amin and me widened even further. I worked constantly on my dissertation, yearning for the day when I would be able to return to America for my Ph.D. I also began writing to Paul. He had become a part of my inner world, and judging by his letters, I had become a part of his. And yet I did not feel that this was a betrayal of Amin. My relationship with Paul was platonic. Amin,

I thought, would always be my husband. This was just a correspondence, a meeting of souls, like the furtive notes prisoners exchange just to know they are making contact with another human being. But gradually our correspondence grew more intense. My letters became X-rays of my inner life, which was struggling to be born.

By this time, Amin and I hardly saw each other. And when we did, we brushed against one another, murmuring polite words. He often took his meals at his parents' home. I was left like a bird in a cage: this little apartment had become a more ominous prison than my parents' home because I held the key. How do you release yourself from such a jail? How do you take the step to leave? And if you do, where do you go? These questions accompanied me everywhere. Finally, I realized that I did not have the courage to ask Amin for a divorce. But I did have an outlet—I could escape. Escape to America as soon as I had completed the writing of my dissertation.

The year 1966 was not a good one to think of going to the United States. Nasser was still fighting the Saudi-backed royalists in Yemen, who were being supported by the United States. President Lyndon Johnson had cut all economic aid to Egypt, so Nasser had appealed to the Soviet Union. The Russians responded by canceling half of Egypt's debt and, more important, by agreeing to finance the Aswan High Dam, which would provide Egypt with the increased energy supply it was in desperate need of. The Americans had turned down Nasser's request in 1956 because Secretary of State John Foster Dulles, among others, was convinced that Nasser was a communist.

However, when Nikita Khrushchev visited Egypt for the inauguration of the second stage of the building of the dam, he and Nasser had a profound disagreement. For Nasser, despite the recent rapprochement with the Soviet Union, Arab nationalism, not communism, was the goal. In his numerous political speeches, Nasser emphasized his policy of nonalignment, which the Russians, like the Americans before them, refused to accept. "Arabs still have one conscience and one mind," he said, his dark eyes burning with anger, his voice compelling, forceful, his presence hypnotic. To make his point even more strongly, Nasser threw almost all Egyptian communists into jail.

Around this time, a nationwide anti-Nasser conspiracy was uncovered by Nasser's secret police. The architects of this conspiracy were members of the Moslem Brotherhood. The brotherhood was an organization established in 1925 to purify Islamic life by protecting it from missionary influences and Western ideas. The founder, Hassan al-Banna, was a schoolteacher who began the organization with only six followers. Four years later, the brotherhood had branches in several towns, including Ismailia and Port Said. In Cairo, Banna launched a program of mosque and school building and began to publish his own magazine. By 1942, the anticolonial and anti-Western appeal of the organization had gained it many new followers. The brotherhood now had its own secret force of armed men. It had also managed to penetrate the army by recruiting sympathizers from within the Free Officers' movement, the group that would oust King Farouk and seize power under Nasser's leadership in 1952. One member of the Free Officers' group who was particularly sympathetic toward the brotherhood, and who even acted as their link with the army, was an obscure officer by the name of Mohammed Anwar al-Sadat.

In 1946, clashes of considerable violence began to take place in the universities between the Moslem extremists and the secular members of the nationalist Wafd party. In 1948, during the first war with Israel, members of the brotherhood volunteered for the Egyptian army and were at the forefront of the troops which fought the Israelis in the Sinai. But they were banned by Farouk when they murdered one of his ministers and Hassan al-Banna was assassinated. In 1951, the ban on the brotherhood was lifted and they resumed their activities with violence directed, this time, against the British. Their activities culminated in the burning of Cairo in January 1952 in protest of British interference in Egypt. It was the burning of Cairo that triggered the coup of July 23, which brought Nasser into power.

The brotherhood was the one political party Nasser permitted to exist. But the organization was discontented with Nasser's secular state, so in October 1954, they attempted to assassinate him. Nasser's reprisal was swift. Brotherhood members were rounded up, jailed, and tortured, and many of their leaders put to death. Nasser's secret police, the *mukhabarat,* were so efficient in tracing them that it was rumored that many of them burned their Korans for fear of being discovered. By 1966, however, they had resurfaced and reorganized. They had also grown in number and influence during their long years underground.

As the Moslem Brotherhood became increasingly powerful, so did the military. The Committee for the Liquidation of Feudalism began to abuse its power by outright seizures of money, homes, and businesses, anything it wished. Nasser saw to it that the military were installed in every conceivable administrative and bureaucratic post. They were even made Egypt's ambassadors and diplomats. Amin belonged to this powerful elite.

And as a member of this elite, it was certainly within his power to keep me from leaving Egypt. It would have been easy for him to convince those in power that his objections to my return to the United States were political—relations between Egypt and the United States were at their worst. But once I announced that I was planning to leave, he did not try to stand in my way. Deep inside, he must have still cared for me and thought this last trip would get America out of my system. He pretended, therefore, that he supported my journey. Now all I had to do was obtain my exit visa.

There is an administrative building called the *mujam'aa,* which looms large in Midan al-Tahrir, Liberation Square, in the center of Cairo. A modern, octagonal edifice about eight stories high, it is divided into countless government cubicles inhabited by pale bureaucrats who seemed to specialize in torturing and humiliating civilians in those days. It was to this building that one went to apply for an exit visa. The visa section was administered by the military and the police.

The ensuing days, weeks, and months of my life were swallowed up by this bureaucratic octopus. In order to get an exit visa, one had to be screened by the Ministry of the Interior and Egyptian Intelligence. These were harrowing procedures that could take months. Once one was through with these, it was then possible to apply for the visa, and the accompanying bureaucratic procedure would be set in motion. At this point, an unimaginable number of papers had to be assembled: papers to prove that you were not a civil servant, papers to prove that you were not serving in the military, papers to prove that you had completed university but that the country did not need your field of specialization, papers to prove that you were not sick or disabled, and papers to prove you had been admitted to a university abroad.

The visa section was constantly swarming with people, passports in hand, pushing, shouting, quarreling, begging for action on their petitions. And it was much easier to get a visa to a "friendly" country, such as the Eastern bloc or nonaligned countries, than it was to get one to an "unfriendly" country like the United States. But I would not be deterred.

The tight security could doubtless be explained by the fact that we were a nation involved in one war and on the brink of another. By the end of 1966, the country was nearly bankrupt because of the vast amounts of money Nasser had poured into the five-year war in Yemen. Egypt's currency reserves were depleted, but this did not seem to matter to the military regime whose only concern was to liberate Yemen from its feudal monarchy and to teach Saudi Arabia—which was backing the royalists and was backed by the United States—a lesson.

Meanwhile, another war was about to be fought. In April 1967, Israel prepared to attack Syria, which had recently taken a radical turn to the left. To the Israelis, Syria was the spiritual father of Al-Fatah, the Palestinian guerrilla organization, which had grown in strength and organization. Moreover, the leftist regime which had come into power in Syria had taken a very aggressive stance toward Israel. On April 7, Israel launched a full-scale attack on Syria with air force, tanks, and artillery. Israel said that this was in retaliation for several incidents on the borders. Abba Eban called for further large-scale retaliatory measures, saying that Israel would have to launch a "decisive blow" against Syria. In an interview with the French paper *La Terre Retrouvée*, Itzhak Rabin declared that until the revolutionary regime in Damascus had been overthrown, no government in the Middle East could feel safe. Then the Israelis concentrated ten of their brigades on the Syrian border, threatening to occupy Damascus. On May 9, the Knesset, Israel's parliament, gave the government permission to take military action against Syria.

By then the entire Arab world believed that an Israeli attack was imminent. To Nasser, the concentration of Israeli forces on the Syrian border was an outright act of provocation and an attempt by the Israelis to "teach the Arabs a good lesson," in the words of Shimon Peres in an interview to the same French paper. On May 15, Egyptian troops, armored cars, and trucks crossed Cairo in the direction of Sinai and the Israeli frontier. Egypt had a defense pact with Syria and we would be obligated to act on its behalf if the Israelis attacked.

The Arab countries, however, were not satisfied with this move to assemble troops in the Sinai. King Hussein of Jordan taunted Nasser and demanded of the leader of the Arab world that he take more stringent measures. Was not Nasser, he asked, hiding behind the cordon of UN troops which prevented Egyptian-Israeli confrontation? Jordan Radio reminded Nasser of the existence of Sharm al-Sheikh, and derided Nasser's inoffensive moves as mere saber rattling. Sharm al-Sheikh commands the Straits of Tiran and hence the outlet from the Gulf of Aqaba to the Red Sea. (In 1956, Sharm al-Sheikh had been conquered by the Israelis and then evacuated under American pressure, and Israeli troops had been replaced by UN ones, so that Israeli ships had been allowed free passage. The closing of the Straits of Tiran to Israeli ships would thus be considered effective retaliation to the presence of Israeli troops on the Syrian border, because the straits, Israel's only outlet to the Red Sea, were considered by them essential to their navigation.) The Syrians were also harassing him. On May 18, the Egyptian ambassador to the UN requested that the UN troops stationed in Egypt along the Sinai border with Israel get out of the way. Nasser explained that the UN had been stationed on the border for eleven years and he suggested that it was time they step over to the Israeli side. Israel refused. To Egypt, this was proof enough that Israel was preparing an attack. On May 19, the last UN observation posts were evacuated. Some Palestinian units from Gaza replaced them alongside Egyptian contingents there. Meanwhile, the Egyptian commander for the Sinai emphasized that only an Israeli attack on Syria would provoke military action. On Sunday, May 21, Egyptian forces replaced the UN troops at Sharm al-Sheikh.

The object of this exercise was to make Israel think twice before attacking Syria. It was not intended as a provocation of war. Why should Egypt grant passage through coastal waters extending less than two miles from its shores to a country with which it was legally at war? asked Nasser. World opinion did not agree. On May 23, Robert Kennedy, addressing B'nai B'rith, demanded that a UN naval force be sent to the Straits of Tiran.

But the Arabs were elated beyond all measure. This diplomatic defeat of Israel also canceled its only gain from the Suez war. Our exaltation was expressed with great braggadocio and our enemy was promised a thousand deaths, exquisitely described. Nasser had fanned a flame which would soon scorch him. The Israelis used our inflammatory statements to prove to the world that their tiny, defenseless state was about to be destroyed by the Arabs.

World opinion was inflamed against Egypt and the Arabs. Meanwhile, Nasser hoped that the matter would be resolved diplomatically. The Soviets urged caution. Johnson asked Nasser not to take any military action until the United States had a chance to mediate between Israel and the Arabs. Egyptian diplomats began to negotiate behind the scenes at the UN on the right of passage through the Straits of Tiran. Zakkaria Muhieddin, the vice-president, was invited to Washington on June 5.

But Nasser's words were menacing. People everywhere took his saber rattling at face value and the pro-Israeli world press took full advantage of it. In reality, though, Nasser hoped that

53

his threats would force Israel to negotiate on all the problems resulting from the creation of the State of Israel, such as the return of the Palestinian refugees, and the territory conquered in 1948. On May 29, Charles Yost, a U.S. State Department adviser, arrived in Cairo to engage in intense negotiations with Nasser. On June 3, Yost left Cairo, having given assurances that Israel would not attack as long as diplomatic negotiations were going on. On June 3, Moshe Dayan gave a press conference in which he spoke of patience and claimed that he would await the outcome of the diplomatic negotiations which were taking place with the Arabs. On Monday, June 5, at dawn, the Israeli air force left the tarmac and within six hours had bombed every important Arab airfield as far apart as Luxor in the south of Egypt and Habbaniya in Iraq.

The attack was a total surprise to the Egyptian army. That very same morning, Abdel Hakim Amer, the commander in chief of the armed forces, had arrived in Sinai on an inspection tour. He was actually in the air when the Israeli attack was taking place, and for about six hours the entire Egyptian army was without orders because there was nowhere he could land.

That Monday morning, on my way to the Dar al-Kotob Archives, I walked across the Kasr-al-Nil Bridge that links the island of Zamalek with the rest of Cairo. There was the usual heavy morning traffic. Scores of little Fiats, donkey carts, bicycles, school buses, tricycles carrying meat and produce—all rushing across the bridge.

Suddenly the sky cracked. Everyone stopped and looked up, as if frozen. "It's our planes attacking Israel," someone shouted. The deafening sound overhead was, in fact, the sound of antiaircraft missiles. It was a sound that would become familiar. The bridge seemed to tilt as everyone tried to get off. I rushed to a nearby kiosk with a radio. A crowd had gathered to listen to the news bulletin. "Fifty more planes shot down ... seventy-three planes shot down ... No, we have just heard that the Egyptian armed forces have shot down a hundred and fifteen Israeli planes," shouted the announcer. People were ecstatic. We were winning the war against Israel. There was so much excitement in the streets that no one went to the air raid shelters. But sirens screeched everywhere. The last thing I heard on the radio before I set off for Zamalek was that Americans were flying the Israeli planes. America was fighting on the Israelis' side.

The panic in the streets had intensified. Members of the Arab Socialist Union were going around in trucks, trying to stave off the panic. All the while, the shouting and screaming of the people mingled with the cracking of antiaircraft batteries.

My heart pounding, I let myself into the apartment and tried the phone. There was no line. With nothing to do but wait, I opened the windows so that the sound of the aircraft would not shatter the glass. Trembling, I sat down. It seemed at that moment that my entire life, like my countrymen's, had been turned upside down. What if Cairo were bombed, destroyed? I went out on the terrace. The Nile glistened indifferently. But somewhere out there, the Egyptian army was being destroyed.

Like the other inhabitants of Zamalek, I was trapped on the island for days. There was no way of communicating with the rest of Cairo. Finally, I was able to reach my parents and in-laws. Amin had sent a message to say he was safe. I was not to move. The streets were barricaded. Curfews were imposed. Egyptian men were dying on the front. We were not winning, we were losing.

At night, the city was silent and dark. Only the voice of the qarawan could be heard. How strange, when I looked out from the terrace, to be greeted with this enveloping blackness. Egypt, Egypt. The name resounded with pain. Silence responded. I knew at that moment that I would never be closer to my country. I knew that my life would always be linked to Egypt. Whatever I did to escape it, or to keep it at an intellectual distance, was useless. I was just a molecule in the atmosphere, one of millions of molecules, but I was inseparable from the rest. Pain binds. Suffering was our adhesive. My life, my pain was insignificant now. All that mattered was Egypt.

•

In the morning I went to the Gezira Club to find out more news about the war. People were gathered around everywhere, exchanging the latest rumors. Families listened attentively to their transistor radios. The atmosphere was filled with tension and frustration.

Suddenly, a well-known Marxist lawyer got to his feet and burst out: "We have lost the war. We have lost the war. Our men are out there, dying in the desert, and we are here, sipping lemonade. Shame, shame!" Then he wept. No one seemed surprised by what he'd said. We had all felt it ourselves. Everyone became silent. I felt like a traitor. The United States, the country I had loved so dearly, was behind all this.

That night as I sat on the terrace I heard the rumbling of large motor vehicles below. The moon revealed a procession of army trucks moving slowly. As they made their way through the tree-shaded streets, I saw that they were covered with canvas sheets, beneath which shapes were piled high. Blood trickled from the truck onto the pavement. I followed the sound of the trucks as they drove into the distance. They were gone, and the silence took over once more—a silence broken only by the occasional lament of the qarawan.

By June 9, we all knew that Egypt had suffered a devastating defeat. The Israelis had done in the air what they had done on the ground—destroyed the Arab forces before they had gotten going. Napalm was the principal weapon. The Israelis had pounded Egyptian armor, transport, and soldiers in the open desert. It seems that they knew all the Egyptian army codes, and with the assistance of the U.S. intelligence ship *The Liberty,* they had sent false orders over Egyptian wavelengths to confuse our divisions in the Sinai and bring them out to exposed positions where the Israelis could get at them easier. Ten thousand Egyptian soldiers were killed or died of thirst in the desert.

Because of the curfews and demonstrations in the streets, it was difficult to get about in the city. I certainly could not go to Heliopolis. So when my mother-in-law asked me over to hear

Nasser speak that evening, I accepted. I did not want to be alone when Nasser announced that we had lost the war.

As I drove the short distance from Zamalek to Garden City, I noticed that there were so many sandbags in front of the Hilton Hotel that its facade was hardly visible. There were sandbags everywhere: on Kasr-al-Nil Bridge, in front of government buildings, and even apartment blocks. I barely recognized my mother-in-law when I saw her. She was not wearing any makeup and her shoulders slumped. Her eyes were clouded with anxiety. I realized how worried about Amin she was. Suddenly I felt a great sense of compassion for her and for all the mothers whose sons were at the front. I was glad I was not a mother at that moment. As I took my place on the couch next to her, in their wood-paneled study, my own thoughts turned to Amin. After all he was my husband. We had been through so much together. I didn't want anything to happen to him.

The Nubian butler brought in two cups of tea on a silver tray. He placed them gravely on the small table before us. My mother-in-law asked him to turn on the television. "He'll be on in a few moments," she said as we listened to the military music coming from the set. Outside, the street was suddenly very quiet. The sound of a transistor radio filtered into the room from the kitchen where the servants were also waiting for the speech.

A few moments later, Nasser's gaunt face appeared on the screen. He spoke slowly and painfully in plain, colloquial Arabic. We had suffered a *nakba,* a setback, he said. Then he began to analyze the events that led up to the attack of June 5. On May 26, President Johnson had warned him that if Egypt struck first, the consequences for us would be serious. The next day, at 3.30 A.M., the Russians cautioned him not to open fire. But Israel had attacked and we had lost the war because the United States had actively helped Israel. The United States, he said, was an imperialistic power which sought to control the world, and to dominate Egypt as well. He was not prepared to accept this. Therefore, he said, and here he wept, he would hand

57

the responsibility of leadership to Zakkaria Muhieddin. He accepted the responsibility for the defeat.

The minute the speech ended, there was a commotion in the streets. I went to the window and looked out. Hundreds of people were running around, shouting, weeping, and waving placards. "I wonder what's happening," I said to my mother-in-law. She was weeping. "He shouldn't have resigned," she said. "The country needs him." I looked at her in astonishment. She used to complain so bitterly about Nasser—he had confiscated her property. And now she was weeping. Yet, I knew her tears were sincere. I went back to the window. Thousands of people were now gathered, all shouting the same refrain: "Nasser, Nasser, Nasser." In that moment my mother-in-law had also become one of the people, and to her, as to millions of Arabs, Nasser was a great leader, a hero, a symbol of Egypt, just like the pharaoh of ancient times.

The uproar outside increased. For seventeen straight hours, the people shouted "Ya, Nasser, Nasser, Nasser, zaim al chaab, ahna m'aak. Lan naqbal al hazima. Nasser, Nasser, Nasser. We will not accept defeat. We are for you."

The Egyptian National Assembly refused to accept Nasser's resignation, but the reality of defeat soon began to sink in. People began to ask why we had been defeated. A series of analytical articles on our defeat appeared in the leading paper *Al-Ahram*. Abdel Hakim Amer, the commander of the armed forces, was arrested on August 26, along with fifty other officers. A tribunal was formed to judge them. In February 1968 massive student demonstrations against the army took place, and in November similar demonstrations took place against the police. Discontent was rampant. Only the most stringent measures by the police kept the country from civil war.

On November 22, 1967, Nasser accepted UN Resolution 242 which stipulated that Egypt, Syria, and Jordan would end the war with Israel, provided that Israel withdraw from all territories occupied in the 1967 war. It also stated that both Israel and the Arabs had a right to live in peace within secure and recognized boundaries. A just settlement of the Palestinian refugee problem was also included. Israel rejected the UN resolution.

My father's health was failing. He, too, was shattered by the defeat. Amin never mentioned the war, but I could sense his despair when he came home each week. Like everybody else, I grew more and more depressed with each passing day. There was a mood of helplessness and frustration which was contaminating everybody. Nasser told us that we must wipe out the traces of the setback, but that is not so easy when people have lost faith in their government, even in themselves.

I felt I was drowning and looked desperately for something to hang on to: my uncompleted degree remained my only salvation. That would mean returning to my once beloved America, now an enemy country.

I LOOKED out of the window of the plane. The glittering aerial view of Cairo had been transformed into a somber wasteland by the blackout. I took a deep breath and sat back in my seat, feeling almost intoxicated by the plastic smell of the jet. Even the safety signals FASTEN SEAT BELTS and NO SMOKING beckoned me to freedom. My spirits soared with the upward motion of the aircraft. I wanted the jet to go faster, faster, to carry me beyond myself, where all would be forgotten, where I would be released from painful memories and dark images.

As the plane began its descent, I felt myself become slightly anxious because I had heard that Arabs were being given a hard time at New York's airport. Once off the plane, I stood in line with the "Non-Citizens." Some of us started to look anxiously in the direction of the glass cubicle where our passports would be screened. Many of the "aliens" looked shabby by comparison to the U.S. citizens in the nearby line. As I got closer to the front of the line, I scrutinized the immigration official within the glass cubicle. Was he Jewish? I wondered. Does he hate Arabs? My turn had come. He knew exactly which way to read the Arabic passport. "Give me your 1-20 form," he snapped. I searched my handbag with a beating heart, thinking I might have lost it. But it was there and I handed it over, only to have him leaf through the passport again. "Is anything wrong?" I asked. Without answering he picked up his rubber stamp and brought it down on my document.

"Anything to declare?" asked the customs official. "No, I'm a student," I said, trying to sound cheerful. "Open your suitcase," he ordered. First one suitcase, then the other, was overturned—books, sweaters, underwear, stockings, pictures of my family poured out. He was searching my luggage, but he should have been searching my heart, for it was there that I concealed my hostility for America. I was no longer the girl who in 1964 so ardently believed in the U.S.A. The 1967 war had changed that. I began to repack my suitcases, hurriedly shoving everything in. Finally, I managed to lock both suitcases and to lug first one and then the other onto the swift conveyer belt.

"Your country is not very popular here at this moment," my academic adviser, looking at me over his bifocals, said. It was a sunless day in November and Urbana was already covered in snow. There was an antiseptic smell, the odor of academe, in his book-strewn office on the second floor of the theater building. The linoleum floor glistened. Professor Charles's face looked unchanged. It was the face of a man in whose life nothing seemed to happen. "Yes, I am told that there is so much hostility that Arabs in America are afraid to admit they are Arabs," I said. He merely smiled. "I'm very glad to see you again, Laila."

That evening I was invited to dinner at his home. His wife, a slender white-haired woman, greeted me with unexpected warmth. When I was in Urbana the first time, she had always been indifferent to me. "We were all wondering if you would make it back," she said. The dinner around the oak table, the log fire, the bookshelves and theater posters welcomed me back into their rarefied world. I looked outside at the white landscape, the wood-framed houses, the pine trees and for the first time in many months, I was filled with peace.

The following day, Professor Charles and I met again in his office. "Your research is exemplary," he said. "But we need more of the plays in translation." "But there are forty plays," I said. "Well, just short excerpts from plays which are representative of each period in Rihani's development is all that is needed," he replied. I must have looked rather glum upon hearing of this time-consuming project. "I have arranged for some financial assistance for you," he continued. "So, I will have to write a second draft, to incorporate all this new material," I said. "Yes," came the answer. "How is your husband?" he asked. I stammered something incoherent. "I hope that you will be able to concentrate on this task. We don't need another student with an uncompleted dissertation," he said. I nodded my head to show him that I understood.

Paul, whom I had contacted upon arrival in the United States, often visited me, commuting the distance between his campus and mine. On the weekends our friendship deepened, and our lives converged. He, too, was an outsider in the Midwest. Paul was a European whom World War II had made a refugee. Sometimes he would recite poetry in his native tongue, moving me with the sadness of his intonation and the tears which inevitably appeared in his eyes.

We would take long walks together in the frozen parks. Warming my hand, he would look into my eyes and tell me over and over again that he loved me, as if to obliterate everything with this redundancy; as if to give me all he knew I missed—my country, my father, my sister, the Nile—with the repetition of the phrase. I could not convince him that in spite of having no family, no friends, no country, no money, I was happy just to be free.

For I did feel happy. I had a purpose in my work—and there was nothing false in my existence now, no pretense, no hypocrisy, no frustration. And besides, I was in love. The man walking beside me in the snow, so different from Amin, was a man I had chosen. There were no priests, no gabanyots, no signatures, no obligations, no codes to be respected, just love.

Back at home we would have long conversations about art, philosophy, theater, and music. We talked about our lives, our marriages, our dreams. And through these conversations I began to define myself. Consciousness illuminated previous instincts and actions, and I began to understand why I had acted the way I had in the past. When we were both too tired to speak any longer, we would curl up on the couch and listen to records, letting the music express our love.

During simple candlelit dinners, he would amuse me with university gossip or tell me the latest news of Egypt and Israel. I was soothed by his political analysis because he was so ardently pro-Arab. Besides, he had become my only link with the outside world. All of my time was spent at home writing my dissertation. But I welcomed this solitude, which gave me time for reflection, self-discovery, and redefinition.

In Paul's arms, I discovered my body. He held me as if every time would be the last, maybe because we had thought we would never see each other again, or because we were aching to express what we had been afraid to even think of in Cairo, or because he, too, was uprooted, a refugee always in search of that eternal place.

The winter passed and the snow gave way to leaves on the trees and the glorious sound of birds. The warmer weather encouraged me to get out, and occasionally I would meet with some of the other Egyptian students on campus. We spoke of nothing but the political situation at home, complaining about the Israeli bias in the American press and how, with the single exception of the *Christian Science Monitor,* we couldn't find a single paper expressing the Arab viewpoint. We protested to the editors of this or that paper or magazine in long letters, which we were too discouraged even to mail. We phoned each other excitedly whenever there was a phone call from Egypt through which political news had been filtered. Or we simply prepared Egyptian food together or told each other the latest political jokes.

My father's correspondence had become increasingly evasive about political matters. He continually wrote things like "Everything is fine," or, "We are all very well." In many of his letters he told me he would come and visit me in America, as if to say I shouldn't think of returning to Egypt just yet. For the situation, judging by the American press, was tense. Nasser was rebuilding the armed forces and had set up a new defense line, which Israel attempted to crush through frequent merciless air raids within Egypt. The Israeli bombings, which succeeded in blowing up an important bridge in upper Egypt and destroying crucial power transformers at Naj Hamadi, demoralized the population. The Israelis even attempted to lay mines at the barrages, the dams below Cairo, thereby threatening our entire irrigation system.

Though the Arab-Israeli conflict was the only political reality for me, I was not entirely oblivious to American politics. This was 1968 and the anti-Vietnam movement was in full gear. I followed these events with particular admiration for those who burned their draft cards. What I appreciated most of all was the freedom of speech. The papers were full of criticism of the president and the war, but the government did nothing to ban it. For me, this was astonishing. In Egypt, these writers and their editors would have been fired or jailed.

One day I heard a lecture on campus by an American Jew, who was, of all things, pro-Arab! His name was Alfred Lilienthal and he was the guest of the Arab student organization on campus. Lilienthal's lecture, "The Other Side of the Coin," packed the student union with Arab and Israeli students. Lilienthal, a thin, graying intellectual, asserted that the prospect of peace between the Arabs and Israel had become an "impossible dream" because of Israel's expansionist policies. He attacked the establishment of a military society in Israel and held it responsible for provoking the 1967 war against the Arabs. The Israeli students booed him, frequently preventing him from continuing his talk. The Arab students cheered. I couldn't believe that he had been "allowed" to talk like this in a pro-Israeli society. It was my first realization that there are American Jews who are not advocates of the Israeli state.

I was also discovering the liberating effect the sixties had on theater. On campus, Megan Terry's *Viet Rock,* an anti-Vietnam play, introduced me to anti-establishment, experimental theater. Traditional conceptions of theater were being reformed in Jean-Claude Van Itallie's *America Hurrah,* a critique of the American dream, and in the "ritual performance" of *The Serpent,* a play about creation which celebrated the original, "religious" function of theater by bringing people together in a communal ceremony where actors and audience participate in a kind of eucharist. In the work of the Living Theatre, there was no plot, no characterizations, nothing but actors confronting their audiences as themselves. The plays of LeRoi Jones (Amiri Baraka) and Ed Bullins added revolution to confrontation.

The radicalization of women had not yet affected me personally in those days, although there was one woman in particular who fascinated me and whose picture I often saw in the comme il faut women's magazines like *Glamour* and *Mademoiselle* which I was reading then. Her name was Gloria Steinem. She wore glasses, and even though she was a model, it was clear she was intelligent. I learned that she was a journalist with a degree from Smith College. If I was leafing through a magazine and saw her picture, I would buy it immediately. The combination of beauty and intellect in her fascinated me. Little did I suspect that one day our realities would converge.

I wondered if my dissertation would ever be ready. I had been working on it day and night for ten months. But one day, "The Development of Comedy in Egypt Before the Revolution" was finally completed. After handing it in to the examining committee, feeling both exhausted and relieved at once, I was asked to appear before the oral panel.

As I walked into the room, I immediately sensed an atmosphere of approval, perhaps because I was one of only two women in the department completing her Ph.D. or because they thought I would not make it. My neatly typed manuscript lay on the table. I had devoted such scholarly attention to Rihani and the other muchakhasatiya of Egyptian theater, but now I wondered if I had managed to capture their spirit in this academic study. I tried to look composed as I sat opposite my professors, some of whom, like Barnard Hewitt, were famous theater historians. Yet I wanted to tell them that four years of my life were in that manuscript—a broken marriage, an abortion, a love affair.

Instead, I answered jargon with jargon, playing academic Ping-Pong with as much skill as I could muster: "How were you able to distinguish the authentic texts from the plagiarized ones?" Line-by-line verification, I answered. "What methodology did you use in your research?" Chronological. "Rihani adapted his plays from other sources. Doesn't that tarnish his validity as the 'creator' of social comedy in Egypt?" Shakespeare worked from adaptations. Does that tarnish his validity? "Did you find Jacob Landau's book, *Studies in the Arab Theatre and Cinema,* a useful source?" It has an excellent bibliography. "Who in the American theater resembles Rihani?" Edward Harrigan. They were pleased.

Two hours later I left the theater building alone, and feeling quite numb. As I stood at the bus stop, I wondered if anyone looking at me could tell that I had just obtained my doctorate.

"Hiya," said the bus driver, who recognized me from my frequent trips between the campus and home. I entered the house where I occupied the small room in which I had done my work. I went to the refrigerator for a glass of water and then I sat down and wept tears of unrestrained joy and triumph. At home, on such an occasion, they would have slaughtered a calf.

"What are your plans now?" everyone asked. I told them I would eventually be returning home, but in the meantime, I asked my professors for letters of recommendation. I was hoping to find a teaching job. "There are no jobs in the theater except in costuming," said the head of the department with a patronizing smile. But I was not discouraged. I had nothing to lose. There were no prospects of a job in Cairo and I had acquired a taste for freedom.

I wrote my father to divulge my plan. My mother wrote back immediately to say that I should return to Cairo, at least for a while to keep up appearances! I did not reply and began to send out letters of application.

A couple of months passed and I received only rejections. The position, they wrote, required someone with experience. But I kept on applying, sending as many as ten letters a week. Paul helped to keep up my spirits during this period. Six months went by and still nothing. In order to support myself, I took a job shelving books in the English department library. Occasionally my father had some money smuggled out of Egypt for me.

By the time April came around, I was full of despair. It was hopeless. Better to admit defeat, I told myself, while I opened the mail which had become so oppressive. Then toward the end of April, I received a letter from Lawrence University in Wisconsin: they were inviting me for an interview. Too good to be true. But true it was.

I got off the plane in a tiny provincial airport feeling nauseated from the flight and nervous as hell. A small delegation awaited me. As we shook hands, I could sense their astonishment. Was I too young, too attractive, too Egyptian? When I took the plane home in the evening, I was drained and anxious.

A couple of weeks went by and I did not hear from them. Despair filled me once more. I would have to return to Egypt; there was no other way to survive. Of course, there was the possibility of marrying Paul, who spoke of leaving his wife and who urged me to divorce Amin. But the concept of marriage was anathema to me. I wanted to earn my own money. I knew this was the secret of a woman's independence.

Then one beautiful spring day, as I sat drinking my coffee, I heard the postman and I rushed downstairs to my mailbox. The letter was there. I brought it back upstairs and left it on the table. I was afraid to open it. I put on a favorite Mozart concerto in the hope that the music would calm my nerves. Then I went up to the letter and picked it up. So what if I didn't get the job? I told myself as I held it in my hand. I *could* return to Egypt, to my father, my mother, my sister, the sunshine. After all, my life in America was unreal. A career, independence, what nonsense. Don't fool yourself, I told myself, it's not the rejection you are afraid of, it's going back to Cairo. But, of course, it's the rejection too. You've become competitive, just like an American. Besides, you have no business staying on. You should return to your country and do something for it.

Then the phone rang. It was Professor Charles wanting to know how I was doing. I opened the letter. "I'm fine," I said. "By the way, I just got a job in Wisconsin."

67

THREE YEARS PASSED. In a small town in Wisconsin, time goes by imperceptibly. But certain things stand out. The first class, the first faculty meeting, the first production I directed, the first walkout by the students in protest of U.S involvement in Cambodia. And the beauty of the Wisconsin landscape remains vivid: the vales, the forests, the rivers, the Indian summer with its crackling leaves, the snow-covered cottages.

I was a demanding teacher and I alienated many students. And being a woman didn't make things easier—the faculty ignored me. Nonetheless, I knew I was being scrutinized, my performance monitored. My first production, *Ring Around the Moon* by Anouilh, was successful, but received mixed reviews. There were those among the radical students who did not feel this farce about the relation of money to happiness was of any relevance to American life in 1969. I advocated the theory that theater must remain above daily events, must retain its purity.

Paul helped me survive this first job with his frequent weekend visits. We had a life of our own now. But we had to conceal it from everyone, for I was still a married woman. My sister Asma kept up a regular correspondence with me and it was she who gave me all the gossip from Cairo. They were saying that I had run away from my husband and that I would not return.

The messy reality I left behind in Cairo did not disturb me on a day-to-day basis. That first year I was absorbed and challenged by my work. To teach *The Voyage of the Beagle* or *The Re-*

public and even such books as *Bury My Heart at Wounded Knee* was engrossing, to say the least, because I had never read such books myself. Then there were endless plays to read and to communicate to my students. They were bright kids, though often cheeky, but I always managed to remain in control. My colleagues in the department were not exactly supportive. One in particular, a homosexual, found me very threatening, and one day I received a note from him informing me that his "balls were still intact." Otherwise, contact with the faculty at Lawrence was thankfully sparse. Gradually, though, I began to make friends in the art department, the music department, and even the English department. Soon I was invited to participate in seminars with such titles as "The Dramatic Elements in Walter Scott's 'The Lady of the Lake.'"

Professionally, things were going well and my relationship with Paul was also deepening. Sex became integral to it and I marveled at the transformation in me since the days when I would lie back frigidly while my husband took his pleasure.

But as the months and then the years went by, I began to realize that something was missing. I had taken refuge from reality, allowing my dreams to guide me; yet, I felt isolated and uprooted. I missed Egypt and felt I had turned my back on it. And I missed my father and Asma terribly. To make matters worse, I experienced hostility from Jewish faculty. Even the civility of academic life cannot conceal such deeply ingrained prejudices. As time went by, I became increasingly alienated. "I will always be a foreigner," I told Paul one day. "We are all foreigners here," came his answer. "Have you forgotten how alienated you were in Cairo?" he added. "But it was different there, I wasn't working," I replied. I at least have a country, I told myself. "You're a product of Nasser's revolution. You're a patriot," Paul said teasingly. "I'm an Egyptian," I replied.

At home, a new kind of war was going on—the "war of attrition," as it was called. In retaliation to the Israeli air raids which had become almost daily occurrences, Nasser had launched a series of guerrilla raids against the Israeli forces in the Sinai. The

Israelis hit back even harder at civilian targets, and not satisfied with having destroyed the Suez Canal towns, they now struck deep into the Egyptian mainland. In January 1970, they bombed a factory just outside Cairo at Abou-Zaabal: seventy workers were killed. In April they bombed a school, killing fifty children.

"They may even go so far as to bomb Cairo," said an Egyptian on campus. Full of panic and anxiety, I tried to get through to my family. It was impossible. I sent a telegram. My father sent one back telling me he would call me on a given day. We had a cousin who worked for the telephone system in Cairo and she was going to help. That day, I sat next to the telephone for hours until it finally rang. "Allo, allo, this is Cairo calling," said a familiarly accented voice. Then my father got on the line, his voice vibrating with emotion: "Everything is fine here. Couldn't be better." Censorship must be at its peak, I thought. "Are you keeping warm? Are you getting enough to eat?" he was asking. Yes, yes, I was. There was barely a minute left and I still had so much to ask. Sensing this my father quickly said, "Asma wants to say hello," and the receiver was passed to Asma who joked and giggled for the remaining minute. "Khalass al-mukalma kholset, the time is up," the operator said. And the line went dead.

But Cairo was in danger. It had no air defense at all, a fact which obviously encouraged the Israelis to accelerate their air raids. In January 1970, Nasser had gone to Moscow to ask the Kremlin to supply Egypt with air defense—missiles, aircraft, and the crews to man them. They were promised for April. Until then, Egypt would lie open to its enemy like a woman about to be raped.

On April 18, the Israelis had their first brush with the newly arrived Russian reconnaissance planes. The signal that the Russians had arrived in Egypt had been received. The Israeli deep-penetration raids were over.

More and more my thoughts were turning to my father. I would think of him in different situations and at different times of his day. In the morning, drinking Turkish coffee and reading *Al-Ahram* cover to cover. At breakfast, drinking heavily saccharined tea with an assortment of no less than twenty sugar-coated pills; at his clinic, wearing his white coat and lead apron, glancing at X rays in the blue light of his laboratory; or writing at his Gothic desk, his two fingers and his entire concentration on the portable Smith-Corona before him.

He was to have a seventieth birthday that summer, and I wrote urging him and my mother to visit me in Wisconsin. They were due to arrive on a warm August day and I felt quite overcome by emotion as I watched the tiny Ozark plane land. My father was wearing his English tweed suit with the waistcoat. He was thin and his face drawn, yet he walked energetically toward me. We hugged each other tightly, unable to speak for the tears. My mother stood behind him, keeping at bay. I went over to her and kissed her dutifully. I returned to my father and asked, "How is your heart?" He replied in English, "Thumping with joy, like a schoolboy's." We laughed and hugged one another again.

"What an impressive automobile," commented my father as we got into my used Camaro. He couldn't believe I could afford a car. At home we sipped tea, while he commented admiringly on how comfortable my apartment was. But soon, inevitably, the conversation turned to politics: "Nasser has destroyed the country. The economy has collapsed, the city has collapsed, and the morale has collapsed." "It's not that bad," said my mother. "Your father as usual is exaggerating." "Then why are thousands, hundreds of thousands, fleeing?" asked my father testily, and then he added, "I only want to live long enough to see the day when Egypt will be delivered from Nasser."

One day, as we were driving home from the supermarket, a news flash on the radio caused me to stop the car almost in the middle of the road. "It has just been learned that Gamal Abdel Nasser, the president of the United Arab Republic, has died." My mother started to weep loudly and I began to feel the tears choking my throat. My father's reaction was very different. He took the news in silence and then after instinctively looking around, for he had once again forgotten that he was not in Egypt and that no one was watching us, he said, "Thank God we are rid of him! This is the best thing that has happened to Egypt in years. Maybe now things will finally change!"

At the airport a couple of weeks later, my father hugged me and urged me to return home—now that the dictator had died, as he put it. I watched the plane take off, wondering if I would ever see my father alive again. I also wondered if things would change for the better in Egypt, as my father had predicted.

On October 15, 1970, the National Assembly elected Mohammed Anwar al-Sadat the new president of Egypt.

It had been a long, dull winter. Paul was becoming possessive, jealous, and we quarreled. I was becoming irritable, and often felt like a dutiful wife. Moreover, the long hours of being locked up in an apartment, an office, or a theater auditorium were starting to make me feel claustrophobic. I yearned for sunshine and the freedom of summer. I was tired of the snow, tired of the monotony of small-town life, tired of the academic angst of the faculty: publish or perish, as if nothing else mattered. Above all, I was tired of the grayness of the indistinguishable lives I saw around me, tired of being an academic wet-nurse and an intellectual nanny.

Then, something happened which restored my energy. When I checked my mailbox at the university I found a telegram from Professor Ramsis, now the dean of the Egyptian Institute of the Theatre in Cairo, offering me a job there. When I got home, Paul was there. He was listening to the sad, haunting Trio in D Major by Beethoven. I sat down next to him on the couch, our silence more articulate than any words could be, our sadness matched only by the music. I did not mention the telegram.

But one evening, I could contain myself no longer. "How would you feel if I returned to Cairo for a while?" Paul looked straight into my eyes, and to avoid his gaze I began to clear the table. "You know I cannot join you there. I have no prospects of a job in Cairo. But I will be due for a sabbatical in two years. Can't you wait? Besides, I thought we were planning to get

married?" "I'm tired of this job, and even if I find a job somewhere else, it will be the same thing. I will just sink into oblivion. Be a nobody. There is a challenge waiting for me in Cairo. I
can feel it in my bones," I replied. "And us?" he said. I did not
reply.

After he was gone, at the end of the weekend, I sat alone with
my thoughts. Did it make any sense to loosen Amin's bonds in
order to acquire Paul's? Marriage—there is such finality in that
word. But why resent a word when one loves the man? It must
be the excitement at the idea of working in the theater in Cairo,
I reasoned. Why not? I had a right to think of my career. I had
paid for it. But my life, even my work, would be empty without
Paul. No, I couldn't give up Paul. But I did not sleep that night.

"April is the cruelest month," wrote Eliot. Yes, April would
be a cruel month. I would have to make a decision. "Breed-
ing / Lilacs out of the dead land, mixing / Memory and desire,
stirring / Dull roots with spring rain." It was Egypt that was
being resurrected within me, Egypt with all its upheavals and
sorrows. It was Egypt that had emerged from the "forgetful"
snow.

One wet, gloomy day that April, during a particularly tedious
departmental meeting my attention began to stray and I looked
out of the chairman's window. A film of snow still covered the
lawn. The winter had been too long. I looked at the impassive
faces of my colleagues and then I asked to be excused.

As I drove home, I looked at the park which led to my apartment building. Suddenly I knew that I would be leaving these
beautiful surroundings and I began to feel sad. Sad at the
knowledge of what I was about to give up.

Paul was at the apartment when I got there. I sat down and
searched for words. "Is something wrong?" he said. I looked up
at him, wondering if anyone would ever know me as well as he
did. I knew no one would. The realization caused me to feel an
almost physical pain in my stomach. But the words had already
been formed and were resounding in the room. "Paul, I have
been offered a job in Cairo and I have decided to accept it." He

said nothing. He went to the bedroom. I thought he was avoiding a discussion. I waited for a few minutes and then I went to him. I found him on the floor. He was slumped over, his head buried in his knees. "Paul," I said softly. He lifted his head without looking at me. His face was drained and he kept staring into space.

As a long-parted mother with her child
Plays fondly with her tears and smiles
  in meeting,
So, weeping, smiling, greet I thee,
  my earth . . .

—Richard II

G OOD AFTERNOON, ladies and gentlemen. Welcome to TWA's flight 748 to Cairo. We will be flying at an altitude of . . ." I sat back in my seat, trying to make myself as comfortable as possible for the twelve-hour flight ahead. "Please fasten your seat belts and observe the no smoking sign." My mind drifted from the metallic voice to my father's letters of the past couple of weeks. The "new man," as my father liked to call Anwar al-Sadat, was changing things for the better. Nasserism was being dismantled.

In December 1970, barely two months after he had come into power, Sadat issued a presidential decree lifting the sequestrations from all those who had their property confiscated by Nasser. It was a move to appease the bourgeoisie, but it was also a step toward democracy. People did not fear him as they feared Nasser, wrote my father, so there was nothing to worry about. The reign of terror had come to an end. My father's letters were filled with optimism. He was sure everything would be set right again and Egypt would be saved. Sadat was rumored to be pro-West. He would open up the country and the people would be free again. As I sat in the airliner, my thoughts churning with memories of the past and visions of the future, I too began to feel optimistic. Maybe a new era was about to begin for Egypt. But I knew with certainty that a new era was about to begin for me. The hours flew as my thoughts ran by with feverish excitement.

"Please fasten your seat belts. We are about to land at Cairo airport. It is seven P.M. and 110 degrees." I braced myself for the descent.

As I stepped off the plane, the hot, dry desert air caressed me. The airport was in semi-darkness and everything looked shabby and poor, but in Egypt, poverty has a smiling face. All around me, I heard "Hamdellah ala al-salama, welcome back." The effects of the war were still visible. Soldiers carrying bayonets could be found at every turn. Sandbags and barbed wire surrounded us. Broken windowpanes, the glass jagged, were still painted blue in case of blackouts. Five years in America had almost erased that reality from my mind. But now I was face-to-face with it again: that dreaded, beloved reality of Egypt.

I was pushed all over the place. There was a continuous flow of commotion as everyone tried to push their way to the inspection window at once. Finally, I reached the officer behind the glass cubicle to whom I could present my passport. He leafed through it. Why had I been away so long? Was I home for good? An endless stream of relevant and irrelevant questions. Finally, the passport was stamped and I was admitted into my country.

The customs official asked to see my passport. "Amreeka, ha," he said sarcastically. Then he asked me to open my suitcases. He inspected my clothes, piece by piece. Then after scrutinizing the titles of my books and periodicals, he nodded his head in satisfaction. "Hamdellah ala al-salama," he said. Seeing my confusion at the strewn belongings, he picked up a few items and helped me lock my suitcase, saying, "Yallah, yallah, come on, come on." As I pushed my cart out of the airport, I was overwhelmed by the screaming mass of people at the gate. Policemen in white uniforms stood at the far end of the gate. I waved my passport and I was allowed to pass. Then I caught sight of my family. Before I knew it I was being shoved from one perspiring embrace to another. "Wahashtina, ya Laila. Ezayek ya rohi, hamdellah ala al-salama. We've missed you. Welcome home." I was in my father's arms. How frail he had become. Every muscle showed through his face. My mother gave me her cheek to kiss and my brother, Nabil, now a tall, young man, shook my hand. Then I was in Asma's arms. As she hugged me her eyes sparkled, her voice vibrated with welcome. Then, all of a sudden, I caught sight of Amin, who was wearing his military uniform. "Have I been forgotten as usual?" he asked. We shook hands as everyone looked away.

As Amin walked ahead with my luggage my mother came up to me and whispered, "We must keep up appearances for the sake of your father's reputation." Amin put my luggage in his car as if nothing had changed. But things had changed. I had changed. I was free now. But the word echoed with mockery as I got into my husband's car.

As Amin brought in my luggage, I looked around at my former cage. Nothing had changed in the Zamalek apartment and yet it no longer seemed threatening. I sat down on the blue couch. My books and records were in place. But I felt freed from them as well. I needed no escape now. I was like a guest checking into a hotel and I knew it was only a matter of time before I would check out. Meanwhile Amin could pretend that his wife had returned to him.

Amin's parents arranged a special lunch. The family silver which had been discreetly locked up in the Nasser days was now displayed in all its sterling grandeur. The vases were filled with gladiolas and roses, and a festive air permeated the catacomb of an apartment with its long winding corridors. As I sat around the table listening to my in-laws, I felt like a complete stranger. But this was a scene which I was compelled to play. I asked polite questions which were replied to with the false British accents characteristic of upper-class Copts with its admixture of Arabic, French, and English. "Of course we're delighted to have the sequestrations lifted," declared my mother-in-law, who was now all sapphired and emeralded again. "I must get a new butler because old A'amed est devenu complètement fou. Khalass, Kharaf khaless." "Old A'amed" was a Nubian who had served the family for over twenty years. "What is going to happen to him?" I asked. "We'll send him back to the village, but Daddy will give him a small pension, won't you, Daddy?" My father-in-law nodded dutifully. "Pass the Gruyère, please, Daddy," she added. Daddy passed the Gruyère. "Are you going away for the summer?" I asked. "I'm thinking of going to Lausanne for the summer and then to Megeve. Netl'aa min albalad di shwaia. Just to get out of this country for a while," added my mother-in-law in English. "Weren't you supposed to visit Cousin Hilda in Paris?" asked one of my husband's cousins. "Je ne sais pas. Ça dépend," came the reply. "It's much easier to get an exit visa these days," chirped my brother-in-law in his pronounced British accent. A thin young man who had grown considerably taller and thinner these past five years, he began to complain about the food in the army where he was serving the compulsory two years. Quite preppie, I thought, as I watched him in his spotlessly clean and pressed white suit. My gaze turned to the servant who was now making his rounds with the second course, his eyes lowered, his turbaned head bowed. As she helped herself to some medium-rare roast beef and Yorkshire pudding, my sister-in-law complained about how boring Cairo was. Amin ate silently. My sister-in-law stopped complaining. I wondered if anyone would inquire about my long absence or whether I had obtained my Ph.D. But no one did. "We ordered the cook to make stuffed grapevine leaves especially for you," said my father-in-law breaking an embarrassing silence.

Things seemed unchanged at the Gezira Club where I went the following day in order to meet Fouad, the university professor who was one of the first people I contacted when I returned to Cairo. Tall, slim, tanned, with silver hair and deep-set eyes, Fouad looked at me through his horn-rimmed glasses, his hand reaching out to touch mine across the table. "Laila, Egypt is changing every second, just like you." "Do you think I've changed?" I asked flirtatiously. After smiling slyly he continued in earnest: "You will see the changes when you start teaching at the institute. The students are more politicized now. Most of them have a brother, an uncle, or a friend at the front. There is ferment in the air and it is up to us to shape the ideas of the new generation," he said, holding my hand tightly. "I'm so glad you're back. Egypt needs you."

"What a pep talk, Fouad," I said laughing, though secretly pleased by what he had said. "Do you know that half the population is now under thirty," he continued undeterred. "They don't have the values you and I have. They were children during the Nasser years and they were cut off from the outside world. It's up to us to give them a sense of direction, ideology, meaning. All they know are the slogans that were pumped into them in primary school. But now slogans have to be replaced with values, for what else is there when society offers no economic opportunities?" I sipped my coffee and looked at him, full of admiration for his ardent nationalism. He leaned over, and speaking passionately, said, "You will meet the sons of peasants, workers, you will know the satisfaction of communicating with them, reaching them. I have no patience with the intellectuals who abandon the country. It's our duty to be here, Laila." I gave him a skeptical look and said, "I think I will be blamed for having spent so much time in the West. I may not even be accepted." "You are an *Egyptian,* Laila," he said, stressing every word.

"Welcome, Dr. Laila," said the president of the Academy of the Arts, extending her hand. Dr. Zeinab, a pioneering Marxist feminist, was the director of the performing arts campus where I was to teach. Her smile was full of the self-assurance of professional women in Egypt. "I will never forget your one-act plays at the Al-Hakim Theater in 1965," she said as I took my seat before her desk. "By the way, mabrouk for the doctora, the Ph.D."

I was then introduced to the other faculty, all males who were outwardly polite but inwardly hostile. They obviously did not like the idea of a Westernized female in their midst. Most of them had been trained in the Soviet Union and other Eastern bloc countries, and I was immediately labeled the "Americaniya."

In spite of this and the fact that the facilities were poor, I left the school feeling quite exhilarated at the prospect of training young actors to become professionals in the Egyptian theater. But classes would not begin until October, which would give me several weeks to rediscover Cairo.

Because of the evacuation of the Suez Canal towns, Cairo now harbored one million refugees who, when lucky enough to find housing, lived two and three families in a room. The housing problem had worsened and all systems—electricity, sewage, transportation, and water—were in poor shape. The streets looked dirtier than I had remembered them and the stores were threadbare by comparison with American shops. Thousands of people made their way to work on foot on broken pavements, while cars raced in the streets, heedless of traffic lights and pedestrians.

Meanwhile, the Israeli bombings continued. It was said that this war of attrition was costing Egypt more than the 1967 war had cost. It was also costing lives. In the middle of 1970, Russian missiles were installed in Egypt by Egyptian civil engineers and workers. Over four thousand of them were killed in daily Israeli raids. It was only after the missiles were installed that Egypt could retaliate, and in the summer of 1970 we learned that six Israeli planes were shot down over the Suez.

The Egyptian army, now reequipped by the Soviet Union, was anxious to fight. The number of Soviet military experts and advisers in Egypt had increased from three thousand to ten thousand. But one month before his death, Nasser had accepted the Rogers Peace Plan which stipulated Israeli withdrawal from territories occupied in 1967 and a ninety-day cease-fire period with the UN mediating a settlement between Egypt, Israel, and the other Arab countries concerned.

Nasser's acceptance of the Rogers Plan had outraged the Palestinians and the other Arab nations, for they, like the army, wanted Egypt to resume the war. The army was discontented. I could sense the frustration everywhere. Fouad became furious when I naively said that the United States was powerless to pressure Israel to withdraw from the occupied territories. "The United States has no intention of pressuring Israel except with conditions that are totally humiliating to the Arabs," he said bitterly. "Israel is perfectly content to allow the war of attrition to continue indefinitely. It is we who are suffering economically, militarily, and psychologically."

The political events of the Arab-Israeli conflict and the internal situation engulfed and overshadowed all our lives. Nonetheless, when I returned home to my Zamalek apartment, a private war of attrition awaited me. The marriage had reached a deadlock but the subject of divorce remained taboo. I decided to get my professional life under control before bringing it up.

One evening I sat with my parents in their garden as my father, in his habitual pajamas, sipped his mint tea. The sun was setting and there was a slight breeze scented by the acacia-mimosa trees. Lying on the table before us was the tape recorder I had brought along to record my father's voice.

Our chatter was aimless family talk. Then suddenly my father asked me how my marriage was going. "Amin and I live like a brother and sister—in every way!" I said, pretending to make a joke of it. My father went pale and said nothing.

When I returned home, I left the tape recorder on the living-room table. Then, after reading a little, I turned off the lights and went to sleep. When I awoke, Amin was gone. I often pretended to be asleep in the mornings in order to avoid conversing with him. In the afternoon, when he came home for lunch, his eyes were full of pain. "What's the matter?" I asked. "I heard the tape," he answered. I was taken aback, but I did not feel guilty. "Amin, this can't go on. I'm sorry," I said. The words had been spoken. I felt that a great weight had been lifted off me. After a moment's silence, he got up and said, "I'm going to see a lawyer tomorrow."

The lawyer, whose office was in a dingy apartment in downtown Cairo, received us in a room lit by neon strips even though it was daylight outside. Sallow, curt, waistcoated, he was careful to avoid emotional subjects. Amin and I sat opposite his desk. Two glasses of lemonade had been set before us. "How long will the divorce take?" I asked. "It will be over very quickly because your husband is initiating and you are both consenting." The office was piled high with dossiers, dust covering the remnants of other arranged marriages. "Of course, you realize that you may never remarry in a Coptic church," he continued. "Your husband has told me that you converted to Protestantism while you were in America. This is an act of denominational betrayal!" "But I only did it to give Amin grounds for divorce," I protested. He raised his hand to silence me, and then getting to his feet, said, "I think that will be all for the time being. I will be in touch with you."

Well, that was very civilized, I thought as I looked at my reflection in the blotched mirror of the elevator which was taking us down. Amin drove me home without uttering a single word.

My family did not oppose the idea of divorce, so I doubted it was they who sent Bishop Samuel, the clergyman who had married us in Washington, to see me one afternoon. If it were not for his long beard, his black robes with their wide sleeves, and his Orthodox, bun-shaped hat, you might never have known that he was a man of the cloth. A former engineer with a theological degree from Princeton, he often had an ironic expression on his face and smiling, mischievous eyes. Bishop Samuel loved food, which made him a great favorite of my father's. The two had many sessions during which matters pertaining to the Coptic community were discussed as they devoured stuffed pigeons or sharkasiva chicken with almond sauce. "Zarna al nabi, the prophet has visited us," my father would say humorously. After the food was brought in, Bishop Samuel would push back his wide sleeves and proceed to eat delectably with his fingers.

Now seated next to me on my couch, he was trying to talk me out of going through with the divorce. "Divorce is strictly forbidden by the Coptic Church," he said. "You will be an outcast from the Coptic community. Marriage is difficult, of course, but when you have children it becomes more tolerable."

I poured him some tea with plenty of sugar in it. Then I offered him a large piece of cake, apologizing for not having more food to offer. He ate the cake quickly and I immediately replaced it. I was actually very fond of Bishop Samuel and admired his crusade to reform the church from within and for his successful social services for the Coptic community: day-care centers, orphanages, schools, and hospitals. He was also a brilliant spokesman for the eight million Copts of Egypt, who he always claimed were suffering a "quiet persecution." But we did not talk about all that now. He was looking at me, expecting my reaction.

"I'm sorry. I must get a divorce," I said almost apologetically. He looked at his watch and then stood, adjusting his leather cross which hung loosely to his waist and beckoning to me majestically. Placing himself in the middle of the room, right in front of my Modigliani prints, he said, "Let us pray to God that He may guide you in your decision." Whereupon a flow of indistinct murmurings issued from his half-closed lips. A few seconds later, he lifted his bowed head and said, "I have to rush now. I have to marry a couple at the Zamalek church. Can you give me a lift? I'm late, you see."

"Laila, you can't let your husband take everything," said my mother on the phone. "You should get to keep the wedding gifts. The silver usually belongs to the wife. Isn't it enough you have returned his shabka—the diamond engagement gift. It's worth a fortune now," she added mournfully. "I don't care about any of that," I said. "I'm even prepared to give him money to get it over with." "Well, I'm coming over to take the German china set I gave you, the dinner set, you remember? I'm not prepared to give it to your husband."

For once I wished I had listened to my mother, for in my haste to free myself of my marriage, I left Amin every single possession we had acquired during our seven-year alliance. Silverware, furniture, linens, and even our American appliances. Property and money were all very far from my mind at that time. The only thing that mattered was to break loose.

The day arrived when Amin knew that I would be leaving the apartment. As he kissed me on the cheeks I saw tears in his eyes.

We told each other we would remain friends. I asked him to ring me up, to keep in touch. I clung to his hand, knowing I would miss him. After he was gone, I packed my suitcases and the few books I would be taking with me. I did not look back as I closed the door behind me for the last time. As I stood on the landing waiting for the elevator, my newly won freedom beckoned me like an enchanting rainbow.

TWO

"I could always live in my art, but not in my life."

—*My Dinner with André*

Sabah al-kheir, good morning, first-year students. Marhaban bikum. Welcome." My first class at the institute was an unforgettable event. I don't ever recall being so nervous. I had prepared for weeks for it, but when I stood before the forty-odd students in the room, my voice quivered. It was as if I had never taught a class before; I desperately wanted them to like me, to accept me.

"Theater is a crucial forum for the communication of ideas," I started to say. They stared at me. I was wearing jeans and my hair was pushed back by my sunglasses—not the usual image of a university teacher in Cairo. I swallowed and continued: "In order to be successful in the theater, you've got to make sacrifices." A young man put up his hand and asked, "Why?" "Because it is a possessive profession, requiring enormous self-discipline and long, long hours. You have got to believe that theater is a *resala,* a mission, and go about it as a missionary would." They looked at me skeptically. I sounded too idealistic, I told myself. "I don't like what's going on in our theaters today—especially in terms of acting styles. Our famous actors and actresses all overact. The melodramatic style is old-fashioned. Have any of you heard of Stanislavsky?" Some of them shook their heads. "Well, I will speak now about his technique involving the realistic style of acting."

I spoke for two hours, after which I felt exhausted. A girl with

87

henna-dyed hair came up to me. "My name is Hoda," she said. "That was a very fine lecture." I smiled in gratitude.

After class I returned to the three-room apartment I had obtained in an apartment building friends of my parents owned. I had made it clear to my family that there would be no question of my returning to live with them, as was customary with divorced women. They did not argue too much. They were eager to show my former in-laws that they could set me up in style. My mother even gave me her Mercedes. An apartment in Garden City and a Mercedes—now that was what comme il faut really was! With my book-lined walls and a new record player, my apartment became a haven, the only place in Cairo where I could unwind.

But people throughout the bourgeois districts of Cairo were shocked, outraged. A divorced woman living alone and driving a Mercedes. What scandal!

The fact that I was being "kept" by my parents bothered me. But my salary at the institute could only pay for food and the utility bills. I yearned nostalgically for my American salary and my used Camaro, paid for with my own money. But since I had become an object of scandal, I resolved to be one in style.

I took my work at the institute very seriously. I announced to my class that we should stage a play. "Let's put on something new, modern," said one of the students. "How about absurdist drama," said another. "Let's do the new Hamlet," said a third. "Why that play?" I asked. "Because it's about young people like us, totally at the mercy of power politics." I was impressed by this analysis and persuaded that Tom Stoppard's play *Rosencrantz and Guildenstern Are Dead,* known to my students as the "new Hamlet," would be an excellent choice.

Since we did not have a fully equipped theater at the institute then, I had to look elsewhere for a stage. It occurred to me that my alma mater, the American University in Cairo, might be a good place to begin the search; and after a couple of meetings with administrators, I was given permission to use the Howard Theatre, a very well-equipped little theater where I had worked in the past. Ecstatic, I told my students the good news, but their reaction was not what I had expected. "Why the American University?" asked one. "Why not?" I replied. My question was greeted with silence. After class, a handful of students came up to me and withdrew from the production. They would not say why.

"Laila, the American University, for these young people, is a bastion of American imperialism," Fouad said later. "They consider it treason even to set foot there. Have you forgotten America's role in the 1967 defeat?" "But AUC is just an academic institution," I protested. "There are rumors that certain of its faculty are CIA agents," he retorted. "This is crazy," I said. "Find another place, Laila; how about Cairo University?" "Their stages are just as poorly equipped as ours," I said in exasperation. "Why is everything so complicated, Fouad?" "You're in Egypt now," he replied.

The American University in Cairo did not make things easier. Special IDs had to be issued for the company and my students were treated as if they were all potential terrorists. More dropped out, but finally, after long weeks of rehearsal, we opened, and I felt as if I had given birth to my first child. We had managed to borrow Elizabethan costumes from the National Theatre, and I used a bare stage. Slides of paintings and drawings by Picasso and Munch were rear-projected at certain intervals of the play in order to emphasize the modernity of the text. The young actors gave compelling performances and were even interviewed on a major talk show. But I had learned a few lessons; above all, that nothing happens in the theatrical life of Cairo which is separable from the political scene. I vowed never again to stage a play at AUC. Nonetheless, by the end of the run, I was triumphant.

"Did you hear the latest joke about Sadat?" asked my sister Asma. "Tell me," I replied. "Well, he's in his limousine and as it approaches a crossroad, the chauffeur asks him which turn he should take. Sadat hesitates for a second and then asks the driver, 'Which one did the late President Nasser, Allah rest his soul, take?' The driver replies without hesitation, 'Left, always left.' So Sadat says, 'In that case, signal left, but turn right!' Asma threw her head back and laughed. She was sitting sideways in an armchair, her legs thrown over one side, her thick, dark, shoulder-length hair hanging loosely about her face, her large brown eyes made up with kohl, sparkling with merriment. That afternoon she wore jeans and an embroidered black shirt. Asma had made a habit of visiting me every day, so I wouldn't get "lonely," as she put it. She did not know how dependent I was becoming on having her in my life.

"There is a new film showing which everybody is talking about," she said after we had stopped laughing. "You must see it, Laila; I will be reviewing it for my journalism class. When it was over, the audience walked away in shock." "Tell me more," I said. "It takes place after the *nakba,* the 1967 defeat, and concerns a group of intellectuals who spend most of their time on a houseboat drinking and taking drugs. One day, a woman journalist is invited to the boat and she is horrified by their political indifference, so she invites them on a picnic. Do you know where she takes them? To the bombed Suez towns! Before this film, the people had never gotten to see what had happened there." She paused to catch her breath. "But there is nothing left of these towns. The Israelis have bombed everything. The intellectuals are shocked out of their lethargy. The journalist preaches at them. They must help rebuild Egypt, she says. But that was done much too propagandistically. There was another scene, which takes place earlier, that was incredible," she continued excitedly. "They leave the houseboat after a night of drinking, to go for a drive at dawn. The car is going very fast on an empty road, when out of the blue, a *fellaha,* a peasant woman, runs across the road. They are too drunk to stop in time, and she is run over and killed." "It sounds very sad," I said. "Do you know what the killing of the fellaha is symbolic of?" "You're impossible," I answered laughingly. "She *is* symbolic of something, you know," Asma said adamantly, "because in our films everything is camouflaged because of censorship. You should go out and see more Egyptian films, Laila," she said with authority. "Well, I'll tell you what the peasant woman's death is symbolic of: do you remember the statue at the entrance of Cairo University, of the Sphinx flanked by a peasant girl with her arm outstretched like this?" She posed for me, her arm positioned as if to keep an imaginary veil from falling. I was trying very hard not to laugh. "*Nahdet Misr* by Mokhtar." I nodded in recollection. "The peasant woman is a symbol of *nahdet misr*, the resurrection of Egypt, and what the film is saying is that a revival of Egypt is still possible, in spite of the 1967 defeat—that is, of course, if people wake up out of their lethargy. Now what do you think of that interpretation?" I was very impressed. When I told her this, Asma was extremely pleased, holding her head up high and pointing her nose into the air in mock conceit. She promised to show me her review later, but then the conversation took an abrupt turn. "Do you think I've lost weight since you saw me last?" she asked. "Pouppa, I saw you yesterday, how can I possibly tell?" I always called her by her nickname when I had no other way of expressing my love for her.

Sadat was becoming increasingly popular. His speeches were candid and he spoke in everyday Arabic rather than literary Arabic as Nasser had usually done. My students at the institute did uncanny imitations of his peasant accent. No one had ever dared to imitate Nasser.

On February 4, I went to my father's home to watch the president deliver a speech to the National Assembly. "This is going to be an important speech," said my father, throwing logs in the fireplace. He was right. Sadat was offering a new initiative to parliament. If Israel would withdraw its forces from the Sinai, he would be willing, he said, to reopen the Suez Canal and to extend the Rogers cease-fire—which had been accepted on August 7, 1970—from three to six months. Then to everybody's astonishment, he went on to say that under these circumstances, he would be willing to restore diplomatic relations with the United States and even to sign a peace agreement with Israel through the intermediary of America. "You see, you see," said my father excitedly, "he wants to build up the country and put an end to this ridiculous war. The man has common sense, not like the other lunatic we had!" My father was never very good at subtle statements. "Drink your mint tea," said my mother. "And don't get so excited. It's not good for your heart."

Fouad was less jubilant when we met a few days later: "If you read the foreign papers, you will discover that Jerusalem has reacted negatively to Sadat's proposal. They have no intention whatsoever of returning to the 1967 borders!"

The man in the street was more positive about Sadat's initiative. As the butcher around the corner put it: "The Soviets do not believe in Allah and besides they are poor and if you are poor you prefer the rich because they can be generous, like Kennedy. Do you remember all the grain we used to get from the Americans then? Let's hope the Americans will bring their wealth here again and it will be good for everyone." Indeed, Cairenes detested the Soviets because their military experts looked down upon the Egyptian military and snubbed the local population. Why didn't they stand beside us like America stood beside Israel, was the rhetorical question asked by all.

On March 7, after receiving no response to his speech of February 4, Sadat appeared on television again to announce that the Rogers cease-fire had expired and that Egypt would no longer be bound to it. On June 5, the anniversary of the 1967 war, Sadat announced that 1971 would be the "year of decision." He vowed that the battle would end one way or another. Then, in a later speech, on the anniversary of the revolution, he proclaimed that "we shall not allow 1971 to pass without deciding the issue through peace or war—even if it means sacrificing one million lives."

But still nothing happened. Sadat was losing credibility. People grew tired of hearing his pronouncements. He became the butt of political jokes. Opposition was growing, especially among the pro-Nasserist Left and the pro-Soviet groups within his cabinet. An influential member of the Executive Committee of the Arab Socialist Union wrote an article in the daily newspaper *Al-Gunhuriya*, in which he denounced all those who "place their hopes in the United States."

Meanwhile the country was being mobilized for war. Black-outs were imposed. There was much talk on TV of how to behave in an air raid. But nothing happened.

On May 2, the newspapers carried a line about the resignation of the vice-president, Ali Sabri. My father phoned me from his clinic. He was very excited: "That's the beginning of the end of that gang, mark my words." He was not the only Egyptian elated by the dismissal of Ali Sabri. People were rejoicing everywhere. The impossible had happened. Ali Sabri, the ogre of the police state, had been sacked. For we all knew that nobody just resigns. Along with other "orthodox" Nasserists, including the minister of the interior, the head of the mukhabarat, the chief of military inelligence, and the former chief of the armed forces, Ali Sabri had spearheaded the opposition to Sadat's presidency, and his powerful clique had refused to resign itself to Sadat's succession. They wanted him to remain the puppet figure he had been under Nasser: a yes-man sent out to inaugurate flower shows.

"But what is *really* behind the opposition against Sadat?" I asked Fouad. We used to meet practically every day now that my academic year had come to an end. "They consider themselves Nasser's rightful heirs. They want power, and they are opposed to Sadat's pro-West leanings, the liberalization programs, the February 4 initiative. They are convinced that Israel will never give up a single inch of the occupied territories, even for a peace treaty with its neighbors. It's a hard line, but it is supported by many students and intellectuals. And, of course, all those who are pro-Palestinian." "I heard rumors that the Soviet Union is behind all this," I said. "Maybe," he replied. "The Gomaa group [Nasserists] would like to see the abolishment of private property." "And Sadat?" I asked. "Sadat is a religious man. Islam protects private property." "What do you think is going to happen now?" "We have to wait and see."

"They have all handed in their resignations," my father said jubilantly as I walked into the house on May 14. "Who?" I

93

asked. "Nasser's men—just like that. But we will know more in a few minutes." We all sat around the TV set to await Sadat's latest speech. "Bismillah, in the name of Allah," said Sadat as soon as he appeared, invoking God before a speech as he usually did. "Bismillah, I will speak to you very frankly, my children, about the events of the past couple of days, which have so shaken our nation. . . ." He had been visited on Thursday night by Nasser's son-in-law, the deputy chief of military intelligence, who informed him of the resignations of the speaker of the National Assembly, the minister of war, the minister of information, the minister of interior, the minister for presidential affairs, and other top political figures. "My children," Sadat said, "it was an attempt to break down the government and to destroy law and order in our country. Well, do you want to know what I did? I accepted their resignations. All of them. It was Allah who guided me in my decision. Then I sent a message to the prime minister to put them all under house arrest. As you know, the telephones are tapped, the mukhabarat taps all our telephones, so I sent my daughter in the middle of the night, with the message to the prime minister!" Sadat then went on to announce that henceforth all tapes of private conversations in the Ministry of Interior would be burned, all political jails would be closed, all political detainees set free, and all arbitrary arrests stopped. It was the most spectacular denunciation of Nasserism that had yet been made.

Later it was rumored that the conspirators had participated in séances with a medium who was supposed to have communicated with the spirit of the late president. Strategic questions were put to the medium: Should Israel be attacked? When should this attack take place? Which one of them should assume power? Natually all of the séances were recorded on tape so that not a word of Nasser's would be lost.

Anwar al-Sadat became the most popular man in Egypt. Many took to the streets in support of the new *rais*, the boss, and the *thawrat al-tashih,* the correction revolution. Political prisoners were set free and the mukhabarat's tapes burned and displayed to the press. But would we really be free? I asked myself as I watched the demonstrators go by.

Fouad smiled cynically when I posed that question to him: "Sadat has had eight thousand people arrested and held for questioning." "What?" I exclaimed. "According to the foreign papers, on that famous Thursday night, a police officer from the Interior Ministry woke up Sadat in the middle of the night with a tape which revealed that the Gomaa group was planning to assassinate him. It was quite a wide-scale conspiracy, by all accounts, and that's why all these people have been arrested," he said with a shrug of his shoulders. "I'm glad Sadat has come out on top of all this," I said, "although it doesn't surprise me that there was a conspiracy to assassinate him. But what I don't understand is how all these political bosses could be set aside without a drop of blood being shed." "Sadat is no fool. He didn't want a civil war on his hands. Besides, who do you think arrested all those thousands? The mukhabarat, of course. He hasn't dismantled the mukhabarat, he's put it at his service. Of course, a part of the secret police was working with the opposition, but another very important part was working *with* Sadat. But Sadat knew he had a winning hand when he was sure of the army's support. That came when he fired Ali Sabri. The army hates the Soviets and he was their man. Firing Sabri must have also pleased the Americans."

On May 20, Sadat ordered the transfer of all his political opponents to the jail at Abou Zaabal. Many prisoners who had just come out of there rejoiced as they witnessed the great and the powerful taken there in chains. Among those who rejoiced the most, because their numbers had filled Nasser's jails, were members of the Moslem Brotherhood.

"Do you speak Arabic?" I asked the European sitting next to me at the dinner table. I had received an unexpected invitation to the home of one of the professors of the American University. Since *Rosencrantz,* I had tried to steer clear of my alma mater. But I accepted this, glad to have a chance to socialize and to be with foreigners. The professor lived with his family in the suburb of Maadi in one of those colonial villas complete with an English garden. The house was furnished in an American style with the occasional arabesque piece of furniture with which transient foreigners reminded themselves that they were in the Arab world.

"No, I don't, although I have spent two years in Algeria as a foreign correspondent," said my neighbor. He was wearing a pink button-down shirt with a dark blue suit. His look was preppie, which was a bit awkward since he was well over fifty. "How can you be a foreign correspondent in the Arab world if you don't know the language?" I asked somewhat contentiously.

I had not succeeded in intimidating him. He looked at me with obvious delight and answered: "I am planning to learn Arabic." Our host intervened at this point to tell me that Mr. Victor worked for a very well-known American paper. I knew the paper well, especially for the anti-Arab stance it took during my student days. "But you are not American," I said, turning to my dinner partner once more. Meanwhile, the Nubian servant came around with the vegetables. "I'm Austrian," he said, helping himself to some sautéed carrots. "But I left Austria a long time ago."

I had to admit to myself as I drove home that I had enjoyed this dinner. The stability of these outsiders' lives had released me from my own world. I had not realized until then how absorbed I had become in the overwhelming political atmosphere of Egypt and in the process of professional survival which had sucked me into its limited world.

"Mr. Victor has an excellent reputation as a foreign correspondent," Asma told me the following afternoon. "He's separated. Why don't you take him on as a boyfriend?" I laughed at her suggestion. "In your position, it's better to have a foreign boyfriend than an Egyptian one." I reminded her that I was a free woman now. "Yes, but an Egyptian will not be discreet while a foreigner might be. Do you want people to gossip?" "No, of course not," I answered. "It would hurt my career."

"He's better than nothing," she added. My mind turned to Paul, with whom I was corresponding, with whom I was still in love. Asma interrupted my thoughts. "Laila, you can't be by yourself all the time," she said in a voice full of concern. "Pouppa, I'm not alone. I have you," I replied. "Besides, why should I need a man?" "Don't be silly, you know why," she answered.

In the ensuing weeks, I plunged into a new project—the preparation of a TV version of the "new Hamlet." But when Fouad called and said he had to see me, that it was urgent, I dropped everything and met him at the club. He looked tired. "I have decided to leave my wife," he said. "As you know, it hasn't been going well for a long time. She accuses me of living in an ivory tower and she cannot forgive me for not earning more money." I was surprised by this turn of events and secretly pleased, but I said, "Women have to be practical; besides, that is what you liked about your wife, that she ran things and was down to earth." He ignored my remark as though he had not heard it. "I don't have the kind of ambitions she admires; I will never be a cabinet minister or an executive . . ." he said, his voice trailing off as if he felt guilty about this. "But, Fouad, that's precisely what's so wonderful about you," I said, unable to contain the warmth in my voice.

A few weeks later, Fouad moved out of his matrimonial home and into a place in the countryside, not too far from Cairo. A whitewashed mud-brick house, designed as an Egyptian peasant home, it had just been completed. It had a large, square living room with a mastaba stone bench running along each side. The high, domelike ceiling was inset with stained glass. The floor was covered with straw mats and there was no furniture except for some chairs and a bookshelf. An occasional handwoven rug was thrown over the mastabas. Fouad put on a record, a Vivaldi violin concerto, and ushered me out into his garden. We sat on the ground, facing the fields, behind us three tall date palms. A village woman came out of the house with a tray of mint tea. She smiled at me as if to say, I am taking care of him now. "Om

Mohammed takes good care of me," Fouad said. Hearing her name, Om Mohammed smiled again. Mohammed was her eldest son. She was named after him.

One day, during one of my visits to Fouad's new home, I asked him if he was happy living alone. "I am at peace," he answered. "And you?" he asked, taking my hand. I yearned for Fouad, but I feared that an involvement would ruin our friendship which had come to mean so much to me. Avoiding his question I said flippantly, "This is scandalous, our being alone here. People will say we are having an affair." "It's already been said," he replied cryptically. We sat there for a long time gazing at the agricultural fields before us and the pyramids in the distance; I too felt suddenly at peace. The din of the city had receded and the moment hung suspended in the eternal landscape.

Moments of peace were few and far between in 1972. To further my career at the institute, I had taken on a double load of teaching, and in February I went into rehearsal with three one-act comedies by Chekhov. Angered by the visibility I received on account of the appearance of the "new Hamlet" on TV, some of my colleagues had accused me of exploiting the students for my personal success. Thus, in order to appease my critics, I agreed to stage the Chekhov plays at the threadbare auditorium there, and then perform them on a proper stage before a public audience.

The search for a theater preoccupied me again. One day a student suggested that we approach the Soviet Cultural Center in Cairo. They had a very well-equipped stage and they were bound to welcome the Chekhov productions. The contact was made and the director of the center gave us the theater free of charge for a whole week as well as unlimited rehearsal time. The Russians also promised to publicize the productions and contribute to the programs. Our own National Theatre gave us nineteenth-century sets and costumes.

My students were overjoyed, especially Hoda, who was to play the lead in two of the three plays. We sent out hundreds of invitations in addition to announcing free admission all over the city. After five weeks of intensive rehearsals, opening night finally arrived. But fifteen minutes before we were due to go on, the auditorium was completely empty. Five minutes before, two rows had filled.

What have I done wrong this time? I wondered as I gave my disappointed company a pep talk. There was nothing American about the Soviet Center! But once again, the answer lay in the political scene. In January 1972, about a month and a half before the Chekhov productions were to open, pro-Palestinian riots had broken out at Cairo University. The demonstrators, protesting the semiwar, semipeace situation, which was frustrating everyone, were calling for war. In a fury, Sadat accused the Soviet Union of instigating these riots. The Egyptian-Soviet friendship had obviously reached a low ebb. But what did that have to do with Chekhov? Apparently everything. People were scared to come near the Soviet Center, as I later learned. The next day, beside myself, I phoned Fouad. "This is the most popular cultural center in town, what's happened?" "Your timing, Laila," came his curt reply. We closed two days later.

Egyptian-Soviet relations grew steadily worse. On July 6, a few months after my production at the Soviet Center, Sadat expelled all fifteen thousand Soviet military experts working in Egypt. He was irritated by the Soviet delay in the delivery of arms and believed that the two superpowers, because of détente, had agreed that there would be no war in the Middle East and that Egypt would be forced to surrender. But as events would prove, Sadat had no intention of surrendering.

In December there were more student demonstrations at Cairo University and several hundred leftist students were rumored to have been arrested. This time Sadat took strong punitive measures against those involved. He was particularly incensed by a declaration signed by a group of five hundred artists and writers stating that "Egyptian culture was dying a slow death because of censorship, religious, social and political bigotry, and graft and corruption."

People everywhere were demoralized by the "no peace, no war" situation. "Sadat keeps saying that the army is ready, then why doesn't he fight those Israelis? Is he scared? Is he a coward?" a taxi driver asked me. Discontent with Sadat's inertia manifested itself dramatically in the beginning of October, when an army captain drove into the religious center of the city with a convoy of armored vehicles and, interrupting the prayers in the Hussein Mosque, demanded immediate war with Israel. The army, the captain said, wanted to "fight, not to eat sand."

In March 1973, Sadat took over the leadership of the armed forces and appointed himself prime minister. The student demonstrations had produced tensions which he said he was determined to contain. A new government post, that of "socialist prosecutor," was created to "protect" society from the crimes of "deviationists." In the meantime, Cairo was once again mobilized for war. Hundreds of young men volunteered to form popular resistance or civilian forces. Basements were cleared for air-raid shelters. A partial blackout was imposed.

My father worried constantly about the future of our family in these uncertain times. One day, a family council was convened. This was an unusual occurrence—democracy was not in the nature of my family. "We are thinking of selling the villa," said my mother. The villa, with its Mediterranean architecture and spacious garden, had become a conspicuous symbol in these days of political instability. It gave us the appearance of wealth when we were not affluent, and if we sold it, we could use the money to live on if the political situation worsened. I encouraged the idea of the sale, though inwardly I knew my father's heart was breaking.

An apartment was found and the process of dismantling the house began to take place. It was up to Asma and my mother, with a little help from me, to pack away thirty-five years of accumulated objects and pieces of furniture into an endless number of carefully labeled cartons. I watched as our old Nubian cook, who had been with my parents even before I was born, put away his pots and pans, packing years of servitude into cartons labeled in Asma's rounded calligraphy.

As I watched Osta Mohamoud, as he was called, I recalled

images of childhood hours spent in his kitchen observing him as he prepared our meals, his nimble fingers swiftly wrapping the stuffed grapevine leaves, or filling the pigeons with the *fereek,* brown rice, or chopping the green leaves which would make the *mulukhia* soup. Now he would be returned to his village, where he would take with him the leftovers of my childhood.

Eventually, the boxes were all packed and piled high in the hallway, waiting to be removed. As the last box was being moved out and the house emptied of it contents, we looked around at the walls, which still belonged to us in spite of their patched nudity. The rooms, too, were still full of us, and clung tenaciously to their familiar odors. As we walked around to be sure that nothing had been forgotten, my mother suddenly cried out: "My plants, my plants!" We had forgotten her plants. She had filled the garden with hundreds of small potted plants, lovingly cultivated over the years. We rushed to the garden with empty cartons to save as many as we could, but most had to be sacrificed because there would be no room for them in the apartment. Later, my mother would take a taxi to secretly collect her forgotten children.

As the family got ready to move into the waiting cars and taxis which were to carry us to the center of the city where the new apartment was waiting for us, I rushed to the basement of the house which had been my playroom as a child. A damp, dark space, with an unforgotten humid smell, welcomed me back. I walked around in the midst of broken rocking chairs, a dislocated swing, worn-out rag dolls, trying to recapture images, moments, which now, more than ever before, had fled.

I WAS DESPERATE for a theater. I had just completed another student production at the institute, but I had nowhere to stage it, and my survival as a director depended on public visibility. I dared not consider the various cultural centers. So where could I find a home for my production? Then, one day, as I was walking in an old quarter of the city, I found it. My theater. It was hidden away in one of those dark alleys of Cairo, concealed between a vegetable market and a garbage lot. From the outside, it looked like a prison with its huge gray, windowless walls. It must have been a fortress of some sort, I surmised as I walked up to the entrance. Large wooden doors were flung open onto the alley, where an assortment of peddlers were noisily selling garlic and tomatoes from their open carts. All trafficked busily, mindless of the beauty inside.

An elaborate wooden screen, densely carved in geometric designs, spanned the doorway and veiled the interior. I edged around the screen and let myself inside. Suddenly the noise outside evaporated, and a marble and stone courtyard with an alabaster fountain, surrounded on all sides by balconies opening onto the courtyard, greeted me. Its beauty took my breath away. Does one fall in love with a building at first sight? Can one feel a sudden bond with stones and wood? Can one feel a sense of elation by just stepping into an open space? The answer was overwhelmingly "yes." The building was obviously hundreds of years old but it was waiting to be discovered. And from the first moment, I knew that I was the one who was going to bring it alive. I was going to let those forgotten stones speak, sing, dance, vibrate. And the courtyard, lying open before me, was going to give my work its shape, its form. Here was the architectual answer to a purely Egyptian theater. I knew it the moment I stepped inside Wekalat al-Ghouri, in the Hussein district of Cairo.

Wekala in Arabic means a market, but this was a caravanserai: a late medieval, Islamic trading center. It was built, as I was to discover, in the sixteenth century by the Mameluke governor of Cairo, Sultan al-Ghouri. Arab tradesmen would come to the wekala from all over the Islamic world, their camels carrying their merchandise. Stepping into the wekala, their camels swaying behind them, the weary merchants would lead their graceful carriers to the fountain to drink. Then they would climb the narrow stairs to the little rooms surrounding the courtyard. I looked up, spellbound by the rows of mashrabiyas, those windows laced with wooden carvings which spanned the courtyard on all four sides. The mashrabiya window is a symbol of the segregation of women, for a woman can look out through them, yet remain concealed from the eyes of men. As I looked up, the thousands of enslaved women's eyes met mine. Stunned, my gaze then traveled from the mashrabiyas to the mosaic-studded fountain and then back again to the rows of little rooms: there must have been hundreds of them concealed behind the windows and doors opening out onto the courtyard. I tried to imagine what went on inside those dark little enclosures hidden so suggestively.

I climbed up to the first balcony encircling the courtyard. The stones of the stairway had been worn down by the feet of travelers. As I moved around the balcony, the fountain beckoned me from all sides, dazzling me with its different perspectives. I tried to open a few of the doors but they were locked. I climbed another dark stairway and wandered around the balcony surrounding the courtyard below. As I climbed each succeeding level, the fountain gained in beauty as it grew more distant and the secret of the building more and more elusive. At the highest tier, the rooms were also closed. I looked at the fountain again; it had become an unattainable marble jewel. There were no balconies at the top of the structure, only the windowed mashrabiyas, closing off those hidden rooms which spanned the courtyard. I made my way beneath those intricately carved windows, keeping close to the edge of the narrow pathway below, fearful that one of the closed doors would suddenly open, and some mysterious arm would push me into a room at the end of the corridor. Shuddering, I ran down the steps. In just a few moments, I was back beside the bewitching fountain, looking up at those haunting rooms above. Already, I could envision my future productions. The fountain could serve as an orchestra pit, the balconies and the mashrabiyas would be the backdrops for the actors. There would be no curtain, no proscenium arch, no fourth wall. I had already been seduced from the Western theater by this intricate, Islamic marvel.

Four hundred years of commerce, of haggling over the price of this stock or the value of that merchandise, had not broken down the aesthetic resilience of Wekalat al-Ghouri. It had endured even when all around it buildings crumbled. It had even endured the nineteenth century when the merchants no longer came, and it was taken over by destitute women as their bordello. It had endured, a reminder of Islamic splendor, long forgotten amid the mud-brick and plaster tenements which house the poor of Cairo. It had endured as only houses of prayer endure in Cairo, waiting for me, its inner life intact.

I returned to my dreams. The audience would sit all around the courtyard and the actors would swing down to the stage on ropes and ladders. And just as in the rural celebrations of Egypt, the audience would encircle us with their warmth and all would join in the communal celebration of theater.

At that moment, a mashrabiya suddenly flew open and angry eyes stared at me. My "Salaam" froze on my lips. No words were spoken and just as suddenly the shutter was closed. If the wekala welcomed merchants and travelers, would it not welcome actors and actresses? A doorkeeper, appearing from nowhere, approached me. I asked him what was inside the rooms at the highest level. "Jinns—ghosts and evil spirits," he warned.

"The Ghouria district would make a very bad beginning for my theatrical debut. No chic people go there," said Hoda when I announced my discovery. "Only clowns, whirling dervishes, and acrobats play there," she added. I tried to reassure her and the rest of the cast that the "proper" audience would be drawn by the performances, but I secretly yearned for a different kind of audience than the one Hoda hoped for. "How we do get the building?" asked a more receptive actor. "Leave it to me," I said.

One week later I was sitting in the office of the undersecretary of the Ministry of Culture who was in charge of the building. It had not been difficult to get an appointment to see him because he had been one of my father's patients. He was a white-haired sculptor whose work decorated important sites in the city. A half-finished bust of Sadat sat on a pedestal next to a bay window. He rang the bell on his desk and asked me what I would like to drink. "Mazbout, please," I said, ordering Turkish coffee. A khaki-dressed attendant came in for the order. "I have been a patient of your father's for many years. I have great respect for him," he said politely. Years of bureaucratic administration had stamped out the expression in his eyes. "I just need the wekala for eight weeks, preferably in the holy month of Ramadan, because that's when everybody goes to the area," I said. He nodded and said, "I understand. But you know that all the plays have to be approved by us as well as the censors. The wekala is surrounded by the religious sites of Cairo." "There will be nothing offensive in my plays," I said to reassure him. "I suppose you have a small budget?" "Very small. I am working with students," I replied. At that he frowned slightly. "We would normally charge you a rental for the building. However," he said after a pause, "we are here to encourage the cultural life of the city and we should stand by you in your efforts." "Thank you, sir, thank you very much. I won't disappoint you. I studied in

America," I said cheerfully. He nodded disinterestedly and began to write something on a pad before him. The attendant reentered with the coffee, which was placed in front of me. I took a sip and waited to be addressed again. "This is an authorization to use the building," he said finally, handing me a paper. "But remember, if there are any damages or any trouble, you will be accountable to me." Overjoyed, I mumbled, "Alf shukr, yafandem, alf shukr, a thousand thanks." "When you go to the wekala, you must give this note to Mr. Afif who is the ministry's representative there. He will formalize the arrangements for you and your troupe to use the building."

The following week, in August 1973, I moved into the wekala with my small band of actors and actresses. But we were not to be its only occupants. The place was swarming with artisans and painters, all employees of the Ministry of Culture, and all allotted rooms which served as their studios. They greeted the company with cold stares. We decided to ignore them and began our rehearsals.

It was not easy. We would be in the middle of rehearsing a scene when suddenly their hammers and chisels would grow loud, in angry metallic cacophony. I would wait for the noise to subside before continuing with the rehearsal. If it didn't, I would shout "Quiet" at the top of my voice. There would be a silence, and then after a while the hammers and chisels would clamor again. "Why are they doing this to us?" I asked Hoda. "They consider the wekala their property. They say we are trying to steal it away from them and they resent our presence in the building," she said. As I turned around, I caught sight of Mr. Afif leaning down on the balustrade of the balcony overlooking the courtyard, smiling with satisfaction.

Our audience for that first production at Wekalat al-Ghouri—an adaptation of Jacinto Benavente's social farce *The Bonds of Interest*—were the people from the Hussein. Small merchants from the nearby tourist bazaar, fruit vendors, hashish peddlers, bedraggled children, a few precious little coins tightly held in the palm of their hand. We were charging about five piasters or pennies, but we often allowed them in for less, for whatever the little palm held. The ones who were turned away because they came without a single piaster would throw rotten tomatoes at the closed wooden doors until they forced them open and rush in screaming with joy at their victory. I would merely throw up my hands in despair and ask them to sit quietly, which they would do, their large brown eyes following the action with fascination.

Opening night I was wild with anxiety. Here was my chance to bring theater to the people, the real people, not the Zamalek bourgeoisie. I wondered as I went about checking the lights and costumes if I had become too Westernized, too sophisticated, to communicate with them. But I needn't have worried. They loved the play, clapping and singing with the music, cheering their favorite personages when they appeared onstage, and boo-ing the villain. At the end of the performance they rushed out into the street singing and shouting refrains from the show.

As she left the wekala after the show, Hoda was met by a band of children, who cheered and clapped and shouted her stage name, "Zanouba hanem," at the top of their lungs. They escorted her to her boyfriend's car, and it was only after she barricaded herself in that they dispersed, still calling "Zanouba! Zanouba!"

Asma was waiting to drive me home. "Mabrouk, you're a great director!" "Come on, Pouppa," I said to her. "It's true. You've made something out of nothing. It was like magic."

But at the institute the next day, my colleagues sneered. I had denigrated my academic status by performing in such an area and by staging an antiliterary play in a nontheater. But at least this time I was not accused of being pro-American or pro-Soviet. The criticism hurt my actors and actresses who sought recognition from the establishment, but they remained loyal. As for me, having found the wekala meant that I had come home.

Around this time I began to see a lot of Kurt Victor, the for-eign correspondent. He had called me soon after we had met at that dinner party and invited me for lunch. The lunch was fol-lowed by dinner the next day, and then lunch again, the day after that. For almost three weeks, we saw each other every day. After a while, it was obvious to both of us that a relationship had developed.

Kurt helped me forget Paul, whose presence in my life had begun to seem like a mirage. Kurt was very different from Paul. He wasn't romantic, intellectual, or poetic. But he was excellent company and he was covering Egypt as only a professional journalist could—with utter dedication and thoroughness. And I was part of the story he was covering. He loved it when I spoke to him about my country and he was always anxious to get my reactions to political events. I soon realized that I was being used, but I used him too. I wanted him to report on Egypt favorably. I even hoped he would become pro-Arab.

Like me, he was lonely. But as the relationship progressed, our loneliness evaporated. Our meetings and phone calls became regular and our communication with one another, stronger. Through him, I was allowed to escape into the Western world, which was still a part of me.

One day, Asma burst into my apartment with the news that she had found a job as a journalist. I was happier that day than when I got my teaching job in Wisconsin. In the last months, since graduating from the American University in Cairo, she had gone from one secretarial job to another. Here, at last, was the possibility of meaningful work.

The job, however, did not turn out to be what we had expected. She had been hired to cover social events for an important daily but her assignments were restricted to weddings and cocktail parties and she hated it. I urged her to stick it out in the hope of a promotion. But as she sat in her favorite armchair in my living room, her legs swung sideways as usual, her hair pushed back by her sunglasses, she said: "It's useless, they've typecast me. I project the image of someone who should be covering the society thing and that's what I will always end up doing. And you know how much I hate this kind of work— especially the weddings." I knew. I also hated weddings.

A couple of months later, she left the newspaper for a job with a German media foundation. She was offered the job by the director, a young man in his thirties. Pouppa loved the idea of the job. "Imagine, they are going to work in family planning and they want me to help them with their research in the villages." "How?" I asked. "They are planning to use video programs to see how they can influence peasant women." "Do they have government authorization?" I inquired a bit skeptically. "Don't worry. They are working with the college of mass media at Cairo University. Dietrich, the director, said I could work with him there, too." The salary was excellent, three times what I was making at the institute.

In a few weeks, Pouppa was a different person—busy, committed, and completely involved in her family-planning videos. She bought herself a used Fiat, which she drove furiously around Cairo. I marveled at what an interesting job can do for a woman.

But all was not perfect. There were pressures at home which were making Asma's life difficult. Pouppa was the baby of the family which meant that she was treated as a child, even after she was grown. But she was also, by virtue of being the youngest female member, its slave. As the youngest daughter in an Arab family she was relegated to the role of housekeeper, private nurse, and errand girl. It was Pouppa who had to be up early to attend to the household, to set the table for meals, to chauffeur our father, and to attend to our parents' slightest whim. It was Pouppa who picked up my brother's socks and saw to it that his room was tidy and his shirts ironed.

When she was born, my father and mother were middle-aged. Asma was a gift from the gods. As a child, she was spoiled, cajoled, but never taken seriously, and as she grew up the family net enmeshed her. She had been placed in a coeducational school as a child, but when she started to fill out, her beauty displaying itself, she was promptly placed in a school run by French nuns. My parents did not wish to make the same mistakes they had made with me.

At school she had to learn a new language and she had to adapt to the customs and manners of religious education. Any other girl would have been suffocated. But not Asma. Even when the nuns humiliated her for wearing her hair too loosely or her skirt too short, her joie de vivre would triumph. She would come home, her tears mingled with laughter and defiance, and later she would nourish her spirit on French love poetry and the Antigones of Anouilh. Or else she would console herself with telephone love affairs and daydreams of the time when she would be released from the family net.

Asma knew she had an ally in me, and this gave her courage. At the same time, I realized that I had grown very dependent on her emotionally. She was becoming more than a sister. She was the child I never had, a mirror in which I saw myself reflected, only younger, more beautiful, unscathed by life's struggles. I loved the way she stole her moments of freedom and laughed away her imprisonment.

I sought comfort in her presence and when she was unable to visit me, I would go over to my parents' new home and visit her. Her room, smaller than the one she had had in our villa in Heliopolis, was untidy as ever. She would dress up for me, trying on new clothes. One shoe would have to be fished out from under the bed, while the other would be somewhere in the bathroom. Drawers would have to be emptied before a pair of stockings could be matched. Lipsticks and rouges and eye makeup filled the corners of her room and I often wondered why she never broke a leg slipping on a rolling tube of mascara.

We would sit cross-legged on her bed, which would be covered with layers of books and magazines, her pictures of Um-Kulthum and Ché Guevara shielding us from the outside world, while we wove and spun Asma's future.

We had been hearing of the impending war with Israel for a long time, but no one took it seriously anymore. Sadat's reputation was at an all-time low. Even my father would occasionally remark that "all the new man is good for is giving speeches." The Arab-Israeli conflict seemed to have reached a permanent deadlock.

The political situation dominated our lives. The minute I walked into my parents' apartment, the conversation would turn to politics. "I was all for kicking out the Soviets—after all, they were occupying the country. But what have the Americans done for us instead? Sadat must be a fool. The Americans have let him down, and wasn't it they who drove us into the arms of the Soviets in the first place, when Dulles refused to finance the High Dam? Laila, these United States of yours don't know what they are doing again!" said my father angrily.

Egyptian students were also disenchanted with America. At Cairo University, where I was teaching a class in American drama, I saw a bloody hand painted on a wall with the American flag superimposed on it. The hand was squashing Egypt. Soon pro-Palestinian demonstrations would take place on campus, once again urging Sadat to war.

On September 20, Sadat gave another speech, this time attacking the United States: "The United States is still under Zionist pressure and is wearing Zionist spectacles. The United States will have to take off these spectacles before they talk to us," he asserted. "Now he's talking," said my father. "America doesn't care for Egypt. It only wants to protect its own interests." Sadat told us that the United States had demanded Egypt's reopening of the Suez Canal as a precondition of any settlement of the Arab-Israeli conflict. "We replied," said Sadat, "and told them that this is a trap. The issue is liberating Arab lands from Israeli aggression, not the opening or closing of the canal." Sadat then went on to talk about internal affairs. He had decided to pardon the leftist intellectuals who had been fired from their jobs for supporting the student riots in January. The students, who were supposed to face trial for these riots, were also pardoned.

The family had a very heated discussion after the speech ended. "Maybe he regrets having thrown out the Soviets," said my mother. "Good thing to free the dissidents," I commented. "The question is whether he is really trying to liberalize the country or just appease the opposition," said my father. "What about the war, are we going to fight or not?" asked Asma. "Forget about the war, he's too cowardly to fight," said my father with conviction in his voice.

Precisely eight days later, on October 6, 1973, Egypt attacked Israel. Our jets launched an air strike against Israeli forces on the east bank of the Suez Canal in a surprise attack planned and led by an unknown air-force general named Hosni Mubarak. During that strike, the Egyptian air force, that same air force which had been destroyed on the ground six years earlier, now successfully attacked all command posts, aerial combat headquarters, missile batteries, and all Israeli gun emplacements in the Sinai.

"Allah-hu-Akhbar, Allah-hu-Akhbar, Allah-hu-Akhbar, La Illah illa Allah, Allah is great and there is no God but Allah," resounded joyously from the tops of Cairo's minarets and echoed through every street and alley. Liberation Square with its circular avenue surrounded by parks filled with people cheering and waving newspapers covered with photographs of our soldiers standing beside the Egyptian flag on the east bank of the canal. Smiling faces greeted you everywhere and children waving small Egyptian flags ran round crying: "Abarna,

abarna, abarna!" We have crossed, we have crossed, we have crossed!

Radios blasted from every kiosk with military bulletins from the front: "Egyptian forces have succeeded in crossing the Suez Canal at all points along the front and have occupied all Israeli positions on the eastern side of the canal." Bystanders greeted this famous communiqué with two words often spoken with tears: "Allah hu-Akhbar."

"I can't believe it, I can't believe it," said Asma, rushing into the apartment with *Al-Ahram*. Then flinging herself across her favorite armchair, she read me the account of the *ubur,* the crossing, in rapid, breathless tones: "The destruction of the Bar-Lev line was accomplished by eight thousand Egyptian commandos who crossed the canal in rubber dinghies, while two thousand howitzers and heavy mortars . . ." Here she paused to ask what a howitzer was. I shrugged and urged her on. ". . . which were concealed in the sand, covered the commandos with a barrage of fire while the crossing took place. The Israelis, who were dug into concrete bunkers on the east side of the canal, were taken in shocked surprise. Imagine the face of the Israeli soldiers as Egyptian commandos climbed up the east bank, carrying ropes, bamboo ladders, and other equipment. In a few minutes our commandos had destroyed Israeli armor on the east bank, aided by a burst of heavy artillery and tank fire from across the canal." "God!" exclaimed Pouppa before going on excitedly: "A second commando attack followed, with our soldiers engaging the Israelis in fierce hand-to-hand combat . . . A few hours later our soldiers had not only broken through the Bar-Lev line, symbol of the Israeli occupation of the canal, but had penetrated the Sinai Desert within ten miles of the canal." Shaking her head in amazement as she put the paper down, Asma said: "Can you believe it? We did it. We did it!" "Mabrouk," I said elatedly.

The whole country was repeating "Mabrouk, congratulations." The crossing of the canal had restored our faith in ourselves, in the army, in our leader, and above all, it gave us back the sense of nationhood which we had lost in 1967.

A few days after the war had begun, Jihan al-Sadat, the president's wife, made an appeal for women volunteers to serve in the hospitals which were receiving the wounded. I offered my assistance to Kasr-al-Aini Hospital, where my father had taught and established an X-ray department thirty-five years before. I asked for night duty, believing that that was when I would be most needed by the wounded.

Kasr-al-Aini is a sprawling, barracklike building where any Egyptian could be treated free of charge. From within its mazelike corridors, I could hear the wheels of stretchers screeching on the tiles or the rumbling motor of a truck in the courtyard below, where it had stopped to be delivered of its cargo of bleeding soldiers.

The first batch of soldiers transported to Kasr-al-Aini were the infantry forces which crossed into the Sinai to confront Israeli tanks. Many of the soldiers had napalm burns of such severity that their flesh was pitch-black and the only indication that a human being lay inside the charcoaled carcass was the eyes: roving silently in the head, staring, pleading, in anguish. I would sit next to one of these soldiers long into the night, hoping to give some small comfort. At daybreak I would be ushered out of the ward. The next evening the bed would often be empty and a tiny Koran would lie on the pillow where the head had been unable to rest.

There were other wards to which I returned each night, such as the ward for spinal injuries: rows of beds in which young men, their arms and legs paralyzed from the shrapnel lodged in the spinal cord, lay. I was assigned to look after a soldier named Hussein. He was handsome, tall, tanned from exposure to the fiery Sinai sun, with hazel-colored eyes and cropped hair. The first thought I had when I saw him was that he would never be able to make love again. But he told me that his wound was insignificant by comparison to our victory.

Meanwhile, the tide of the war was turning. The Israelis had made desperate calls from Tel Aviv to Washington to "save Israel" by stepping in on their behalf. The United States began airlifting arms to the Israeli army straight to the front line at Al-Arish. These airlifts were to reverse the course of the war. On October 16, the Israelis succeeded in creating a gap between our second and third armies, forming a kind of bridgehead which came to be known as the Deversoir Bulge. On October 17, military communiqués revealed that the enemy had sneaked across the Bitter Lakes north of the canal, with seven tanks, in an attempt to raid certain positions on the west bank. The next day, a military spokesman told us that this force had been wiped out. But the rumors confirming the Israeli thrust were overwhelmingly strong.

On October 22, Sadat accepted the UN–sponsored cease-fire. "With a heart that bled I have accepted the call for a cease-fire. I am willing to fight Israel, no matter how long, but never the United States. Besides, I won't ever again allow my armed forces to be destroyed or my people to suffer another debacle," he told us in a speech from the National Assembly.

Two hours after it had been imposed, the cease-fire was broken by Israel, so that by the night of October 23, Israel had encircled our third army to the east of the canal. The road to Suez, our only supply line, was in Israeli hands. Meanwhile, another cease-fire was imposed, but Israel refused to return to the October 22 lines. Had Sadat been duped into accepting this cease-fire? we wondered.

In the corridors of the Kasr-al-Aini Hospital, soldiers stood and wept out of frustration and anger when they heard about the cease-fire. "We have been betrayed," they cried. "We could have gone on fighting. The army, down to the very last man, wants to go on fighting. We could have destroyed the bridgehead."

Meanwhile, we heard accounts in Cairo of how the Israeli army was refusing to allow supplies to reach the besieged third army. Even plasma was poured out into the desert sand.

"Sadat had to stop fighting. There was no point in penetrating farther into the Sinai and losing air cover of the SAM missiles," said Fouad.

We were at the club where, as usual, everything was impervious to the realities outside. The Nubian servants, cool in their white *galabiyas* and black turbans, were as bored as ever. The swimming pool gurgled with turquoise water, while European women in bikinis sunbathed beside it in the crisp October sunshine. Gardeners clipped the manicured lawns and nipped the weeds from the elaborate flower beds.

Fighting the exhaustion of yet another sleepless night at the hospital, I was barely listening as Fouad spoke. "Maybe you should stop these visits to the hospital," he said as he saw my eyes closing. "Do you think all this fighting, all this killing, will ever come to an end?" I asked wearily. "The war was inevitable. It was brilliant strategy. The only way Sadat could have shaken the United States and Russia out of the lethargy of détente. The only way to make America reassess its position toward the Arabs. It was brilliant arm-twisting," he asserted. "But what a price to pay," I said. He smiled and said: "We had no choice. We have to fight to get our land back because the Israelis only understand the language of force." I nodded and said, "But the Israelis also paid a price. In a few weeks of fighting they have lost thousands of men and their myth of an invincible military has been shattered." "Now you're talking!" he said. "Egyptians have proved that they are fighters and also masters of modern warfare. The crossing of the canal and the destruction of the Bar-Lev line were strategies of military genius."

A Nubian waiter had set two cups of Turkish coffee before us. I took a sip of mine. Fouad leaned forward in his chair, his white cap low on his forehead, his skin bronzed from his daily swim. "Do you know that on October 17, the OPEC countries met in Kuwait and decided to reduce all oil production by five percent until Israel withdraws from the occupied territories?" I shook my head. "This is the *first time in history* that the Arabs have realized the power of the oil weapon to pressure the West." "But the OPEC countries have not paid in men's lives, as we have," I answered. "What does it matter? They are standing beside us. That's what's important," he replied.

On March 14, 1974, the Arab oil embargo was lifted. The increase in the oil prices and the cuts in oil production had provided staggering profits for the Arab countries, as well as for the American oil companies. But the lifting of the embargo did not coincide with the timetable for the withdrawal of Israel from the occupied territories—as it was originally meant to.

Unable to bear the daily suffering any longer, I stopped going to the hospital and decided to go back to the theater. Since the outbreak of the war, all schools and universities had been closed and all normal life had ceased. But after the cease-fire, things began to go slowly back to normal. I summoned my troupe and urged them to donate blood. I knew, however, that this was not enough. I would have to engage them in a more enduring way. It was then that it occurred to me to stage the previous season's production of *Dunia al-Masaleh* (the Bonds of Interest), the Benavente adaptation, for the soldiers at Kasr-al-Aini Hospital. Special permission was quickly obtained from Yussef al-Sebaii, the minister of culture, who was enthusiastic about my request to do something for the soldiers.

It was agreed that the hospital dining room would become our theater: the dining-room tables, our scaffold; the chairs, our stalls. On the day of the performance the soldiers sat everywhere: on the windowsills, on the floor, and on the stage. Some of them were in wheelchairs, some had crutches, and others had arms in slings or legs in casts. But they were all in good spirits, and when I arrived, I could hardly reach the stage for the jostling and pushing and laughing all around me. Finally, I made my way to the tables, which I climbed up on in order to get the attention of the audience. For the first few moments the sight of me up there seemed only to increase the volume, but soon one of the male nurses took pity on me and shouted at everybody to keep quiet so that the "doctora" could make an announcement.

I rapidly told them the name of the play and the names of the actors and actresses. They applauded after each name, as if my performers were celebrities. Then, as the company walked toward the stage, the soldiers broke into applause, catcalls, and whistles. The troupe climbed on the stage and the first actor tried to make his opening line heard, straining to no avail. The moment he started to speak, the cheering grew louder and the applause more vehement. To salute the audience, he bowed, as is customary in old-fashioned theater, but the uproar continued. Finally, he had no choice but to wave his arms and to shout that he was about to begin acting. The crowd simmered down a bit but the moment Hoda took her place onstage, the hall swelled into a paroxysm of clapping, whistling, and shouting. Hoda looked in my direction with desperation. I waved to her to go on. She waited quietly and then suddenly began to sing. The audience grew quiet, applauded at the end of the song, and waited for her to begin her lines.

I quickly realized that the audience had been reacting to the physical presence of the actors onstage, their faces, movements, and gestures, instead of their words because most of the soldiers had known only the circus, the clowns of rural entertainments, and the traveling ballad singers. As I watched them respond, I became convinced that in order to reach the masses, Egyptian theater must retain its indigenous roots, must remain visual, physical, and musical. From that moment on, I made up my mind that I would strive to create a theater which would reach audiences like the one at Kasr-al-Aini. My resala, my mission, would be the creation of a folk theater—a theater for the people.

By this time, late October, the cease-fire had, for the most part, quieted the war, although there was sporadic fighting until the first disengagement of forces between Egypt and Israel in January 1974. As normalcy was beginning to reassert itself, the schools and universities reopened. Curfews and blackouts, however, continued to be imposed and it would be many months before our lives would return to normal.

My life was, at least, restored to its working routine, a routine which stabilized my existence and without which I was always at a loss.

PAUL HAD BEEN sending desperate messages during the war, but he now belonged to another universe—the psychological distance between us had grown even wider than the geographical. It was Kurt who now filled my days and my nights. We had become closer than ever, and the reality of Egypt, which we shared, strengthened the bond between us.

We had seen very little of each other during the war, but he would call me every day, and a couple of weeks after the ceasefire, he invited me to lunch at a restaurant where we had often met before the war. It sat right on the bank of the Nile, shielding us from the traffic noises, the crowds, and the pollution of downtown Cairo.

The restaurant offered a view unmarred by the concrete conglomerations of the city. Nubian waiters clad in baggy fisherman's trousers would stand about murmuring quietly, while a couple of stray dogs would wag their tails in welcome and then lie back in the winter sun.

As we walked into the restaurant, I reprimanded Kurt for having neglected me during the war. He mumbled an excuse, something about how busy he was covering the Kissinger-Sadat disengagement talks. We were ushered to a table next to the Nile. The water glistened in the sunshine. For a while as we sat gazing at the river, the war seemed remote. I watched some boatmen who were preparing to launch their feluccas, or sailboats, on the waterway. One of these boats was carrying a cargo of limestone which is used as building material in Egypt. I watched the boatman climb the tall, wooden mast with expert agility, his naked, mud-cracked legs swiftly reaching the top of the sail. Then, unaided by anyone, he unwound the white linen cloth for the waiting breeze to guide on its course; while below, another boatman lifted the anchor, steadying the boat for the final loads of stone which were being carried onto the felucca on the backs of laborers. How harsh the life of the boatman is, I thought.

A few minutes later, the fully loaded felucca glided onto the river, the wind compassing its course, the boatmen standing majestically beside the masts, their brown skin contrasting with the white sails. These boatmen's lives had not changed for thousands of years. Yet I found a strange comfort in observing the life of my ancestors reassert itself with primeval confidence, the still point of Egypt.

Our meal of grilled sea bass was brought to us with a bottle of white wine. The fish lay on one side, its spinal cord a clean white bone shining in the sun. "I have asked my wife to join me in Cairo," said Kurt suddenly, coldly. I stared at him in paralyzed silence. "I have decided to bring the family together," he added. I kept my eyes on the plate before me, unable to say anything. Finally I mumbled something about the promise he had made to me, never to bring his wife to Cairo. He shrugged his shoulders, but his mouth remained closed, the lips gripping one another firmly. I lifted my eyes from the plate, pleadingly. "I'm sorry," he said, lowering his head. As I walked swiftly out of the restaurant, he did not try to stop me.

The following day he phoned to say he would like to save "our friendship." I asked him not to call again, for I wanted to banish him from my life. But even as I put down the receiver, I knew this would not be easy. I had grown dependent on Kurt; he had become more than a lover, he had become a presence in my life, someone who could ease my anxieties over a cup of coffee or a glass of wine. I had become dependent on his early-morning telephone calls, his smiling hellos, the grip of his hand, the scent of his freshly laundered shirts, the sound of his car engine driving up late at night. But I refused to yield, to accept the contingencies of love, to share him with another woman. Years later, it was this pain that made me realize what it must be like for an Arab woman to discover that her husband has taken another wife with whom he wishes to be shared.

The cultural establishment had been insistently calling upon artists and intellectuals to create works dealing with the October war. Ordinarily I would have resisted such propaganda, but the war had left such deep personal and professional marks on me that I decided to collaborate with the Ministry of Culture and direct something for television.

I had read a play, *Milad Batal*, by the famous playwright, journalist, essayist, and novelist Tewfik al-Hakim, which seemed appropriate. A philosophical one-acter, it was originally written about the 1948 war with Israel. I commissioned a script-writer to update it, since the basic theme—military heroism— would also be relevant to the recent war. The new version was about a young officer who is among those who lead Egyptian soldiers in the crossing of the canal and the onslaught on the Bar-Lev line. He is wounded and taken to a hospital where he has a chance to meditate about his life and the war that is going on. When he is well enough to leave the hospital, he chooses to return to the front, instead of taking home leave.

At the front, he meets up with his military commander, who applauds his decision to return to the fighting. The war becomes more ferocious as the Egyptian army tries to thrust itself into the occupied Sinai desert. During a moment of calm during which he is lying in the sand near his commander, he is asked whether the civilians in Cairo have changed as the army has. He answers in one syllable: yes. A few hours later he is killed in a mine explosion.

The day it was shown, the whole family sat in front of the TV set, waiting anxiously for the play to come on. Asma invited all her friends so that I could have a live audience. When it came on, announced by the music from Beethoven's *Eroica*, they all applauded, the ovation growing louder as my name appeared in the credits. When it was over, my father grumbled something about its being too short. It had been an hour-long special.

Time magazine included me in an article on Egypt, in which I was called a "filmmaker." They even showed a picture of me looking through my movie camera! Typically, my colleagues at the institute sneered and the leftist establishment denounced me for working on commission to the Ministry of Culture. The Left still opposed Sadat, especially after the war, which they claimed he had bungled by the cease-fire. One of them even claimed that Sadat had accepted the cease-fire at the instruction of the CIA.

"The Left," said Fouad when I visited him a few days later, "opposes the rapprochement with the United States which Kissinger's shuttle diplomacy is bringing about." "But why?" I asked. "Laila, it's been only seven months since the American airlift to Israel at Al-Arish, one month since the oil embargo has been lifted, and the Israelis have not budged from the occupied territories."

None of this deterred me from directing another play for the Ministry of Culture. This one was to be staged at the wekala. It too concerned the October war, and was based on the true story of Om Hamada, mother of Hamada, whose son had been taken prisoner by the Israelis in 1967. An exchange of prisoners takes place in 1974 and Om Hamada waits for her son to return. She spends her days and nights next to the phone, waiting for him to call. But he does not call. She grows bitter with the gradual realization of his death and denounces the war in an impassioned monologue. Her neighbors try to console her with the victory of the ubur, the crossing, and the prospect of peace that it implies.

One day, as I was rehearsing a dance number which involved a sheikh, an Islamic man of the cloth who appears frequently in the play to preach patience and submission to God to Om Hamada and her neighbors, one of the mashrabiya windows of the wekala flew open and someone stuck out his head and screamed, "Stop the music and dancing!" I looked up inquiringly. A bearded head glared at me. "It is forbidden in Islam to show a sheikh dancing," he shouted. "Jesus Christ dances in musical plays," I replied as audibly as I could. Two glaring eyes stared at me and then the mashrabiya was slammed shut as quickly as it had been opened.

The next day I received a call from Mr. Hassan, the author of the short story of Om Hamada, himself an important official in the Ministry of Culture. "I don't recall a dancing sheikh in my story," he said quietly. "But you do have a sheikh; all I did was include him in the choreography. After all, he's an important part of the community and they all get up and jump around when they hear about the ubur," I continued in my own defense. "Kindly remove him from such festivities," came the reply. "All right," I sighed.

A few days later the author phoned me again: "Is the word 'Allah' being used in songs accompanied by electronic music?" "Yes," I replied. "What does it matter?" "It is causing offense," he said. "To whom?" I asked sharply. "Either the word 'Allah' or the electronic instruments have to be removed," he answered coldly. "I assure you," I said, "there is no offense meant whatsoever. The electronic music is essential to the contemporary sound to the play . . . after all, this is the seventies and the Egyptian army made use of electronic equipment, tanks, howitzers . . ." I said, unable to control my temper. There was a brief silence on the other side of the line, then the word, "All right."

Finally we opened—to two excellent reviews in *Al-Ahram* and *Al-Akhbar*, the other leading paper. I was overjoyed. By now the wekala was becoming a popular place and the audiences packed it. Also, the Ministry of Culture sent schoolchildren, factory workers, and other groups to see the show.

One evening, as I walked around the courtyard during the intermission, I caught sight of a familiar face. It was one of the soldiers from the Kasr-al-Aini Hospital. His handsome face was no longer scorched, but raw and peeling. I went up to him, welcoming him to the wekala with unconcealed emotion. "Are you enjoying the play?" I asked. "Yes," he replied. "What are your plans now?" I asked. "Mrs. Jihan al-Sadat is sending me and other soldiers to Germany for further treatment," he replied.

We stood together for a few moments in which I felt totally overcome by emotion. Finally I was able to say: "I just want to say it's a great honor, sharaf lina, to have you here."

The success of *Om Hamada* took my mind off my private life, at least temporarily. And when the show closed in November 1974, I decided to throw myself into another production. Fortuitously, the Italian Cultural Institute approached me to direct a production of Pirandello's *Enrico IV*. It is a play about a contemporary Italian nobleman who loses his memory in a fall during a masquerade in which he impersonates Henry IV, the Holy Roman Emperor of the eleventh century. When he recovers he continues in his impersonation, thus causing his family to believe that he has gone mad. He is locked in a mansion where he is surrounded by a staff which also pretends that he is emperor. At the end of the play, even when he does have a chance through the intervention of shock treatment to break out of his mask, he chooses to remain, fixed forever in the character of Henry IV.

Life slips through our fingers without our perceiving it, the play says. But art, theater, captures life and imprisons it everlastingly in a frozen moment. I sought consolation in that theme, as well as in the artistic process which directing it involved. Gradually, my work became the center of my existence again, and the bruising clashes with reality were dissolved in the reaffirmation of my faith in the theater.

One afternoon, during rehearsal, I received a phone call from Asma: "Has anybody called you yet? Have you heard what's happened?" she asked frantically. "Heard what?" I asked. "About Kurt's wife," she said. "Kurt's wife has committed suicide!" I was speechless. When I recovered my voice, I said, "Are you sure?" "Of course I'm sure. I'm surprised you didn't know...." "Thank you for telling me, Pouppa," I responded. "I'll see you later," I added, and put down the receiver. I sat down in a nearby chair and grappled with my emotions. Finally, I was able to get up and go back to the rehearsal.

A few days later, I mustered the courage to call Kurt.

"Hello," he said, his voice unchanged. "Why didn't you call me about what happened?" I said emotionally. He did not reply. "What happened?" I said to break the silence. "It was an accident. She accidentally took an overdose of sleeping pills. It wasn't the drinking," he added calmly. "Oh," I said, pretending to believe it. "I just wanted you to know how sorry I am." The dreaded conversation was over. I lit a cigarette. My hand shook. Suddenly I realized that it wasn't Kurt I was feeling sorry for, but his wife. This is pure catharsis, I thought, for I realized how fortunate I was to have escaped from my own unhappy marriage alive.

The death of Kurt's wife did not leave me for many weeks. But that night, as I watched the rehearsal from the darkened auditorium of the Al-Hakim Theater, I was barely able to concentrate. My mind flitted continuously to that woman, who could have been me. As I sat there, my life crystallized for me. I became aware as never before what my work would signify: not a refuge from daily reality, or an escape, but the sum total of my life.

MEANWHILE, life was filled with the changes of Egypt. In the aftermath of the October war, a semblance of parliamentary life was, at last, beginning to assert itself. Nasser's Arab Socialist Union was dissolved in favor of *nawabir,* or forums approximating political parties: one for the Right, one for the Left, and one for the center to be headed by the prime minister. Liberalization of travel restrictions occurred and the nightmarish visa was no longer a requirement for leaving the country. An Egyptian court decreed that it was "unconstitutional" for the state to implement Nasser's military decree of 1961, legalizing the seizure of private property. Slowly a revitalization of the private sector began to take place. People began to go into entrepreneurial projects. Many were able to buy their first TV, refrigerator, or car. Previously confiscated companies were returned to their owners. Foreign investment was encouraged.

But as a consequence of four wars with Israel and one with royalist Yemen, all taking place within thirty years, Egypt was still an impoverished country. To make matters worse, there was a population explosion, which had begun in the Nasser days, but which had been left unattended because of the preoccupation with foreign policy. Each year, there were a million new mouths to feed. But now there were debates initiated by Mrs. Jihan al-Sadat, an activist, and, in her own way, a feminist. Mrs. Sadat had started to emerge as a public figure in her own right during the October war, when she played a major role in mobilizing the public to provide social and medical services for the wounded. She frequently appeared on television in debates about reforming the *sharia,* or religious-inspired Family Law which governs the status of women in Egypt.

I had never heard of the Family Law before it was brought to my attention by Jihan al-Sadat's debates. It was this Family Law which prescribed the inferiority of women, and that established the social and cultural norms which Christian and Moslem women alike were subjected to.

According to that law, a civil code, which had not been amended since 1929, a man is entitled to have four wives simultaneously. If a woman abandons her husband he is entitled to bring her home forcibly with the help of the police. By uttering "I divorce thee" thrice before a witness, a man is entitled to divorce his wife. A woman can ask for divorce only by court procedure, and only if she can prove that her husband in impotent, mentally ill, or serving a lengthy jail sentence. A divorced woman is stripped of a son over seven and a daughter over nine. A woman cannot travel without her husband's or father's consent. A woman inherits half as much as a man, and a widow like Om Abdou inherits but an eighth of her husband's property. In court, a woman's testimony is given half the weight of a man's.

Mrs. Sadat decided that it was time to reform this Family Law. In addition to television debates, she instigated the publication of countless articles in the papers and programs on the radio. In order to mobilize women further, she gave public lectures and met as often as she could with women's groups in order to discuss the most expedient way to amend the law. I was not involved in any of these activities, but I supported them wholeheartedly. But then, one day something happened which made me join the battle in my own way.

"They are demonstrating against Mrs. Sadat at Al-Azhar University," Hoda cried as she burst into the courtyard at the wekala, where I was discussing a scene with one of my other actresses. "What?" I asked incredulously. For in Egypt people do not demonstrate against their leaders. "It's not a political demonstration, it's a religious one by veiled women, Islamic sisters or something!" Hoda said, half out of breath. "But why are they demonstrating against Mrs. Sadat?" "Because of the Family Law. They are saying that her proposed amendments are against Islam. They are calling her every name in the book!" "Women—are you sure there are women among the demonstrators?" I persisted. "They are all women; I saw them with my own eyes," she said. "What amendments are they protesting?" I asked Hoda, who was now smoking a cigarette with her characteristic flourish. "Oh," she said, "nothing drastic. . . . A man is to marry in court if he takes a second or third wife, instead of just having a religious ceremony. And child custody should go to the mother, at least until the children are older. Arbitrary divorce should be abolished and a man should only divorce his wife before a judge, when tempers have cooled," she said, obviously amused. "And oh, yes," she added, "a woman should be allowed to travel without male authorization."

Suddenly the other actress burst out, saying, "Mrs. Sadat is defying Islam with all this. You must not tamper with or interpret sharia. It is Islamic law. It is revealed by God!" "But Mrs. Sadat is only trying to amend a civil law which is influenced by religious law," I argued. "No," asserted my actress, herself a repudiated woman. "Sharia is the revealed law of Islam." I did not reply.

A couple of days later, my student assistant and I made our way through the Khan Khalili bazaar opposite the wekala to al-Fishawi café for tea. We walked past the small tourist shops with their camel saddles, leather cushions, and handwoven rugs; past the more expensive shops with silver piled high in the windows, then through a winding alley till we reached al-Fishawi, with its famous gilded mirrors. Here a woman is allowed to sit because it is a tourist spot. "What will you have, ya doctora?" asked the waiter in striped calico galabiya. It pleased me more to be recognized here than in the drawing rooms of Cairo. We ordered mint tea. Adel lit a cigarette and offered me one. A familiar tune was playing. "What's that song, Adel?" I asked. The male singer intoned the southern *saidi* accent of Om Abdou, an accent she was never able to lose, even after she moved to Cairo. "That's the ballad of 'Chafeeka wa Metwalli,'" he said. I vaguely recalled the story of the ballad. "Isn't that the one about the brother who murders his sister because she dishonored him?" I asked mischievously. "His sister became a prostitute," Adel replied with a bashful look. "Is it heroic to kill a prostitute?" I asked. "Of course. Metwalli had to do it because of his *ird*, his honor," he replied. "You mean his honor lies in the chastity of his sister?" I argued. "Of course," replied my young assistant.

Adel brought a cassette version of the ballad to the theater, and we listened to it together the following day. It was mostly about the brother, Metwalli, his suffering and his determination to wash away the disgrace his sister had brought upon him. But there was practically nothing about her. Her name was mentioned only twice. I researched the story and discovered that it was based on an actual crime which took place in the twenties. Chafeeka had been seduced by the mayor's son, who had refused to marry her when she became pregnant. She was introduced to prostitution by the procuress of her abortion. Central to this rural Egyptian story was the moral that a girl who loses her virginity is likely to be killed by her clan.

My assistant and I discussed the ballad extensively. I asked him if he would have done the same as Metwalli, if it had been his sister. He scratched his head and said quickly, almost apologetically, "I would not be able to show my face in the neighborhood if I didn't kill her." "But, Adel," I began. "Doctora," he interrupted me, "society even forgives crimes of honor. Metwalli's sentence was suspended and he returned to his village a hero."

I was horrified by Adel's words and by the conviction with which he spoke. But the conversation had given me the idea for a play. I realized that the story of Chafeeka touched the core of an ethos—that code implicit in the Family Law which assumes male ownership of women. When a female disgraced her clan, she was challenging that ownership. Therefore, she had to be destroyed. "What do you do when a branch of your tree grows into the neighbor's yard?" Metwalli asks the judge who is about to sentence him. "You cut it off," he asserts.

"Do you know, Adel, this simple folktale is symbolic of the condition of women in our society." He looked at me with considerable incredulity. "If I used the ballad form, I could tell Chafeeka's story and maybe people would listen," I continued. He nodded his head dubiously. "Let's rewrite the ballad from the girl's point of view and dramatize it," I went on. "What for?" he asked. "This is Women's Year. It would be a way of contributing something," I replied. "What's Women's Year?" he asked. "In Egypt, it is . . ." I searched for the words carefully. ". . . the year to fight for women's legal and human rights. Like Jihan al-Sadat is doing." "For you, doctora, I would do anything," he said, smiling.

In the next four weeks, an increasingly enthusiastic Adel, along with a team of student writers, dramatized the episode and rewrote the ballad. The opening lines of the new ballad resounded in the wekala:

> The most beautiful words on Honor
> Have been spoken a long time ago.
> Let us repeat them tonight
> But in a completely different way.
> Approach, people, and hear what we have to say. . . .

The scenes were tailored to the caravanserai. Each stanza of the ballad was sung from a different corner of the wekala. The ballad singer and his musicians would follow the action on-stage, or move up to the balconies, or sit in the fountain. Different scenes took place in different locations of the theater. Chafeeka's bordello was located beneath a mashrabiya window at the highest tier. Below, Metwalli plans his revenge. Chafeeka leans out of a mashrabiya to beckon a client while her brother beckons to the relatives who will assist him in the slaughter. The audience is caught in-between the two actions, the two predicaments.

I had recruited some actors from the neighborhood. One of them, Bulbul, was obese and mentally retarded. We cast him in the role of village idiot, but he is the only person who recognizes Chafeeka's suffering. When Chafeeka discovers that she is pregnant, a spotlight catches Bulbul looking at her in mute anguish.

We rehearsed for weeks in the unbearable July heat. It was the holy month of Ramadan. The troupe grumbled a lot because they were fasting and they were not even allowed to drink. They waited impatiently for sunset and the muezzin's voice calling, "Allah-hu-Akhbar, Allah-hu-Akhbar, Allah-hu-Akhbar," to announce the breaking of the fast. As they rushed out to eat and drink, the muezzin's call would be joined by other voices ringing from the mosques, the atmosphere resounding with their powerful cacophony.

I would finally have a chance to sit down and rest in the mesmerizing quiet of the wekala, the only sound that of the trickling fountain. After spending a few minutes thinking about the rehearsal, I would usually step outside for a pack of cigarettes. On the way, I would be greeted by the leather-faced garlic vendor who would say, "Itfadali, ya doctora," as he offered me his bowl of foul beans. Farther on, straw mats and newspapers would have been spread on the ground, while men and women, rich and poor, sat side by side to partake of the *iftar*—the breaking of the fast. The intoxicating smell of fried onions and garlic would fill the air. Still farther, the more affluent would sit at long tables, feasting on broiled lamb kebab and tehina or sesame salad. Nearby a confectioner would proudly display his baklava trays, the flies buzzing over them greedily. Next to the confectioner, the butcher, his decapitated carcasses oozing blood. "Ahlan, ya doctora," said the butcher, with whom I had made a deal. He would get a free ticket to the show in exchange for the use of his largest knife. Metwalli murdered his sister with a butcher's knife.

By the time I had bought my cigarettes and returned to the wekala, the troupe would be back full of energy for the next rehearsal, and the almost unreal stillness of before would seem an illusion.

The rehearsals were going so well that I decided to call on my contacts in the Ministry of Culture to see if they would help finance the play. I was referred to Mr. Mohammed Saad, a former general with a sallow complexion and a military mustache. He listened politely to what I told him about the new version and asked me to return in a couple of days. When I did, we had coffee and made small talk, a process which was repeated a couple of times before he informed me that it was against the rules to finance or release equipment to a company which was not affiliated with the state. I reminded him that I had worked with the state in previous productions. He asked me to return in a few days.

When I arrived, Mr. Mohammed Saad greeted me with great excitement. "I have moved mountains for you!" he announced. "We will give you the equipment and the stage!" I was beside myself with joy—until I met the official in charge of the ministry's warehouses. He greeted me sullenly. "Come back in a week," he said. "But Mr. Mohammed Saad said I could have the equipment right away," I said in complete exasperation. "Mr. Mohammed doesn't know this is inventory time," he barked.

Almost in tears, I returned to the office of the ex-general. "You must be patient," he said paternalistically. "This is not America."

Meanwhile, we forged ahead with our rehearsals. But I was in a state of despair. Adel suggested we go begging at the other theaters in Cairo, and we did just that, but no one would give us a projector or a platform. Finally, we ended up at the television building, where we were told we might get something. While Adel and I negotiated with one of the bureaucrats there, a tall, well-built man in his fifties, with a wide forehead and horn-rimmed glasses, emerged. It was Said Adham, the foremost theater director of the sixties. He walked slowly, coolly, a young actor following him worshipfully. I watched him in envy: all he would have to do is lift a finger and the state would put all its lighting equipment and stages at his disposal—even though he was a Nasserist. As he approached, I greeted him. He nodded his head, and stopped to talk with me. I told him about my difficulties. "It's the infrastructure, the infrastructure has collapsed," and saying this he moved on majestically, his follower tripping behind. Little did I suspect, as I watched him go, that one day we would work together.

Finally the equipment was released and we opened on schedule. Because of its economical staging, *Chafeeka* had a lyrical simplicity. The ballad was accompanied by a solitary reed flute that any villager can play, and was sung by a single voice. When Chafeeka was about to be killed, her heartbeat was syncopated with the beat of a leather drum. When she pleads for her life, explaining that she had no choice, a rural *mizmar*, or oboe, echoes her cries while a single spotlight illuminates her. One light, one voice, one oboe, one flute and the subdued indignation of women for thousands of years: *Chafeeka* in 1975, Women's Year.

My father was unable to see *Chafeeka* because of his health. But he read all the reviews out loud to me, even though they had already been read to me by Asma, and when it was later taped and aired on Egyptian television, he watched it with great solemnity.

A couple of weeks after the production closed, I received an invitation to lecture on the Egyptian theater and cinema at several U.S. universities. The prospect of it filled me with dread. Hadn't my daily struggles in the Hussein and my serpentine meanderings in the bureaucracy rendered me academically unfit? What would I wear? I had no academically respectable clothes, no suits, no skirts. What would I say? I was filled with angst, but I accepted the invitation.

This time there was no need to apply for an exit visa. All I had to do was show my passport at the airport, and the officer in charge would wave a hand and say, "M'aa al-salama, go in peace." But leaving my father worried me. He quieted my fears by saying, "Don't be silly. Go and give your lectures and make me proud of you."

When I arrived at JFK, I received a friendly smile from the customs official. "What do you have in there, hashish from

Egypt?" Very different from the last time. "Going to the Big Apple?" asked the cabbie as he took my luggage. I stretched my legs in the spacious car. The driver grinned into the mirror. "Where you from?" he asked. "The Middle East," I replied. "Israel?" he asked hopefully. "Egypt," I answered. "Sadat," he commented after a moment's pause. As we sped along the familiar expressway, the Manhattan skyline in all its geometric splendor welcomed me to America.

The Roosevelt, a second-rate hotel with its red and gold lobby, looked unimaginably opulent. I went immediately to the coffee shop and ordered a hamburger, and marveled at the size of a neighbor's ice cream. I bought a pack of my favorite mentholated cigarettes, unavailable in Cairo, lit one and inhaled deeply as I partook of the pleasures of the consumer society unabashedly.

"Paul, it's Laila," I said over the long-distance line. It seemed the most natural thing in the world to call him now that I was in America. "Laila, you're back. I can't believe it. Have you come back to me?" he asked. "Paul, can you meet my plane on Friday?" I said, avoiding his question. "Of course I will. I've missed you so much. So much." "I've missed you too," I said, not realizing until that moment that I had. "Have you?" he persisted. "Yes, it's just that Cairo is so crazy—I don't have time to think—of anything," I replied apologetically.

The next couple of weeks were to be filled with academic activity. I was scheduled to lecture at New York University, Columbia University, then the University of North Carolina, the University of Colorado, UCLA, Harvard University, and even the University of Toronto. The routine of the lecture tour gave me that sense of stability which American academic life invariably provides. Breakfast at eight, a lecture at nine, coffee break at ten, a panel followed by lunch where there would be a name to indicate my place. The afternoon session would follow the same neat pattern, so different from life in Cairo which defied any pattern. The days thus went by very quickly, but at night my thoughts returned to Paul in anticipation of seeing him.

He was waiting for me at the airport and took me in his arms for a long kiss the moment he saw me. I tried to push him away, feeling a strange embarrassment as I did. "You're looking beautiful," he said. "I've just lost a bit of weight. There are no Mars bars in Cairo," I replied, and we both laughed, breaking the tension. As we walked, he held on to my arm, and while we waited for my luggage, he kissed me again. "Paul, someone might see us," I said. "This isn't Cairo, Laila."

In the car I began to chat about my work. He drove silently. Do I still love him? I wondered.

Back at his apartment, he had prepared a candlelit dinner. As soon as he sat down, he told me he had left his wife, and was living alone. His eyes were full of pain and reproach, but at the same time he reached for my hand across the table. I continued making small talk, trying to sound casual. "You must stay here now," he said urgently. "I miss you. I need you." "I need you too," I replied, "but I have learned to . . ." I faltered, ". . . to suppress my needs. Besides, Cairo, the war, have changed me. I'm more involved in my work. My father is ill. I cannot leave." I sound too apologetic, I thought. He came toward me and took me in his arms again. I stiffened. "Have you been involved with another man?" he asked. "No," I lied. Later in his arms, I realized that I had forgotten how to love, and I surrendered myself to him knowing it would be the last time.

"Dr. Laila, that was a very interesting lecture," said an Egyptian man, about fifty, with thick glasses. It was Sayed Moussa, a prominent politician and lawyer who, it was rumored in Cairo, would become the next minister of justice. He was a guest lecturer at the University of California at Los Angeles. We talked for a while and then he asked me to have a cup of coffee with him.

Over American coffee, he told me he had seen *Milad Batal* on TV. Then we discussed Sadat's liberalization of the media. There had been much talk in Cairo recently of relaxing theatrical censorship. He suggested we meet again in Washington, where we were both going next.

The moment I stepped into my Washington hotel room, the telephone rang. It was Mr. Moussa. "Would you like to come to a reception at the Egyptian embassy tonight? I would like to introduce you to the ambassador," he said. I told him I would love to come.

As I entered the elegant drawing room of the ambassador's residence, Sayed Moussa came up to me, and smiling at me from behind his thick glasses, guided me gently to the ambassador. The ambassador was no stranger. I had seen his face frequently on American television these past weeks. "Your excellency," I said as I shook hands. "Welcome, Dr. Laila," he said cordially. His wife gave me a condescending smile. Moussa stood by me for a few polite moments, then he left me alone to mingle with a group of diplomats. An Egyptian woman historian who was now teaching in the United States approached me. "I heard your lecture here," she said, and then added in a stern voice, "However, I would think twice before exposing our problems to the West." "Those of us who live in Egypt at least try to do something about our problems," I answered. She gave me a cold stare and walked way. Moussa returned to my side. "I hope you are enjoying yourself?" he said.

When I returned to New York a couple of days later, I found a message from Professor Edward Said of Columbia University, inviting me to his home for dinner. He greeted me in Arabic as I walked into his modest Riverside Drive apartment. He introduced me to his wife, who was preparing food in the kitchen, and then led me to his study. "You know, I knew your sister in high school in Cairo," I said as I took my seat. "Yes, I know that. I've been wanting to meet you. I have read your excellent study of Rihani," he said warmly. "And I've been wanting to meet you, too," I said. "When I was a student here in the sixties, I was very much influenced by your articles on the image of the Arabs in the American media. I agree with you that we still need to do so much to humanize that image for American audiences." He nodded adamantly. "Have you read my books on

Conrad?" he asked. "I'm afraid not, but I certainly plan to," I added.

The conversation then turned to what it was like being an Arab in New York—a favorite subject of Said's—to the intellectual life in Egypt, and then to the Middle Eastern situation. As we talked, I found myself drawn to this dashing Arab intellectual. The affinity I had with him lay in the fact that we were both exiles of a sort: we both lived with one foot in the Arab world, another in the West. We thought in English, but conversed in Arabic, and we shared an uneasiness with both these cultures. As we parted, I felt that the problem of identity was as unresolved for him as it was for me.

The next day I was invited for dinner to the home of Jacob Hurewitz, a well-known Middle Eastern historian at Columbia University. And I was slightly surprised by the warmth with which I was received by him and Miriam, his wife. I had been accustomed to nothing but hostility from Jewish faculty in the sixties, but this was different. At dinner, the subject invariably turned to Middle Eastern politics. Hurewitz struck me as unopinionated, even objective. And he made a point of enumerating his various friends in Cairo.

As he saw me to the elevator at the end of the evening, Hurewitz said, "Let's keep in touch, and if you should return to New York, let me know so that you can give another talk at Columbia."

Things had certainly changed since the sixties.

CONVEYER BELTS had been installed for baggage at Cairo airport. The building had been modernized and reorganized. This was one of the many signs of the open-door policy. Customs officials smiled at the "Nothing to Declare" travelers and welcomed them with a warm "Hamdellah ala al-salama."

My parents, Asma, and Nabil, my brother, were waiting for me—a familiar scene. My father wore his white sharkskin, double-breasted jacket. He held a white linen handkerchief with an *N* embroidered on it to wipe the perspiration from his face. Although it was mid-November, it was still very hot. "We've been waiting for two hours," said my mother, as my father hugged me as if I had been away for years instead of weeks. Asma hovered over us, bombarding me with questions, not waiting for any of the answers. She wore tight blue jeans and her favorite black shirt. Her eyes sparkled, her voice resounded joyfully, and people stared at her in admiration as we made our way through the crowd.

The sky over the desert road which leads into Cairo was red with the sunset. As we drove, a soft breeze came through the window. The dry air was soothing; everything was familiar, warm. Even the bumps in the road. I looked at my father, noticing how his cheekbones protruded. Sensing my concern, he pressed my hand with strong fingers. I shuddered at my morbidity.

A white linen tablecloth had been laid at home with all my

favorite dishes—stuffed grapevine leaves with yogurt salad, roast lamb and tehina, stuffed pigeons and chicken with walnut sharkasiya sauce. It was useless explaining that I had eaten on the plane. As I ate, my father asked me questions about the universities I had visited. "Harvard! Columbia! Marvelous, bravo," he said when I told him where I had been.

After the meal, the conversation turned to politics and "this new man," as my father persisted in calling Sadat. "This new man is not in control internally. He is letting people get away with everything. No one stops at the traffic lights anymore. The other day, I almost had a little heart attack, and when I tried the oxygen flasks for my breathing, they were full of air instead of oxygen! It's because the company that makes them is owned by the government. Anything that's run by the government is hopeless!" I tried to conceal my smile. "And the streets are so crowded," he went on. "There is no space to park anymore! Many of my clients have stopped coming to the clinic because they have nowhere to park. Of course, these young doctors have stolen some of my clients. I only get the difficult cases—the ones nobody can solve. You know these young doctors today, they don't know a thing about medicine. All they care about is to make money fast. In my day you went into the medical profession for the sake of science," he said passionately. "Nessim," interrupted my mother, "you're seventy-five. You have no business working at all, let alone complaining you're not getting enough cases." "Let's go to the balcony, Laila," said my father, taking me by the hand.

As I sat down on the terrace, he told me that my mother didn't understand him: "She doesn't understand that my life is my work." Then he added, "Do you know where I want to die, Laila? At my clinic. Close to my X-ray machines." I protested at this turn in the conversation and he became silent, his hands folded beneath his chin, his forehead furrowed in deep concentration. I watched him, my heart full of unspoken words. The thumb of one of his hands moved up and down on the palm of the other as if he were summing up, evaluating his life.

Soon it had grown dark on the terrace. There was a cool

breeze from the Nile. The water shimmered with the evening lights. The noise of the city had subsided. Now and then we would hear the lament of a stray dog. My father's breathing, which had come in spasmodic rasps before, was more even now. As his breathing became easier, the muscles in his face relaxed. Suddenly he got up and announced that he would change into a fresh pair of pajamas. He returned a little while later, the smell of his cologne filling the air, his thick white mane neatly combed. He declared that he felt as "good as new." I reassured him by telling him that he looked very dashing. "As dashing as those movie stars you used to have a crush on?" he asked. "You look even better than Clark Gable," I said.

At my apartment everything was the same as I had left it: a bathroom cabinet with half-empty bottles, a hairbrush to which strands of my hair still clung, a pair of slippers, half-finished letters, my eyedrops next to the bed. Everything was there exactly as I had left it, waiting for me like old, neglected friends.

As I drove to the institute the next day, I noticed the Coca-Cola and Seven-Up billboards everywhere. The Marlboro and Kent ads stole the show because they were larger than all the other ones. Hundreds of small boutiques and kiosks had sprung up. They were no longer illegal as they had been in the Nasser days. They flaunted their new Western goods—TVs, washing machines, refrigerators, electric fans—on the sidewalks for everyone to see. A sign of a new consumer era. But Cairo's buses seemed more overcrowded than ever; people hung on to the doors, while others grabbed on to the back fenders. This sight, a strong visual reminder of the population explosion, contrasted sharply with the brand-new cars and the new products in the boutiques.

So did the surrounding poverty.

G<small>UESS WHAT</small>?" said Asma on the phone, her voice vibrating with excitement. "What?" I inquired. "Dietrich has asked me to marry him." "That's wonderful. Are you happy, Pouppa?" I asked. "Yes, very happy. I'll come over later and I'll tell you all about it." But as I put the receiver down I knew there would be trouble.

My mother was beside herself. "It's all your fault, Laila. It's your terrible influence on your sister that's brought this on us. Freedom, career, Western ideas—that's why Asma wants to marry a foreigner." "Do you know anything about him?" asked my father somewhat more calmly. I shook my head. My brother, who was also present at this council, commented that "Dietrich is short, much too short for Pouppa." "I think we can still stop this relationship from going any further," declared my mother. "She will just have to stop seeing him."

From then on, Asma had to return home immediately after work. Her telephone calls were monitored, her outings curfewed. Naturally, her German suitor became even more adamant. The pressures on Asma must have been overwhelming. She could not conceive of defying the family. She needed their approval, their blessing. Yet she always smiled, always gave the impression of lightheartedness. No one would have known she was distraught.

But one day, sitting in her favorite armchair, her eyes overcast with worry, she said, "If I don't get married now, I'll never get out of their grip. They have refused to let me study abroad and they will continue to refuse. I will never be free unless I get married. Besides, Dietrich has been good for me." She lit a cigarette. She was smoking too much. "But do you love him?" I asked. "It doesn't matter. He loves me. He's devoted to me and I need that. I need loving. And he encourages my work. With him I could be free and have a career. But if I were to marry an Egyptian . . ." I nodded in understanding. "If it doesn't work out, I could always leave him. All I really want is a career, like you, Laila." If only I could do something to ease her problem, I thought. But I could only give her moral support. "You are right," I said. "The marriage is a way out, a good strategy."

Meanwhile, my mother's campaign was becoming a full-scale war. Uncles, aunts, cousins, friends were all mobilized to dissaude her from marrying the foreigner. My brother, who was now twenty-five, was eager to assert his manhood, so he became the missile with which the relationship was attacked. This tribal onslaught became even too much for Asma to bear. It was she who was being devastated by it. She lost weight; her movements became frenzied, almost furtive.

The tension at home became unbearable. My father's health grew steadily worse. But instead of resting at home, he insisted on spending longer hours than ever at his clinic.

Around Christmastime, Dietrich announced that his parents had come to Egypt and wanted a meeting. Begrudgingly, a dinner was given in their honor. Bearing flowers, and in compliance with our customs, they officially requested Asma's hand for their son. It was all very formal, very comme il faut. They were obviously wealthy and belonged to the German business elite. A lot of hints were dropped about country houses and vacations in the South Seas. Asma's future mother-in-law wore expensive jewelry and a fur jacket. Their son, too, was breaking convention by marrying a non-German, she explained. By the end of the dinner it was settled. Asma would marry Dietrich by the summer.

After they left, my father had a heart attack.

Asma had filled the house with youthful laughter. Now he

would be surrounded with the silence of an empty house. How hollow the echo of these rooms would be without her. I tried to reassure my father by telling him that I would always be there. But his eyes told me that he knew that I had left a long time ago.

My father always sought refuge in his clinic—it was there that he tried to protect himself from the adversities of life. There he could defend himself from these assaults, immuring himself behind his massive desk, his Smith-Corona before him, X-ray machines next door, his seven degrees behind him. Here his life was preserved in all its pristine glory.

One day, after a heated family discussion about Dietrich, with my mother complaining as usual, he put on his clothes and left for the clinic.

I was assigned the task of bringing him home. The moment I entered the clinic, I sensed the permutations of his soul roaming happily in that space. "You can't spend the night here," I said. "You must come home with me." He gave me an ironical smile. Home? it seemed to say. What was home to a man whose very being inhabited these rooms he called his clinic? Was this not his home? The home I proposed was a cluttered apartment where hearts and tongues continuously clashed. Domestic life peels away the layers of the personality until at last nothing but a kernel, an exposed nerve, remains. It takes resilience to hang on to that bare core. My father did this by his retreats to his clinic. There he could be the man he truly was, rather than the husband or the father. There he could really be himself, he seemed to be saying as he sat facing me across his desk, thus barricaded, thus preserved, thus intact.

The clock on a nearby shelf ticked loudly, filling the space around us. Photographs of his father and mother smiled at us from other worlds. The noise of the city outside was muted by the shut windows. Occasionally the air conditioning grumbled. "Please come home," I repeated. He sighed and stood up. While he went into the next room to change his long white coat for his sharkskin jacket, I remained in the office, where even the air, molecule by molecule, was filled with his presence.

"I'm ready now," he said, reentering the office. He winked at me and began to hum one of his favorite songs: "I am he who has lost a lifetime in illusions, ana mann day'aa fil awhami 'umran." Then he took my arm for support. We waited for the elevator on the tiled landing, but the elevator was not working, so we had to take the stairs. The Nubian doorman shuffled to his feet when he saw my father walking slowly down the last steps into the lobby. My car was parked in front of the building. As my father and I walked toward it, someone called to him: "Salamat, ya doctor." He waved his arm and smiled his broad smile and then he got into the car.

A few days later he collapsed. An intern from a nearby hospital was rushed over to administer oxygen to him. Then my mother, brother, Asma, and I sat in his room until dawn. Occasionally my father would raise his hand as if to acknowledge our presence. But the hand would soon drop listlessly to his side.

The apartment was transformed into a sickroom. His bed was removed to the living room because of its sunny exposure. The sofas and chairs were pushed next to the walls and covered with white sheets to protect them from the dust. The room took on a morguelike appearance. Everywhere, tables were strewn with medications, and empty oxygen flasks waited to be taken away. Two nurses moved silently about at all hours. At one point, my father called one of them over and said, "This is the famous Dr. Laila, my daughter." The nurse nodded deferentially. For many hours I sat by his side, murmuring words of comfort. When he could muster the strength to speak he said, "I'm going to die, you know. I'm a doctor, I know my condition." I got up in order to hide my tears. He called my name. I returned and held his hand. My mother entered the room half dazed. Her eyes roamed wildly and the lines of grief were already etched into her face.

After several days of sitting by his bedside my father insisted that we all "carry on" with our work. Asma returned to her office, I to my classes. Meanwhile the house filled with visitors from my father's vast extended family. They would all bend down and kiss him on the forehead or the cheek, then they would wait patiently for a sign of recognition from him. Even in such moments, he fulfilled his obligation as the head of the clan: he would smile or his hand would clasp that of a favorite niece.

When they were all gone, we would sit in silent vigil by his side. He spoke in hoarse, barely audible tones. I would have to bend down to hear him: "Did I ever tell you that I never saw my father on his deathbed?" I tried to smile. He had told me this a hundred times. "I was in England. He died the moment I set foot on Egyptian soil."

As time went by, his heart grew so weak that it could pump up the energy to digest only yogurt. My mother would spoon-feed him and as she did he would murmur, "Isn't this ridiculous. At my age." And at moments like these, I would tell myself that he would pull through. I refused to believe that he was dying.

On the morning of December 31, I told my father that I wanted to celebrate the New Year with him. That evening, wearing a fresh pair of pajamas, he was helped into his armchair by one of his nurses. He asked for his cologne. I was sure this meant that he was recovering. Then he asked for a bottle of Napoleon brandy he kept for special occasions. We were all alone. The nurse had disappeared, Asma and Nabil had gone off to a party, and my mother, who did not drink, was busy around the house.

"This brandy is at least forty years old," he said feebly. It was only ten in the evening but we decided to toast the New Year anyway. He took the glass I held out to him and sniffed it, and swirled its contents. He was enjoying the ritual. His eyes sparkled again for the first time since he was taken ill. He laughed ever so faintly and lifting his glass said, "Happy New Year, darling. . . ." "Fi sehatek, ya papi, wa kul sana wa enta tayeb. Your health," I replied. We each took a sip of the soothing Napoleon V.S.O.P. I told him we should start making plans for the summer. Maybe we could go to the Swiss Alps as we did when I was a child. He said nothing. Occasionally he took a small sip of the brandy, lifting his glass each time, saying, "Happy New Year."

A few days later, he could hardly speak at all. My mother, who never left his side, kept holding his hand. Now and then he opened his eyes and smiled at us with a visible effort. The room was still, his irregular breathing the only sound. It seemed to come from the very core of his being. The nurse checked his pulse at regular intervals. Hours went by as quickly as seconds. My existence was suspended between his inhaling and exhaling breaths. He will recover, I told myself. He will recover. His belongings flung around the room also waited for him to recover: his slippers next to his bed, his bathrobe placed on a chair, his hairbrush, his bottle of cologne on a nearby table, his gold watch ticking, ticking.

Returning home from class a couple of days later, the doorman greeted me with, "Al bakia fi hayatek," words of condolence. Frantically, I rushed upstairs. My father was lying still on the bed. I called out his name, but he did not answer. My mother's head was buried in his shoulder.

The house immediately began to fill with relatives in black. The women surrounded my father's bed, wailing rhythmically. The next day his body was lowered into an ebony coffin by some of the male members of the family. Then it was placed on the shoulders of two men from the funeral parlor. They were dressed in worn-out tuxedos, their hair polished by Brilliantine. They looked like music-hall performers.

My brother, Asma, and I followed the coffin as it was borne down the stairs. In the street, a black car with large glass windows waited to receive it. Two women appeared on the balcony of a nearby house and watched indifferently.

Bishop Samuel waited outside the Coptic Cathedral on Ramsis Street, to pay his respects to the family. By the time the ebony box was carried inside, the benches had filled with men on one side of the aisle, and women, their hair concealed beneath black scarves, on the other. The family sat on the front bench. Asma and my mother on the women's side, my brother and I on the men's.

Bishop Samuel's voice was mournful as he spoke. He recalled the various episodes of the "doctor's" life, as he called my father.

His humble beginnings, his struggle to open a practice in Cairo, his long years of service to the Faculty of Medicine at Cairo University, his establishment of the X-ray department there. He spoke of his loyalty and assistance to the Coptic community and his contributions to the poor. He spoke of him as a *rajul esami*, a self-made man.

When the service was over, the church was bathed in incense. The choir intoned a sad, nasal lament. The coffin was borne down the aisle, my brother and other male members of the family holding it up. We stood at the entrance of the church to shake the hands of all those who had come. "Al bakia fi hayatek, al bakia fi hatatkum" was murmured over and over.

A long procession of cars drove to the graveyard on the outskirts of the city, which is surrounded by nothing but sand hills as far as the eye can see. Inside a high stone fence was a church, flanked on all sides by small mausoleums which held the bodies of prominent and wealthy Copts. The iron gates, usually closed to people of different class or religion, were now wide open. Women in black stood everywhere. A couple of elderly beggar women, shrouded in tattered, black galabiyas, descended upon the mourners, screeching with outstretched palms—vultures waiting to pick at the residue of sorrow.

The crowd moved slowly behind the coffin. Ornamental plaster angels, from the mausoleums on either side, gazed on. Someone began to wail rhythmically.

Inside the church, workmen were trying to loosen the marble vault in which the coffin would be placed, the voice of their hammers and chisels drowning out the nasal chants of the priest. When his chanting ceased, the coffin was placed in the vault. The workmen who had shut the lid of the vault were now busy cementing it. They worked swiftly, professionally. As I watched them, I wondered how we would be able to differentiate the vault in which my father lay from the other vaults in the crypt. I took out a picture of him that I had always kept in my purse and placed it between the handle and the white marble. By now everyone had left. The cold marble returned my touch. Yet the sound of my father's voice as he sang his favorite refrain was still in my ears: "I am he who has lost a lifetime in illusions. . . ."

The ancient Egyptians refuted death; to them it was merely an interruption of life. A dead person survives intellectually and emotionally—indelible proof of the afterlife. The ancient Egyptians communicated regularly with their dead. They even wrote letters to them. On feast days they visited their tombs, a tradition which is practiced to this very day. They take food with them and have a meal at which the dead are supposedly present. Ancient Egyptian tombs are covered with reliefs depicting life's necessities. They often contain inscriptions addressed to the occasional passerby, invoking his attention to the person buried in that tomb:

> O ye who live and exist, who love life and hate death. Whosoever shall pass by this tomb, as ye love life and hate death, so ye shall offer to me that which is in your hands. If naught is in your hands, ye shall speak thus with your mouth: a thousand bottles of Napoleon brandy, a thousand white linen handkerchiefs initialed *N,* a thousand white sharkskin jackets, a thousand of all pure things, to the revered Nessim, son of Soliman.

For weeks, I was unable to see anyone, unable to function. I just remained alone in my apartment. Even Asma, who visited me regularly, could not alleviate the emotional devastation I felt.

A month after my father's death, I returned to the institute. I even made an attempt at teaching. Another month went by and I was still not functioning. I knew that only the most strenuous work would bring me back to the living. Before my father's death, I had agreed to direct a comedy for the Italian Cultural Institute. With the help of Asma, I managed to pull myself together enough to pay my patrons a visit.

The Italian embassy is located in the fashionable quarter of Garden City, on the Nile Corniche. Nubian doormen dressed in black suits announce you, while diplomats in gray silk and Italian shoes walk by in a cloud of elegance. My sponsor was the cultural counselor, Mr. Stephano Vincenzi, a chubby, middle-aged man who was writing a book on Louis XIII, with whom he claimed he had continual conversations. His face lit up as I was ushered into his mahogany-paneled office which was lined with leather-bound books. "La belle Laila," he said, kissing my hand.

After a quarter of an hour, the exchange of compliments was over and we finally got down to business. "Have you decided which one?" he asked, as if it were a secret between us. *"La Locandiera—The Mistress of the Inn,"* I said. "Of course. Bravissimo. And you will play la Mirandolina, the mistress." I had not thought of acting, but now I found myself seduced by the idea. Blushing, I replied, "Do you think I will make a good Mirandolina?" "Perfect," he replied. "Then we can count on your financial backing?" I asked, seizing the moment. "But of course, we will have a good budget for you," he said, taking my hand and kissing it again. "If I act . . ." I said. "But you must," he interrupted. "Thank you. That means I will have to hire a first-rate director to mount the play. C'est indispensable," I remarked. "Naturellement, ma chère amie, you have carte blanche," he announced, standing up, obviously in a hurry to return to Louis XIII. As he ushered me to the door, he kissed my hand again and said, "A trés bientôt."

From the embassy, I dashed to the nearest phone. I was able to get through to Said Adham, the famous director of the sixties, on the first try. I wondered if he still had the assistant tripping behind him. "Would you like to direct a Goldoni?" I asked, the excitement in my voice impossible to conceal. "Come see me tomorrow at the office. We'll discuss it then," he replied without conveying any emotion. Adham had directed a famous production of Goldoni's *The Servant of Two Masters* in the sixties, and as well as having studied in Italy, he was regarded as the Egyptian Goldoni specialist. His acceptance of the job would add prestige to the production.

He smiled patronizingly as I entered his small office in the government building for theater administration. Then he lit a cigarette and sat back eyeing me. "Dr. Laila, I envy your enthusiasm," he said from behind his cluttered aluminum desk. "But I enjoy it too, as I am enjoying you." I ignored the pass. "Let me think your proposition over," he went on with a wave of his hand. My face fell. "I have so much government work," he added. He was heading one of the state-subsidized theaters. As we shook hands, he told me to get in touch with him in a couple of days.

Later that week I was again seated before the aluminum desk. "Why Mirandolina?" he asked. "Because it's a play about the rise of a new class, the middle class, with its sense of survival, its instinct for business . . . in effect, the *infitah* [Sadat's economic open-door policy]." He stiffened at the mention of infitah. Had I said the wrong thing? "You are an advocate of the infitah?" he asked. "Well," I said, trying to choose my words, "I believe in the vitality of the mercantile class. We Arabs have always been wonderful merchants. . . ." My voice trailed off. Had I forgotten I was talking to a man of the sixties? "Mirandolina, the hotel owner, represents the new bourgeoisie in Italy in the eighteenth century. She is pitted against the aristocracy, the feudal elite." Adham began to nod in approval. I was getting close. "It's an anti-aristocratic play." His nod was more definite this time. I heaved a sigh of relief. "I have always wanted to stage it," he declared. "Who will play Mirandolina?" But before I could answer he looked at me searchingly and said, "You want to do the part?" I shifted uneasily in my chair and said, "Only if you think I can, if I am suitable." After a long pause I detected a smile. "Why do you want to do it?" I was pleased by the question and yet irritated at the same time. I felt like a student at an audition. "Mirandolina is in many ways a feminist. She is a working woman who is trying to survive in a man's world. It's not easy. Her customers think of only one thing: how to get into her bed. She, on the other hand, thinks of how to keep her hotel running, of how to make money, of how to survive." "Hmm," he said, "where will you stage it?" I suggested a production in the round, preferably in a real hotel. The idea appealed to him.

The Meridien Hotel—located practically in the middle of the

Nile—was the setting I chose for the play. A few days later, we sat on the terrace which jutted out into the water. In the background, an Egyptian *qanoun* or harp played a melancholy tune. I had just shown him the banquet room which he approved for a theater. Now, nursing his Scotch, he informed me that he had thought my proposal over and decided to accept it.

Later, alone in my apartment, I paced up and down in excitement. This was the big time! My collaboration with Adham would open all the doors of the professional theater which had hitherto been closed to me.

The first preproduction meeting was held in my apartment. He stood in front of my bookshelves, scrutinizing the many books. "Your books are mostly in English," he said in an accusing tone. Then he turned around and added, "They say you are American." "I have lived and studied in America but that doesn't make me an American," I replied. "America is a reactionary superpower which exploits the Third World," he said. "And what about the Soviet Union?" I asked. "The Soviet system, socialism, the five-year plan, approximate the needs of our country better than capitalism and the materialistic values of America." I quickly turned our conversation to the play.

At our next meeting, Adham suggested we make an adaptation of the play in order to bring it closer to Egyptian audiences. I suggested Farouk Helw, a comic writer who had just had an enormous hit in the commercial theater. The moment I mentioned his name, Adham froze. Helw's play concerned the expulsion of the Soviet experts from Egypt. The experts were portrayed in a farcical fashion: fat, red in the face, always in shorts, and always accompanied by a translator even though they all spoke Arabic. The plot was about how these experts interfered in the affairs of an Egyptian village and the villagers' decision to kick them out—after making complete fools of them. The message, of course, was Egypt for the Egyptians, but the play's treatment of the Soviets was considered insulting by their diplomats in Cairo and the embassy protested officially. Their protest fell on President Sadat's deaf ears. The play was allowed to continue its run, with official blessing.

Adham cringed at the idea of a collaboration with a right-winger like Helw, but I managed to talk him into it because I knew Helw would be ideal for Goldoni.

I went to see Helw at his theater which had a small proscenium stage and the look of a cheap music-hall. A dusty canvas tent covered the dirt floor and straw chairs. I was ushered into Helw's dressing room. "Itfadali, ya doctora," he said, pointing to a chair next to where he sat, having his makeup put on. He was fleshy, bald, extremely nearsighted. He squinted periodically behind his thick glasses. His voice had the hoarse quality of a hashish smoker. He had come into the theater late in life, via a legal background, journalism, and marriage to a famous belly dancer.

The makeup artist had placed a huge, upturned mustache on his face and Helw was busy smoothing it over with his hand. It looked so inconsistent with his bald head and glasses that I had a difficult time concealing my smile. I began to talk about the play. He was extremely flattered at the idea of working with an intellectual like Adham. "You have read Goldoni, of course?" I asked him. He nodded his head quickly, eager to appear knowledgeable. "Then you will do the adaptation?" I said. He nodded again, while holding on to his mustache with two chubby fingers.

A month later, he had rewritten Goldoni's play, adapting the eighteenth-century plot to Nasser's Egypt in 1965. Goldoni's rigid and decaying aristocracy became the powerful, corrosive military elite of the police state. The misogynist whom the mistress of the inn tricks into falling in love with her is a retired general of the Egyptian army. Thus it was not just the woman-hater who was being humiliated in Helw's version, but an entire regime. By this time, Adham was so absorbed in our work that he pretended not to object to the political nuances. In reality, however, he was trying to ingratiate himself with the Sadat regime.

The adaptation became instantly controversial. On the day of our final rehearsal, we were served a court order to halt the production. "Do you know of a good lawyer?" asked Adham, his face yellow as a lemon. "Someone is accusing us of plagiarism!" We looked at each other in disbelief. "Yes, let's get on the phone," I said.

Early the next morning we stood in court in a special session, a famous lawyer, Labib Moawad, defending our case. Holding a history of the theater in his hands, the lawyer said: "Your Honor, according to our copyright laws, anyone is entitled to translate or adapt a work by an author who has been dead for over a hundred years. According to this history text, the author in question, Carlo Goldoni, has been dead for over *a hundred and fifty years.* This means that even you, Your Honor, should you wish, are entitled to translate and adapt the plays of said author!" The judge ruled in our favor and we opened on schedule.

It was a triumphant opening. The events of the court suit had increased our publicity. The banquet hall was packed. Cameras flashed everywhere, and after Act 1 scores of people came backstage to congratulate us. Among them was Sayed Moussa, the politician I had met in the United States. He had been promoted, not to minister of justice, but to minister of culture and information. His presence, therefore, impressed many, especially Adham. Smiling at me from behind his horn-rimmed glasses, Moussa shook my hand and said, "Bravo, Dr. Laila."

A week after the production closed, I received a phone call from Paul. He was calling from Cairo where he had come to spend the Easter break. "I thought I'd surprise you. I have two weeks' vacation and I wanted to see you," he said with warmth. I was pleased to hear from him, even happy—the kind of happiness one feels when reunited with a member of one's family.

The moment he entered the apartment he tried to take me in his arms. I mumbled something and gently pushed him away. His face changed color with the rejection. It irritated me that he could summon sexual desire on the spur of the moment. "Let's go for a bite," I said, smiling as brightly as I could.

We walked to a restaurant in a building opposite the Nile. A highway separated the restaurant from the river. We could see red and green lights reflected on the water. A soft breeze blew and mingled with the sound of car horns. Our wine was brought before us and we sat silently as the waiter uncorked it. "About your father," he said, breaking the silence, "I have no words. I know how much he meant to you." I nodded my head. "Are you happy in Egypt?" Paul then said. The question sounded like a reproach. "Yes. Professionally. The production I have just finished has put me on the map. I was working with the best professionals. The critics reviewed it well, except the Left, of course." But Paul wasn't listening, so I stopped talking. "What about your priorities?" he said, an edge in his voice. Our food had been brought and set on the table. The memory of the hundreds of meals we had shared made him suddenly overwhelmingly close. I wanted to reach across the table and touch his hand. "Besides, I've heard rumors that you are having an affair with the director who staged the play," he said. I broke a piece of bread and dipped it into the tehina salad. We began to eat our meal. The silence between us was interrupted only by the intermittent sound of car horns. Soon he was gone.

Asma's marriage had been postponed because of our father's death. My mother, therefore, was in a position to exert more control over Asma than ever. A whole new campaign of hostilities was waged. Asma and Dietrich had to hide their meetings, and much of their relationship had to be confined to letters. "I have been hearing things right and left against a common life between us: that is to say, the disadvantages of living in Germany," she wrote to him. "There are many who add that I am good and wonderful enough to marry a prince. The more I hear negative remarks, the more I want 'us'! I have been suppressed all my life by my mother and father. My life, no matter how much I was able to lead it my own way, was in the greater portion dedicated to them. I need to begin living in a more relaxed way. I need to have someone who will help my psyche relax. To stop having to be alert, always having to be there because this or that person expects it. I need to discuss everything with the person I care for, little things and big things, to exchange views from chocolate to politics. I need to stimulate the needs of my intellect. If I don't continue to fight for something in life, I'll wither away and become very old, even if my skin is still fresh."

But then, a few months after our father died, Asma burst into my apartment, and bubbling with excitement, held out her hand. "My shabka," she announced. Dietrich, in compliance with our customs, had bought her an expensive wedding ring. The wedding would soon take place.

The Mistress of the Inn had helped to take my mind off my father's death. But as soon as the production was over, the pain returned with even more ferocity than before. Everything I did seemed to be futile because he wasn't there to share it. Even my work seemed to diminish in importance, because he wasn't there to applaud it. My mother was hostile to the theater and she so resented my taking on an acting role that she hadn't even come to the production. The family became a group of people I tried to avoid. Only Asma tied me to them and the countless aunts and uncles to whom I had long since become an object of scandal. I searched, in vain, for an ally among them, but none was to be found. I would return to my apartment, to sit opposite my father's smiling photograph—alone.

During its run, the Goldoni play had been taped by Egyptian television, but two months after the production had closed, it had still not been aired. I decided to try to speed up the bureaucratic process by speaking to the officials in charge at the television building.

Finally, I ended up in the office of the censorship committee. It was a small office, with a window overlooking a courtyard. A severe-looking woman, wearing an Islamic hair cover in the shape of a turban, sat behind one of three desks. Many women were now wearing these turbans instead of the more cumbersome veil. "We have your request," she said, looking at my jeans disapprovingly. Then she returned to the newspaper she was reading. Not realizing that I had been dismissed, I stood there. Finally, she looked at me and snapped, "Come back in a week!"

When I returned, two more bureaucrats were occupying the other two desks and they were all chattering busily. The turbaned censor briskly asked me to sit down. "We are having problems with your play," she said in an officious voice. "What kind of problems?" I asked. "The script is full of lewdness. We cannot possibly air it in this condition. You will have to rewrite and reshoot." "That's impossible," I said, louder than I had intended. She gave me a glacial look. "What are the scenes that displease you?" I asked, trying to speak as calmly as possible. "All those scenes with the consumption of alcohol in them," she said. "But that's the entire second act," I gasped. "The word 'general' has to be eliminated as well." "The general is a major character who appears throughout the play. We can't possibly eliminate him," I protested. "Parodies on the military are unacceptable on television," she declared indignantly. "Look," I said, "this is an adaptation of an Italian play. I assure you there are no malicious implications for the military in our society." "I'm sorry, the general will have to go," she insisted. "But that's unreasonable. Totally unreasonable," I cried, raising my voice. The two other bureaucrats stopped chatting and looked at me in disdain. "We can try to edit out the word 'general,' I said faintly. "All right, we'll see the tapes after you have done so, but I don't promise anything."

When I returned to inquire if she would review the tapes now that they had been "cleansed," she asked me to return in a week. When she finally viewed the tapes, she informed me that "the wine bottle was still there." "Of course it's still there," I said, losing my patience. "The heroine tries to get the general drunk as part of the seduction." She stared at me in utter contempt. "The consumption of alcohol is forbidden on television," she said. "I will bring the whole matter before *the director of television,*" she informed me.

As I left the building, I wondered what would have been the outcome if my father were still alive. I could see him, smiling and saying, "Cheer up, I have a friend in television. He will fix everything." And the next day everything would be fixed. . . . Maybe they all knew, I thought as I got into my car, that I had no man to back me up. Maybe that was it. Or maybe things in Egypt were changing again.

HAVE YOU HEARD that Mrs. Sadat has initiated a new draft of the amendment of the Family Law?" said Asma as she sat in my apartment. "No, I've been so busy with the Goldoni, I've been completely out of things," I answered. "I gather it's not going to be televised," she said. "Tell me about the draft law," I said, anxious to change the subject. "Do you remember the Azhar demonstration last year?" I nodded my head. "Well, this time she managed to get the support of the head of Al-Azhar University, and you know, he is the most powerful Islamic leader in the country," she added. "Fantastic," I said. "And what I've heard is that the new draft gives women the right to sue for divorce if their husband takes a second wife." "Well, that's something," I said jokingly. "Don't laugh! You know that women are not allowed to initiate divorce except for impossible reasons. Besides, this is supposed to discourage unilateral divorce, polygamy and so on," she said with conviction. "That's all wonderful," I said, "but does it really make a difference when most of our women are too poor and illiterate even to know their legal rights?" "Laila, how can you say that?" she said indignantly. "Egyptian women are fighters, even when they are illiterate. Om Abdou barely knew how to read or write, but she knew how to stand up for her rights . . . or have you forgotten?" "Quite, absolutely," I remarked, then a thought suddenly came to me. "What are you thinking of?" she asked. "You've just given me an idea for my next production," I said. "What?" she asked gleefully. "It's a ballad based on a true story called 'Hassan wa Naima,' about an illiterate peasant girl who fights for her rights." "Terrific. Tell me about it later. Now I have to rush. I'm having lunch with Dietrich." And giving me a hug, she ran out, her perfume lingering behind her.

As the door closed, I picked up the phone and rang Samir Abdel Halim, one of the foremost experts on Middle Eastern folklore. He was also a playwright who, in the sixties, had done several dramatizations of folk ballads, including "Hassan wa Naima." "Dr. Laila, what a nice surprise." "Thank you," I replied. "Do you remember we met when you were staging your plays in 1965?" he asked. "Of course, of course," I said. "I was hoping you'd remember." "I also enjoyed your 'New Hamlet' on TV." "Thank you, so kind of you to say so. I was wondering if we could meet sometime soon. I have an idea for a play that I would like to discuss with you," I said.

Samir Abdel Halim ushered me into a darkened room filled with ancient Egyptian masks, pottery, and books. "So you're a collector?" I commented. "Only of our ancient heritage," he said, offering me a seat. "I'm a great admirer of your volume on Egyptian folk ballads," I started to say. "But how is someone like you, Americanized, Westernized, interested in the peasants?" he asked. "My grandmother was a peasant," I remarked. "Is that why you are interested in folklore?" "That's one part of it," I murmured. "The peasants are neglected by the Cairenes," he said, rolling a cigarette and offering it to me. "Is that hashish?" I asked. He nodded with a smile. "Some other time," I said, not wishing to offend him. "You learn to smoke this stuff in jail," he said. "Yes, I understand that you were jailed by Nasser for communism," I said. "Let's talk about something else," he said. "Let's take the condition of the peasants," he began. "Do you include women in your peasant category?" I asked a bit sarcastically. "Of course. But once the revolution takes place, the condition of women will automatically improve." "The condition of women hasn't improved in most Eastern bloc countries, or where socialism exists," I commented. He looked at me impatiently. "You have to look at it within the economic context: that's the only way. Most of our industry is based on agricultural raw materials which go into industrial raw materials which go into industrial export products. The fellahin, therefore, earn eighty percent of our hard currency, but the government keeps them in poverty by its outrageous exploitation of them. For instance, since ancient times the Egyptian peasant has been *forced* by the government to grow cotton. If they don't, they are fined. And, of course, it is the government which sets the price it will pay for this cotton. The government then is the capitalist class which exploits the peasants who are the real proletariat class of this country," he said. "You mean the government cheats them by forcing them to sell at reduced rates?" I asked. He nodded his head. "It's up to us to politicize the peasants. That's why I write peasant dramas."

I listened to him in admiration for his ideological commitment, but I knew it would obviously be difficult to mobilize him for the women's issue. I lit one of my cigarettes and began to smoke. Then I said, "You are the only one who can understand why I too want to produce a peasant drama, as you put it. You're the best man in town for the job. I don't want a piece of propaganda for the women's cause, I want a real play by a playwright of your stature." "Thank you," he replied. "You staged *Chafeeka* in a feminist fashion, didn't you?" he added, a note of cynicism in his voice. "Fifty percent of the country is female, and in the rural countryside they are an unpaid labor force. Isn't that also exploitation?" I asked, trying to sound convincing. "Of course," he said. "Good," I replied. "Then you will listen to my conception of Hassan wa Naima?"

He did not protest as I launched into my description, but it was clear from the expression on his face that he was humoring me. It was an expression I was to see on the faces of many men—right, left, or center—when I talked about women's rights. "This girl Naima, who ran away with a singer in defiance of all traditions and then denounced her parents to the police when they murdered him, is quite extraordinary. In your version, she is a symbol of the Egyptian people: passive, lethargic. I

would like her to be more fleshed out, a realistic characteriza-
tion, not symbolic, mind you. I want to stress the qualities of
anger and rebellion in her. I am proposing an image of women
who make their own choices," I said forcefully. "Men own
women in our culture, and that is why they dictate sexual behavior to them. If women realized this, however uneducated
they may be, they would demand their rights. Even those of us
who are educated are at the mercy of this code of ethics. I, too,
once upon a time was a piece of property, and I was passed over
from my family to my husband exactly like merchandise."

Halim smiled and leaned over in his chair. "Tell me more
about your marriage," he said. "Some other time," I said. "Do
you remember the scene in the ballad when Naima is examined
by midwives in front of the whole village to find out if she is a
virgin or not?" "Yes, I do." "That scene is not even included in
your version, and if I recall correctly, she doesn't even denounce
her parents to the police." "Ballads are there to be interpreted,"
he protested. "Fine. Well, in my version that scene must be included. It's intrinsic. That scene could have happened to my
own grandmother or even to me, if I lived in the south." He
nodded in acknowledgment of this. "It's capitalism. If a woman
loses her virginity she cannot be sold in marriage. Men cannot
increase their property by owning such women," I asserted.
"You're going too far, she was a girl in love," he said. "No," I
argued, "she was an assertive woman, a rebellious woman in a
culture where women have no business being one or the other."

After a few more such discussions, I finally managed to convince Abdel Halim to collaborate with me on a new version of
the play. The virginity examination and the denunciation of the
parents to the police were included. Moreover, Naima became
not the victimized, passive, mute-like girl who watches helplessly as her parents murder her lover, but a militant apasion-
aria who travels with Hassan to Egyptian villages in order to
rouse the peasants with revolutionary songs.

While Abdel Halim and I were working on the play, I managed to get an appointment to see Mr. Sayed Moussa, the minister of culture and information. He had a large, carpeted office,

with a glassed-in balcony overlooking the Nile on the top floor of the television building. The minister came from behind his desk to shake my hand. "Your Excellency, thank you for receiving me," I said. "Don't speak like that, we're old friends," he said. "Before I tell you the purpose of this visit, I would like to congratulate you on the political debates you have allowed on television," I said. "In the past political discussions were never allowed. Sadat really believes in democracy," he said, "and you cannot have democracy if you have a censored media." "Yes, we talked about this in the United States," I reminded him. "I am convinced that Sadat is trying to liberalize the country, the media, the economy," he commented; "that's why I accepted this post." "Let us hope that Sadat is successful," I said. "In-shallah," he replied. "Now what can I do for you?"

I told him about *Hassan wa Naima*. "And how are the rehearsals going?" he asked. "We haven't started because we don't have a budget. And last year when I applied for one I was turned down," I added. "Aren't you a civil servant?" he asked. "Of course, I teach in a government institute." "Then there should be no problem. How much do you need?" he asked. "About ten thousand pounds," I said. "Consider it done," he replied, writing something on a pad. "Thank you," I stammered. He got up and held out his hand. "Why do you support me?" I asked, unable to believe my good luck. "It's my job. My job is to encourage the cultural life of this country," he replied.

Eight weeks later, we opened at the wekala. After the performance, Abdel Halim and I were pushed onstage by the rest of the cast, while the audience gave us a standing ovation. The next day, a review appeared in one of the dailies: "This production," it ended, "has taken the Egyptian theater one step forward. It is indeed ironical that theater in Egypt has made this progress in the hands of a woman."

One evening after the final ovation, my gaze met a familiar pair of eyes. It was Paul, standing in a corner of the wekala with a well-known leftist critic. Paul barely smiled as I walked up to him. "I did not know you were here," I said, very much taken aback. "Did you like the play?" I asked. He nodded but did not say a word. I excused myself and left. I was never to see him again.

"The auditorium is full of security agents," Halim whispered to me as I watched the play one night toward the end of the run. "Don't be paranoid, Abdel Halim," I whispered back. "I can smell them a mile away," he insisted. "But why would they come here?" I whispered back. "It's the fun the actors are poking at Sadat's reelection," he answered. Sadat had just been reelected with a 99.9 percent majority, and, as is frequently the case in popular theater, the actors were ad-libbing on this occurrence and the fact that no one ran against Sadat. "We should tell the actors to stop ad-libbing," said Abdel Halim in hushed tones. "Don't be silly," I whispered back, "these are not the Nasser days."

C AIRO IS BURNING, Cairo is burning!" was the cry heard everywhere as thousands of rioters and demonstrators filled the streets. "Ya batal al-ubur, fein al futur?" they cried: "O hero of the crossing, where is our food?" And "Jihan, Jihan, al cha'ab ga'an": "Jihan, Jihan, the people are hungry." Then for seventy-two hours they destroyed movie houses, theaters, restaurants, cafés, Coca-Cola, Seven-Up, Marlboro, and other such billboards—anything, in fact, which evoked the consumer or infitah era. The city blazed. Curfews were imposed. Thousands were arrested.

"What's happened?" we asked one another on the phone. But it was only much later that the events of January 17, 18, and 19, 1977, were explained. Apparently a delegation of factory workers had made their way to President Sadat's offices at Abdine Palace to protest his decision to halve the government subsidies on bread, sugar, rice, oil, meat, and soap. The president had decided to reduce the subsidies for those commodities in order to reduce Egypt's enormous foreign debt. The factory workers wanted to discuss this with the president, but when they approached the palace, they were threatened by security forces and told to disperse. Angry and frustrated they went on to Liberation Square, where they were joined along the way by other angry Egyptians. They brandished newspapers, and clamored for attention. But the authorities paid no attention to them. Suddenly the mass was transformed into an angry mob that sought to destroy everything that represented affluence and Westernization in Egypt.

"Laila, stay home," Asma advised me sternly. "They are still arresting people and there are rumors that many of these are students and writers and journalists." "But why?" I asked. "I'll tell you tomorrow when I see you," she replied.

"People everywhere are saying that it is the communists who are behind this," she said the next day when she came to see me. "But the communists wouldn't burn theaters, movie houses," I replied. "You have a point. Anyway that's what the government is claiming." "You know, Pouppa, all this reminds me of similar riots which took place also in January. But it was 1952. You were just a baby. The demonstrators burned everything in sight—shops, hotels, cars—but only in the western area of the city. It was called 'Black Saturday' and started off as an anti-British demonstration. But everyone knew who was behind the rioters who burned Cairo on January 25, 1952." "Who?" she asked. "The Moslem Brotherhood."

A week later, the curfews were lifted and I was able to go to the institute again. But the streets were still full of policemen holding their bayonets in readiness. And at almost every street corner, an armored vehicle stood in wait.

The faces of my colleagues looked drawn. The institute as well as Cairo University had been ordered to suspend teaching. No one from the institute was arrested, but there were rumors that there were still arrests being made. As I drove by Cairo University on my way home, I noticed that the entrance was cordoned off by policemen and that the building was surrounded by army trucks.

"It was a power struggle," said my brother Nabil from the head of the table, as we were having lunch the next day. "They tried to topple the Sadat regime." "Who?" I asked. "The Nasserists, the leftists, and all those who oppose Sadat's open-door economic policies." "I heard a different story," said my mother, piling food on my brother's plate, "and that is that the Moslem Brotherhood took advantage of the whole situation in order to bring about a revolution." "What do you think, Laila?" asked my brother. "I smell America behind this somewhere," I said. "I read that it was the International Monetary Fund that advised Sadat to lift the food subsidies." "Since when are you *anti-*American?" asked my brother sarcastically. "I'm not. Even America can make mistakes. Millions of people depend on the food subsidies, and for them, even a piaster makes a difference," I asserted. "Laila is becoming a leftist," said my brother, cutting into a filet mignon.

"Sadat's economic policies have not worked," snapped Jean-Pierre, a French journalist and family friend who lived and worked in Cairo. We were sitting on a velvet couch in his spacious apartment overlooking the Garden City corniche, that avenue that accompanies the Nile on its course through the city. Green plants were strewn all over the room and bookshelves lined the cream-colored walls. A Nubian servant, with the lines of his race etched into his gaunt face, brought in a silver tray with a cup of coffee on it.

Jean-Pierre, who was about forty, tall, with an ascetically shaven head, had been a loyal friend to Asma and me over the past six years. We also relied on him as a source of information, for he always knew what was happening in Egypt, even when nothing was reported in our newspapers. The bureaucracy tried to have him removed several times, because his articles were unsparingly critical. Yet he loved Egypt with a passion, and he believed that his articles could contribute to change. He was also the only correspondent in the city who regularly reported on the problems of the Coptic minority and women. But above all, he was a friend, and as later events were to prove, the kind of friend one could always count on.

"Why do you think the infitah has not worked?" I asked, taking a few sips of Turkish coffee served in a fine French porcelain cup. "Almost immediately after the infitah laws were promulgated, there occurred an inflation of twenty-five percent, aided, of course, by world inflation. The price of land in Cairo skyrocketed. Rents spiraled. Thirty-five percent of the young people of this city are unable to get married because they cannot afford the rents," he said with indignation in his voice. "I know all that," I said impatiently. "Just look around you: hundreds, thousands of people standing in line for food outside the state-owned co-ops while frenzied buying is taking place in private boutiques where a dress costs more than six months of a civil servant's salary," he continued. "But, Jean-Pierre, I still remember the time when a roll of toilet paper was an item of luxury in Cairo," I reminded him. "But for whom? For the bourgeoisie?" he asked ironically. "You're a fine one to talk," I said. "Look at the way you live. Anyway, our economic problems stem from the West," I said, trying to sound patriotic. He smiled. "You're right, the West is partially to blame. Sadat's open-door policy was supposed to encourage Western investment in Egypt, but no one has invested here." "Why not?" I asked. "The bureaucracy, of course. How can anybody be expected to get around that antiquated monster?" "It's not Sadat's fault that he has inherited a decaying infrastructure," I said. "I agree with you. He has also inherited corruption. I happen to know that between 1960 and 1965, about forty percent of all Egyptian investment funds made their way into private hands through subcontracting." "And all those wars with Israel, they, too, drained the economy," I added. "Yes, they cost Egypt more than one hundred billion dollars," he said. I tried to imagine how many homes, schools, hospitals could have been built with all that money. "There's also the population problem," Jean-Pierre said quietly.

After I left Jean-Pierre's apartment, I crossed to the opposite side of the street where my car was parked. The traffic was bumper to bumper. Fiats, Peugeots, Mercedes, trying to outmaster each other. Suddenly, a man in a wooden cart pulled by two shaggy donkeys tried to find a passageway between the cars. The blindered donkeys heaved under their cargo. The driver whipped them and cursed while a man driving a shiny new BMW looked indifferently on.

Two weeks after the January riots, Sadat gave an angry speech at the National Assembly. "There is no difference between the communists and those who call themselves Nasser's heirs," he declared, reaching for a glass of water. "Is surveillance what you want? What did Nasser achieve? Expropriation? Detention camps? Arab unity the Nasser way? Turning Egypt into a loudspeaker for the Arabs?" He drank some more water and took out his handkerchief to wipe his forehead. "The difference between me and Nasser is that I have abolished the emergency laws. I believe in freedom," he said, banging on the podium. But at the end of the speech, he announced that he would cancel his decision to lift the food subsidies.

For Egyptians, Sadat's declaration to allow the food subsidies to continue meant that a loaf of bread would once again cost one piaster instead of two. Sadat had given in to the demonstrators. But he retaliated against the Left. In March a referendum passed by the National Assembly made "participation in organizations hostile to the social system" punishable by life imprisonment with hard labor. "Demonstrating with intent to destroy public property" or the "participation in a gathering which would endanger public security" also became punishable in this way. Then, in order to silence the opposition, Sadat transferred some of his men to key media positions.

But Egypt's economic problems remained. And the other Arab nations did nothing to help Sadat. An article in one of the dailies reminded us that one of the oil-producing countries was so rich that if it diverted just one-third of a single year's revenue to us, it would settle all of Egypt's outstanding debts.

THE INSTITUTE reopened and everything seemed to return to normal. I began rehearsing an absurdist play by Ionesco entitled *Jack, or the Submission*. In order to emphasize the grotesqueness of Ionesco's parody on marriage and family, the all-male cast had their faces made up like circus clowns. The characters in Ionesco's play are like puppets, and speak in nonsense syllables. Their movements and gestures are robotlike. And yet this caricatured reality represented a world that was more comprehensible to me than the reality of the food riots that had exploded around me.

At the opening of the production, which took place in a confiscated villa owned by the Ministry of Culture, I sighted Abdel Halim in the audience. We embraced warmly; we had become comrades, at least in theatrical terms. Lighting one of his customary cigarettes, he informed me that he had a surprise for me. He pulled out a folded newspaper hidden underneath his coat. "What's this? Concealing arms now?" I joked. "It's my new play," he announced proudly. "I want you to direct it." It's dangerous to collaborate with leftists, I told myself as I took it. But when I went home, I could not resist it.

The play was made to order for the wekala—and it was obviously the caravanserai that Abdel Halim had in mind when he wrote it. The theme of the play was also perfect—it summed up all my ideas for the creation of Egyptian folk theater. The plot concerned a folk road-troupe which was unable to make ends meet. The young man who runs it decides to save the group by selling his father, an old actor, at an auction sale. The father reluctantly accepts and the sale takes place. Swinging down from the rope ladders, the clowns, belly dancers, acrobats, fire-eaters, jugglers, and storytellers all beckon the audience to the "occasione." "Who will bid the highest for this magnificent heritage? Who will buy this ancient old father?" they ask.

The father is then wheeled into the wekala on a garlic cart, decorated with balloons and pushed by a *ghazzia*, a belly dancer. The cart is paraded on all four sides of the building and followed by the singing troupe. "Stop," says a *ma'allam*, a prosperous entrepreneur, a fat cat of the infitah. "Stop. I'll take the whole lot. And throw in that belly dancer." "Ala una, ala duoa, ala tre. Gone to Mr. Toyota," declares the son.

The troupe is hurtled to Cairo's cabaret districts where they are made over as Western entertainers, complete with tuxedos and Charleston dresses. The folk ballads they used to sing have been replaced by pop hits and the jerk and the twist. But soon, unable to stand it anymore, the old father escapes to the village—symbolized by the wekala—and the others soon join him. Folk artists are not dead, and neither is folk art, Abdel Halim is saying.

In form and content, *Occasione* was the perfect folk play—the play I had always dreamed of finding. Yet, there was a snag: it was obviously a satire on Sadat's infitah—the open-door policy. But I couldn't resist it.

The theatrical censor, a young woman not unlike the television censor, wearing glasses and a scarf to conceal her hair, stared at both of us from across her desk but addressed only Abdel Halim: "Your play has been rejected, Mr. Abdel Halim, because it has been judged dangerous for the youth of this country." Abdel Halim squirmed in his seat. "Why dangerous?" I asked. "A young actor auctioning his father off in order to raise money for his theatrical troupe is a morally dangerous idea. It sets a bad example for the young. After seeing your play, my son might come up to me and say, I would like to put up my father for sale." Abdel Halim coughed. I moved uneasily in my chair.

"Look," I said, "this plot is allegorical. The father here is sup-posed to represent our folkloric heritage, which is about to be-come extinct because we are turning to Western forms of entertainment like TV, cabarets, pop music, and discos." I stopped there, for she was giving me a look which clearly meant: don't bullshit me. "The father," she sniffed, "is a symbol of the fatherland and here he is being sold to the West. Moreover, President Sadat refers to himself as the 'father of the Egyptian family.' Abdel Halim coughed again. "This is a real folktale, I assure you," he said. "No offense meant whatsoever at the rais." She now fixed him with the same gaze I had received a moment ago. "All right, let's forget it," I said, getting up. Then Abdel Halim kicked me gently. "Dr. Laila, you go home and I will ex-plain things to Madam here." Knowing that he was a past mas-ter at negotiating with censors, I left.

The negotiations went on for two months. Abdel Halim was forced to make several cuts and changes. Finally, when we were both in utter despair, the play was approved. But this was only the beginning of our battle.

The play was to be produced by one of the state-subsidized theaters, headed by Ahmed Daeel, a skinny, bald-headed direc-tor in his forties who had made his reputation on bedroom farces. An appointment was set, but when I arrived at his office, he was not there. "Try his wives," suggested one of his numerous assistants. "His what?" I asked. "He has two wives. Sometimes he is with one and sometimes with the other," said the assistant mockingly. Very funny, I thought. But I did try both numbers, though to no avail. I returned to the assistant, hoping to get more information from him. "We can't give you his girlfriend's number, now can we?" he said.

Finally I found Ahmed Daeel at his office. "Mr. Daeel, I have an opening date, I have to start casting, rehearsing," I said, barely able to control my rage. He rang a bell and another as-sistant, a sour-faced young man, was ordered to "stand by me."

A couple of days later, the assistant informed me that none of the actors I had requested were available. I went to see Mr.

Daeel: "Why are your performers boycotting my play? If you had instructed them to cooperate, they would have!" "Now, now," he said, "don't forget you are a woman. These are top-notch professionals. They don't like to take orders from a woman." "Then how are we going to get this play done?" I said, not wanting to engage him in a conversation on the merits of professional women. "Leave it to me," he said.

A week later a cast was assembled, but by the next day they had all disappeared. "What's happening?" I barked at the assistant. He just shrugged. I rushed back to see Daeel. "Sit down," he said. "Have a lemonade, or would you prefer some coffee?" "What the hell is going on?" I said, no longer willing to be polite. He opened a drawer and took out a sheet of paper with a long list of names. "This is a list of artists who are blacklisted. Abdel Halim is right here," he said, pointing to a particular spot on the page with great emphasis. "*Leftist.* I have my orders." "Then why did you accept the text in the first place?" I asked, completely bewildered. "I didn't think you would get censorship approval. As a matter of fact, I tried to circumvent that approval, but you and your author were too stubborn," he said angrily. I looked at him in amazement. "I'll give you another play to direct," he said after a few moments. "I don't play that game," I said. "I'm going ahead. Even if I have to use amateurs." "By the way," he said as I was preparing to leave, "we won't be able to give you the auditorium to rehearse in."

So we rehearsed in the garden of one of the state museums. The parts were filled by students, but when it became apparent that we would open, some professionals joined the cast. One of them was a famous leftist poet, actor, and director of the sixties, Najib Serour. He was diabetic and an alcoholic, but he was also one of the most talented and beloved actors of the Egyptian theater. He had recently been ostracized by the cultural establishment because of his outspokenness in unpublished limericks and colloquial poetry which were circulated orally all over Cairo. I welcomed him with open arms because he was an artist any director would wish to work with—totally dedicated to the theater. "All I want, Laila, is to be onstage once more," he told me.

Two weeks before opening, Daeel gave in and allowed us to move equipment to the wekala. I had lost fifteen pounds and felt ill, but we managed to open—on schedule. The performance opened with a prologue written and delivered by Serour, in which he satirized commercial, Westernized theater, pop singers, and TV ads. One of the ads he satirized was for a deodorant called "Mum." Serour would point to his armpits and then take one hand and raise it to his mouth, saying, "We all want mum." "Mum" was a colloquial way of referring to food. It brought the house down. The theater was packed every night. Many people came just to see Serour.

Then one day I was summoned to the office of one of the highly placed officials of the ministry. "Mr. Daeel," he said, "tells me that your actors improvise, tell jokes against the regime, indulge in dialogue which has not been approved by the censors." "That's not true," I replied. "Only Serour improvises." I was sorry the moment I had said it. "Get rid of Serour," he said. "Fire him from the play." "No, I'm sorry, I can't do that," I replied. I knew it would kill Serour if I did.

When I returned to the wekala that evening, I found a notice from the ministry banning Serour *and* me from entering the theater.

I ran to my lawyer, Labib Moawad, and told him what had happened. "You can take it to court," he said, trying to calm me. "As long as the play runs, you, as director, have artistic ownership of it." "When can we get a hearing?" I asked. "In a couple of days," he replied.

The day of the hearing, I met my lawyer outside a small district court with white plaster walls. There were people everywhere, crowding and jostling one another as they entered the courthouse. As we pushed our way up the stairway which overlooked a rubbish dump, I urged him again to be sure to tell the judge that it was a matter of artistic freedom, the right of the artist to express himself. My words got lost in the shouting and commotion at the top of the stairs.

•

"You've won your case," said Labib Moawad a few days later. "You can go back to the wekala tonight. I'll send a clerk with you to show them the court order. Take Serour." "I can't believe it," I said. "It's the supremacy of the law," he answered. "Sadat believes in the supremacy of the law."

I phoned Serour with the good news and asked him to join me at the wekala that night. But he was too depressed and disillusioned to do so, so I entered the wekala alone. The show had already begun, but I found a seat in the dark and watched the play. I knew my play inside out, but this was not my play. Scenes had been reblocked, choreography altered, and dialogue omitted. That night when I returned home I wept as if someone I loved had died.

In the morning, I went to see Mr. Daeel. He flew into a rage. "I'll throttle that lawyer of yours. How dare he get an injunction against the ministry?" "I wish to redirect the play," I said quietly but firmly. "You will do no such thing! We are closing it down. It is a commercial failure!" he roared.

Two days later, *Auction Sale* was dismantled. Not long after, Najib Serour committed suicide.

L IFE HAS a way of catching you unaware. Suddenly a year has gone by or many years and you hadn't noticed it. Suddenly you realize that your hair has grown white and you hadn't noticed it. Or that another life is being planned; unseen activities which touch upon your life, but go unperceived. And suddenly someone is getting married and it is your little sister, and you are watching her look into the future with large, round, sparkling eyes; you were too busy with the mechanics of life to notice the movements of her heart, the undulations of her soul, and the explosion of her happiness. It is August 14, 1977, her wedding day.

"Don't forget, tomorrow is the wedding," Asma had reminded me the day before the ceremony. "Asma, how could I forget?" I had asked. "You've been out of this world with *Auction Sale*—besides, you're capable of absolutely anything."

Hers was a European ceremony, very different from mine. A Protestant priest wearing a black suit officiated in English. The church, an austere Anglican structure, was a reminder of the colonial days. Byzantine madonnas did not stare out at you from the walls. The air was not filled with incense or the nasal chants of the *chamasin* singing "Kyrie eleison." The altar was undecorated. Everything was Western, brief.

As I sat there, I wanted to protest out loud, to say, "You can't take Asma away from us like this." My mother looked elegant but sad, my brother, self-important. They sat in the front row, silently, disapprovingly.

After the wedding came the cutting of a large, layered cake at Dietrich's villa and a toast with champagne. German friends and relatives mingled with Egyptian cousins, uncles, and aunts. "Isn't she beautiful?" everyone was saying. "I wish they'd stop saying that," said an aunt, "they'll give her the evil eye."

Then the party was over, people started to leave. "Mabrouk, alf mabrouk, a thousand mabrouks—congratulations." I nodded politely as I shook their hands. It was hot and I was perspiring. Sounds of cars starting, cheerful voices, music, the rattling of glasses. "Come and visit us, Laila. Why do you keep away from the family?" a relative was saying. "Fil afrah, dayman, only happy times," was heard over and over as they got into their cars.

Western music was pounding in the background. The remaining people, mostly friends, had begun to dance. Asma came up to me radiant, breathless. "How was it?" she asked. "Perfect," I replied, "and you look gorgeous." She smiled and hugged me. "There are so many flower baskets, why don't you take some home with you?" As Asma rushed off, I noticed my mother sitting in a corner with my brother Nabil. They were a couple already. Around me people were still saying "Mabrouk, mabrouk." The long white-clad tables were starting to look creased and stuffed grapevine leaves rolled about here and there. The Nubian waiters in their European tuxedos looked uncomfortable. August is too hot for tuxedos; they should have been allowed to wear their galabiyas. I began to choose the flower baskets I would be taking with me; gladiola and red roses. Then I said my good-byes.

As soon as I reached my apartment, I watered the flowers and began to distribute them all over the living room. Many of them had already started to wilt from the oppressive heat. If they would only last until tomorrow, I thought, as I continued to scatter them about. The apartment looked like a funeral parlor. I reached out for another glass of wine, telling myself that I already had had too much to drink. A few moments later, I stumbled to bed.

Asma's visits became less frequent. She was extremely busy with her work, as well as with her new husband. The weeks after the wedding were filled with a new loneliness. Moreover, the closing of *Auction Sale* had left me too depressed to summon up the energy for another project.

One night, one very hot night, I awoke to the most terrible abdominal pain. I managed to get a doctor over to examine me and he prescribed a painkiller. But the pain did not disappear and only grew worse. In the morning, I was in agony, barely able to stumble to the phone to call Asma. "Why didn't you call me last night?" she asked with concern. "I didn't want to disturb you," I replied. "Oh, Laila. I'll be right there."

By the time she got to the apartment, I was in such pain I could hardly speak. She helped me dress and took me to a hospital, where a famous surgeon, a friend of my father's, was told that we would be coming. The examination took seconds. "You are bleeding internally. You have an ovarian cyst which must be removed immediately," he said brusquely. "But I am not prepared for . . ." I began to protest. "I'll get your things from the flat," said Asma, who was standing by. The next thing I knew, a stretcher was brought into the doctor's office, I was placed on it, and wheeled to the operating amphitheater.

"What's an ovarian cyst?" I asked the anesthesiologist who was standing beside me. "It's a gynecological disorder which usually occurs when women do not have pregnancies," he said professionally. "Is it a cancer growth?" I said in a panic. "Give me your arm, please. Bad veins, very bad veins," he murmured without answering my question. I'm going to die, I thought. The smell of ether was overpowering. "Please don't hurt me," I pleaded with the doctor. As the syringe found its vein, darkness, then oblivion, mercifully engulfed me.

"Laila? Are you all right?" asked Asma, bending over my hospital bed. I nodded. "If I hadn't taken you to the hospital in the nick of time, and if Dr. Halim hadn't cut the red tape and operated at once, your cyst would have burst and you would have died," she said. I reached for her hand. "You saved my life, Pouppa." "You have to sleep now. They've given you a tranquilizer. Are you in pain?" I nodded. "Very bad?" she asked. I nodded again. "I'll stay here until you go to sleep. Don't worry," she said, as if she were talking to a child. Then she took my hand and held it tightly.

Asma visited me every day at the hospital. The first couple of days after the surgery, I was in such pain that I was put to sleep most of the time. Gradually, the incision in my abdomen began to heal and I began to notice her again. She was always gay and full of laughter. Her clothes were all in reds and greens and oranges. My hospital room vibrated with her presence. Perfume filled the air and the clinking of her jewelry resonated gaily, banishing my depression. At every visit she brought flowers, arranging them in vases of whites and reds and pinks. She would sit with me for hours, chattering away about her new teaching job at Cairo University. "The only way for Egypt to solve its population problem is through the media. But when we have workshops with TV personalities, they act as if they have just discovered we have a population problem. This is not what we should be discussing in a communications session!" she said decisively. "What should you be discussing?" I inquired. "Communications, of course. Seventy-five percent of our women are illiterate. How do you reach them?" she said. "How?" I asked. "On the radio," she said, and her voice went on excitedly, interrupted only by the chirping of birds coming through the window of the hospital room.

My spirits would rise dramatically when Asma was with me, but when she left, I would become morbid again. When the surgery was over, I had asked the nurse if my ovaries had been removed. "The doctor will tell you," came the stern reply. When the doctor came the next day he brought a jar with him. I cringed in recollection when I saw it. But it was just dead tissue. "Here are your cysts," the doctor said with medical pride; "as you can see they were very large." I looked at the jar, in revulsion at the female condition. The creased, grayish tissue quivered in the water—a reminder of a dead past. The doctor placed it on the table next to my bed.

After he left, I looked at it again. My abortion suddenly seemed as vivid as if it had happened yesterday. I was reminded that I could still have children. Up until now, I had not given it a thought. I had been too busy. But maybe soon, or else it would be too late. But even if it was too late, so what? Because of my abortion, I had been given life. I had no regrets.

I looked again at the jar. The dead tissue glared at me in all its torn ugliness. It seemed to grimace—but it was only a chunk of flesh. Don't be afraid of this tissue, I told myself. It is not nature you have offended. It is society, its traditions, its laws. Society might never forgive, but nature will. I stared again at the jar: the gray, veinless tissue no longer seemed so ominous. It was dead and I was alive—alive and well.

IT WAS a cool afternoon in November. I was convalescing from my surgery at home. The doorbell rang. I went to open it, walking slowly, because my stomach was still full of stitches. The ringing became insistent. I heard Asma's voice from the landing. "Laila, Laila," she was calling. As I opened the door, she rushed into the room, saying, "Sadat has gone to Jerusalem!" "He's done what?" I asked incredulously. "He's on a plane to Jerusalem," she said, as if she could hardly believe it herself. "Where did you hear this?" I asked. "On the radio; he's going to give a speech to the Knesset." I was completely dumbfounded. My generation, the Nasser generation, believed that Israel would be our enemy for centuries to come. It was impossible to conceive that in my lifetime, or even the lifetime of the next generation, this enmity would end. "Peace is in the air," Asma was now saying. Peace? But at what price? I thought. Wasn't peace the "impossible dream" Lilienthal had spoken of almost ten years ago?

Riveted in front of my television, I listened to Sadat's speech from Jerusalem:

"Peace for us all, of the Arab lands and in Israel, as well as in every part of this big world, which is beset by conflicts, perturbed by its deep contradictions, menaced now and then by destructive wars launched by man to annihilate his fellow men. Any life that is lost in war is a human life, be it that of an Arab or an Israeli. For the sake of all the lives of our sisters and brothers—for that I have made my decision to come to you, despite all the hazards, to deliver my address. First of all I have not come here for a separate agreement between Egypt and Israel. The problem is not that of Egypt and Israel. If peace between all the confrontational states and Israel were achieved in the absence of a just solution to the Palestinian problem, never will there be that durable and just peace upon which the entire world insists. I hail the Israeli voices that call for the recognition of the Palestinian people's right to achieve and safeguard peace. Here I tell you, ladies and gentlemen, that it is no use to refrain from recognizing the Palestinian people and their right to statehood, their right of return.

"I have chosen to set aside all precedents and traditions known by warring nations. In spite of the fact that occupation of Arab countries is still there, the declaration of my readiness to proceed to Israel came as a great surprise that stirred many feelings and confounded many minds. Some of them even doubted its intent."

On his return from Jerusalem, Sadat was given a hero's welcome. At the airport and all through the streets of Cairo, banners read: IN OUR BLOOD AND SPIRIT WE SHALL SACRIFICE OURSELVES FOR YOU, O SADAT. Policemen lined the streets all along the route to the presidential palace. "Yehia batal al-salam," cheered the masses. "Long live the hero of peace." "Yehia batal al-salama," they cheered again, as each man in the crowd jostled for the best view of the rais, the leader, the hero of peace.

To the average Egyptian, peace meant prosperity and an end to an expensive war. Our newspapers reminded us repeatedly that in addition to costing the lives of 100,000 Egyptian men, the four wars with Israel had cost Egypt 250 billion pounds. If we made peace with Israel, this money would be spent on rebuilding the country.

For days, Cairo sparkled with decorations and lights. The poor hung paper lanterns with candles in them. But many of Cairo's fifteen thousand mosques were dark, and in subsequent weeks, zealous sheikhs warned their congregations against the evil of rapprochement with Israel. And like the Egyptian leftist party, they denounced Sadat's visit to Jerusalem as a betrayal of the Palestinian cause.

Upon his return from Jerusalem, Sadat had invited the UN, Syria, Jordan, and the PLO to attend a conference in Cairo in preparation for the conference to be held in Geneva with these and other Arab countries. Arafat declined the invitation. To the PLO, Sadat's visit to Jerusalem was a "defilement of the blood of the hundreds and thousands of martyrs who died for Palestine."

THREE

Shed no tear, O shed no tear.
The flower will bloom another year.

—Shelley

A COUPLE OF DAYS after Sadat's return from Jerusalem, Asma announced that she and Dietrich were making a trip to the western desert of Egypt. She was planning to investigate the status of women among the Bedouin communities there. It would be an "adventurous trip," as she put it, because they were going to live in tents in the desert. Before returning to Cairo, they were going to make their way to Om Abdou's southern village and spend the night in Om Abdou's house. Our mother would meet Dietrich, Asma, and their party there. "Drive carefully," I told her as we said good-bye. "Don't worry," she replied, "I can't run into anything in the middle of the desert," and she rushed out with only the familiar scent of her perfume lingering after her.

Three days later, my brother came to visit me. "Well, what do you think of Sadat's visit to Jerusalem?" I said, trying to goad him. He did not reply. He just stood in the middle of the room, looking at me with his dark brown eyes. "What's the matter?" I asked. As he spoke the world seemed to stop moving, even though I could hear children laughing, a donkey braying, and cars hooting in the street below. My mind, too, seemed to have come to a halt, but a few seconds later, I could hear myself scream. I felt as if my retinas had been torn from the sockets, or as if my eyes were jerked inward to gaze at my spinal cord dangling with bare nerves. Before me was an inward inferno where my heart was a gaping void and gray intestines were strangling my throat. I was seeing madness. Asma was dead.

My brother's voice now seemed as if it were coming from the depths of an abyss. There had been an accident. Asma was driving. Dietrich, who had survived, phoned to say that they would be sending her home tonight. She's dead, Laila, he repeated. Be brave. God is with us. You dare mention God, I cried.

Late that night, I lay awake, waiting for Asma. I knew it was she the moment I heard the sound of the engine in the quiet street below. When I went downstairs I saw a hastily made wooden box in the back of a truck. I stifled my grief and directed the driver and his companion to carry the box to my apartment. They carried it up the four stories on their shoulders and placed it in the center of the living room—the room that had so often been filled with Asma's laughter. They were opening the box. "Do you recognize her?" one of them asked. I nodded. "She's in good condition, considering," said the other. "Is there someone here to sign this paper saying that the body has been received?" I stared at him in a daze. "The man of the family, maybe?" he inquired. "I'll phone my brother, he lives nearby." After I made the phone call, I went back to the box and asked them to lift Asma out of it. A few moments later, my brother entered the apartment and signed the form. He gave the two men a gratuity. "May God give you a long life," they said, thanking him.

"Can you clean her up a little?" said my brother. "I'll be back later."

Alone with Asma, I pulled her from the floor to the bed, holding her under her arms. I looked into her eyes. What have you done to yourself, Pouppa? She wore her jeans and her favorite black shirt. They were all full of blood. The bedroom was dark so I could not see her face. She lay there quietly as if she were asleep. But I could not hear her breathing. Weeping, I began to speak to her. I held her hand. Was she clasping mine? Had I gone mad? What have you done to yourself? I asked her again. But mine was the only voice in the room. Asma, Asma, my little sister, with her dreams for the future, her beauty, her warmth, her infectious laughter—reduced to this? My voice echoed back at me in the dark room. I waited for Asma to show some sign of life. But she remained quiet.

Dawn crept into the room. I had been talking to Asma all through the night. Then I saw her face. I rushed to my bathroom cabinet and brought out a box of theatrical makeup. With great care, I began to obscure the traces of the accident: a little masking cream to hide the broken nose, rouge to highlight the cheeks and make them glow again, lipstick to bring the smile back on her face. I combed out her hair and then I brushed it. It looked alive and fluffy again. Then I removed her clothes and wrapped them in a newspaper. I took a clean white caftan which I knew she liked and put it on her. I poured perfume all over her, and I washed her hands with it, for they were still bloodstained. Her nails were freshly painted with red polish. Were you in pain, Pouppa? I asked her. But she did not answer. I sat down on the floor next to the bed, where I had kept my vigil all night, and took her hand once more into mine.

An hour later, my brother returned. "We must bury her at once. I've made all the arrangements," he said. "No!" I shouted. "We are entitled to keep her for three days. I know the customs. Besides, we must wait for Mother." "She must go now," said my brother insistently. He was full of self-righteousness. Then he said, "Mother will have a stroke if she sees her." "She won't," I replied feebly. I knew that my mother would want to see her child one last time. "I make the decisions, I give the orders," my brother said quietly, ominously. When he left the room, I locked the door from the inside, barricading myself in with Asma.

The family had gathered like a flock of vultures when they smell a corpse: aunts, uncles, cousins, all in black again. As they filed into the bedroom one by one, many began to wail. They wanted to have a look at Asma, to say good-bye, they said. But I felt that they were defiling her with their eyes. "Do what your brother wants," they urged. "He is now the head of the family. He is the *man*. He knows best." An aunt came up to me, whispering, "If you keep her the body will smell." "I don't care," I replied. "She's my sister." She looked at me as if I were mad. The others looked at me that way, too. Their eyes said I was crazy. I was a free woman, an artist. And now I wanted to keep the body! they whispered. Finally, they left the bedroom and huddled together in the living room. "Do you have any coffee, Laila?" said one of them. "No. Please leave us alone," I pleaded. But they ignored me and peered curiously at my belongings. "Please leave us alone," I said again. When they did not, I locked the bedroom door from the inside. My brother and his clan began to pound on it from the other side. They shouted that they wanted to be let in. It sounded as if they were about to break the lock. "Open the door," shouted my brother. His zeal was not a funerary one, I thought, as I sat quietly on the floor.

I had shamed my brother before the tribe and that is why the door was about to be broken and Asma to be dragged into an ebony box. "Go away, all of you," I shouted. "She's gone completely mad," I heard someone say. Then a voice I did not recognize called my name. "It is the *assis*, the priest, wishing to speak to you," said my brother. "Tell him I don't want to speak to him," I responded. There was a shocked silence on the other side of the door. "My daughter, open the door," said the assis. "Go away, Father," I replied. Another silence. They stopped hammering. My brother spoke in quiet tones. He would not take Asma away if I unlocked the door. I opened the door. "You have offended the family," he said as he took me aside. "To hell with them!" I said. "But she's just a corpse now," he continued. "Get out," I told him. The family stared at me through the doorway. A cousin of my mother's glared at me through mascaraed eyes. Finally, they vacated the bedroom and left me alone.

When Dietrich arrived, he rushed into the bedroom and the family all rushed back after him. They stretched their necks to catch a glimpse of the scene, as if they were watching a Grand Guignol spectacle. "Get out, all of you," I screamed. "Poor thing, she's lost her mind," they murmured loud enough for me to hear. And then they made for the door, the Coptic priest waddling after them. "I will be receiving condolences at my mother's apartment," my brother announced, drawing himself up as he said it.

The room was dark. Dietrich was holding Asma in his arms. I could hear voices in the street and the subdued sound of traffic. "She bled to death," Dietrich said quietly. "The nearest hospital was miles away. She kept bleeding all the time. She had been driving too fast. She wanted to get to Om Abdou's village in a hurry, to see your mother. She did not see the rock in the middle of the highway. The sun had blinded her. She was thrown through the windshield. She hit her head on the pavement. When we arrived at the hospital they said she was—dead."

A commotion was stirring outside. My mother had arrived. The family gathered again at the bedroom door in anticipation of the spectacle. As my mother made her way to the room, they all trailed her. The scene resembled a parade. Their insatiable appetites for other people's grief had been whetted by my mother's arrival. Now they waited for the ultimate scene: a mother about to receive her child's body. "Get out, all of you," I screamed as loudly as I could. They scattered in every direction like vultures: scavengers of grief, rapacious gluttons of other people's agony.

The room was quiet as my mother took Asma in her arms, weeping words of comfort to her all through the long night. It was still in that darkened room and the quiet street below echoed our grief. Asma was still, too. Only her perfume reminded us of the days when she lived. On her face there was an expression of distaste, which even a mother's weeping could not dispel.

In the morning, they put Asma in a polished ebony coffin. My mother was injected with Valium but her eyes told me that I had done the right thing.

The church was packed with real mourners—Asma's friends, who could not believe she was no longer with us. Bishop Samuel's soft tones made waves in the still air: "Behold, I show you a mystery: we shall not all sleep, but we shall all be changed. For the corruptible shall be made incorruptible, and the mortal shall be made model immortal, then shall be brought to pass the saying, that is written, Death is swallowed up in victory." Asma's death a victory? What was he saying? I tried to keep my eyes away from the wooden box. My gaze roamed the walls of the church: oval paintings of two-dimensional madonnas stared back at me through bored eyes. Jesus sat on their laps, too plump, too well-fed. Bishop Samuel now murmured mechanically: "And when Jesus came into the ruler's house and saw the minstrels and the people making a noise, He said unto them, give place for the maid is not dead, but sleepeth." I kept my eyes on Bishop Samuel. He bent over the wooden box saying the final prayer. He alone retained the dignity of a medieval faith which had peeled away like the plaster walls.

The coffin was carried out, borne by the men of the family. Women in black streamed out of the church, crying loudly, the street noises mingling with the sound of grief.

We made our way to the cemetery where my father was buried. The sand path to the vault had been newly swept and the cactus plants had been watered to welcome Asma. The aroma of roses mixed with incense filled the air. Someone, I don't know who, held my arm. I looked in my mother's direction. She was weeping bitterly, in spite of the Valium. I turned to Asma's coffin. I could not look as they put her in the vault.

Outside the sun was unmerciful, the flies tormenting. A desert landscape glared at us, broken only by the women in black and the persistent, dehydrated wailing of a voice coming from nowhere.

IN MY SOCIETY death, like birth, is the business of women. My parents' apartment started to fill up with women whose purpose was to mourn with us for forty days, the death of Asma. I resented this ancient tradition because I wanted to be alone with my grief. My brother returned to his work immediately after the funeral, but because I was female I was obligated to remain at home with my mother to receive the mourners.

Day after day, the house was filled with women in black who sat for hours silently sipping Turkish coffee, or weeping into their handkerchiefs. A professional mourner was brought to chant Biblical verses, her droning voice muting even the street noises. As the days passed, I started to get accustomed to those empty hours of sipping coffee and staring at nothing. It was as if I had become frozen into this Byzantine tapestry of stylized grief. Gradually, though, I devised a way of abstracting myself from the mourners. I would make them talk about their lives and I would listen. In this way, I could convince myself that I was not a part of this female ghetto.

The older women, their hair tied in black scarves, said nothing, mourning passively with hands folded in their laps. For them it was too late for words or even for regrets. But the younger women talked, as they had never talked before. Asma's death had served as a psychological wailing wall which they came to with their own inner deaths. Here at last was a feminist communion: women sharing their lives against the backdrop of sorrow and mourning. It was as if only death could make them face the deaths inside, evoke the sorrows within.

As I listened to these stories unfold, I began to feel a bond with these women which I had never felt before. I was awed by the strength and dignity with which they bore their burdens or the way that they turned their personal failures into professional successes. Sonia, one of Asma's best friends, told me about her divorce. Her husband had left her and taken their one-year-old child with him to one of the other Arab countries. According to the Family Law she was entitled to keep her child until he reached the age of seven, so she went to court and managed to get a court order to get her child back. But her husband found ways of evading her. "Even if I did get my child back, what use would it be, since I would still have to give him up again after six years?" she told me. "So I went back to school for a B.A. in social science, and now I have a job which takes me to the villages. Still, every single second of the day, I am reminded of my baby. But one day, I will get my baby back. One mustn't lose hope. After all, life is a struggle, isn't it?" she said with determination.

"I am married to a man with a second wife," said another woman who was a famous lawyer. "But he encouraged me to work. So I have supported the family, even his other wife. I find great fulfillment in my work and in helping other women to fight the Family Law." "How many women go to court because of the Family Law?" I asked. "There are at least three million cases a year," she replied. "And most of them are women who are fighting for child custody and child support. Or simply trying to get their husbands to divorce them."

"When my husband died," said one of my cousins, whose marriage had been arranged when she was sixteen, "I had no education of any kind. He left a pharmacy, but according to the Family Law, a widow with five children is not allowed to administer her husband's affairs. They were going to take the pharmacy away from us and have one of the male members of the family run it. But I wouldn't have it. I used to get up every day at six in the morning to open the pharmacy. I became the saleswoman and cashier, everything. Then I hired a doctor to prepare the prescriptions. It wasn't easy. But I kept the pharmacy this way, and I was able to support the family. We have even shown profits. And my eldest boy, Sameh, will graduate from pharmacological school in four years. Then he can take over," she said, smiling. "Would you ever marry again?" I asked her, for she was only thirty-five. "Never. I like being independent," she replied.

Another woman said, "My husband had a flower store and one day when he fell ill, I went over and ran the place. Soon, I began to ship and sell flowers all over the world. It became a big business. Sometimes I work twenty-four hours a day," she declared proudly. "And your husband?" I asked. "After I became so successful, my husband handed the business to me and even left his other wife to live with me."

Nagwa, a friend of Asma's, told me about her parents' attempts to arrange her marriage. "I was officially engaged to a man for a year, and during that year we were always accompanied by a chaperone. Then one day we managed to evade the chaperone and we had our first date. It was quite a shock. He told me that as of that moment I must accept his judgments because he was the man. I'll never forget what he said that day: if a wall is black but I say it's white, then white it must be because I am the man and the man knows best," laughed Nagwa. "I gave up all notions of marriage, and then I obtained a degree in French. I earn my living teaching. Of course, I live with my father and mother."

Before the forty days of mourning were over, I had decided to make a documentary on Egyptian women. I approached the women who had talked so openly and asked them if they would agree to be interviewed on film. Many of them accepted. The woman lawyer suggested I also interview some leading feminists in order to find out more about the Family Law. This led me to a conference which was attended by many feminists who were lobbying for the amendment of the Family Law. I managed to assemble a film crew and to scrape up enough money to purchase film stock and to pay for a week of shooting.

The large conference hall was half empty when we arrived to set up our lights. "Stand by . . . Roll," I said for the first time in my life and the first feet of film began to be shot. We filmed an Islamic scholar who was saying that the Koran is filled with verses which indicate the equality of men and women, as, for instance, the verse: "But the believers who do good, whether men or women, shall enter the gardens of paradise." The speaker went on to explain that though the Koran itself was just to women, the present Family Law was based on an interpretation of Koranic texts made three hundred years ago by Islamic scholars and jurists. The injustice to women stems from the *judicial* interpretation of Islamic sharia and not from the *spirit* or *text* of the Koran. The scholar continued by saying that at the time that these jurists codified sharia, they operated with a pre-Islamic mentality that was strongly rooted in the culture and ethos of the Arabs, even after the birth of Islam in the sixth century. He concluded that in order to amend the Family Law, sharia or Islamic law had to be reinterpreted.

After the lecture was over, I asked the white-haired speaker if he would allow me to interview him. He nodded and a few minutes later, I was doing my first interview: "Is it difficult to reinterpret sharia?" I asked. "Very difficult," he replied. "Why?" I prodded. "Because many would consider this an act of apostasy. You see, the ninth-century jurists who codified the sharia declared that there could be no further reinterpretation of Islam after their own legislation based on Koranic law, sharia, had taken place. Henceforth, only precedent counted, and the sharia or Koranic law became rigidly defined." "Who were the jurists who codified the sharia?" I asked the scholar. "The sharia was codified by four jurists who died between A.D. 767 and 855. By the ninth century all the components of Koranic or sharia law were established." "And what are these components?" I asked. "Sharia law is composed of the Koran as revealed to Mohammed, of the *Sunna* or trodden path of a devout Moslem which is based on what has orally been transmitted of the Prophet's practices and actions, of the *hadith* or personal sayings of the Prophet, and lastly of the *tradition* of the four caliphs descended from Mohammed. All these components were codified with commentaries and then the jurists agreed among themselves, without consulting the community, that henceforth no reinterpretation of the Koranic law would be permissible." "Was this decision opposed at all?" I inquired. "Yes, by moderates and reformists. Bloody feuds occurred and the dissidents were defeated. Sharia has not been challenged since the Middle Ages."

"Religion is a taboo subject. Keep away from it, Laila," Fouad said when I called him the next day. "I don't want to delve into religion. I am certainly not attacking Islam—all I am interested in is that civil code known as the Family Law," I replied impatiently. "Let's have a cup of coffee at the club," he said. "Wonderful, it will be like old times."

The palm trees swayed gently and the air was filled with the scent of flowers as people played polo at the Gezira Club. "You've grown so thin, Laila," said Fouad. Then he added quickly, "But it suits you." A woman walking her poodle sauntered by and I stared at her. As if reading my thoughts, Fouad said, "You are looking at the world through the eyes of grief, Laila." Then he reached across the table and pressed my hand. I fumbled in my purse for a handkerchief. He pressed my hand again as if to say: be strong. "Fouad, I'm making this film for Asma. It will have a dedication to her," I said. "I am afraid for you, he said," his forehead wrinkled with worry. "Questioning Islam is a dangerous thing because you are a Copt. It will be misinterpreted." "The Family Law affects us all," I replied. He nodded. "Of course," he said, "I personally believe that the Family Law should be reformed, but you must understand that every Koranic verse is, to a believer, the revelation of God, and therefore it cannot be altered or interpreted. The Koran says, for instance, that men have authority over women because Allah has made the one to excel the other and because they spend their wealth to maintain them. It also says, and here I quote, 'Good women are obedient. They guard their unseen parts because Allah has guarded them. As for those from whom you feel disobedience, admonish them to beds apart and beat them.' " "The Bible is full of verses discriminating against women, but . . ." "In Islam," Fouad interrupted, "there are no buts. To a true believer, these are God's words. And this is an Islamic country."

The following day I arranged to meet Cessa Nabarawi, one of the last surviving feminists of the pioneering movement launched in the twenties. The movement came about in the wake of a national uprising in 1919 in which women demonstrated alongside men against the British occupation of Egypt. Cessa was a slim, white-haired woman, with a fair complexion and European features. She lived in Maadi, a suburb of Cairo, completely alone but for a maid who came to cook her meals. Her sparsely furnished apartment was filled with magazines, books, and photographs of her feminist companion Hoda Chaarawi with whom she had founded the Feminist Union in 1923. As soon as we sat down on her faded couch, she began to talk about the beginnings of the feminist movement in Egypt.

"The first thing we did was to remove the veil," she said, her voice full of childlike excitement. "The year was 1923. Hoda Chaarawi's husband had just died and we had been invited to attend the Congress of the International Feminist Alliance in Rome. So I told Hoda Chaarawi, 'Here we are two feminists about to go to an international congress and we are wearing veils!' You know the veil was compulsory in those days. Anyhow, we removed our veils in Rome, but on our way home, we put them on again. On the train back to Cairo, I asked Hoda Chaarawi if it were not time for us to remove our veils in Egypt as well. And, of course, she agreed because now that her husband was dead, she was no longer accountable to any man. So, upon arriving at Cairo station—even before shaking hands with the ladies' delegation waiting for us—we removed our veils! For a moment there was a stunned silence. Then all the other women started taking off their *yashmaks* [veil worn over the mouth] one by one." Cessa smiled triumphantly here, her eyes taking on a special glow. "The next day it was all over the press. They even came to take our photographs and we posed, unveiled, of course. That's how the feminist movement started."

"Did you fight for the amendment of the Family Law?" I asked. "Of course we did—way back in the twenties and thirties. We were never able to change the divorce laws but we did manage to get a law passed making education compulsory for women and sixteen the legal age for marriage. You know before that girls were married off at twelve, or thirteen. Hoda Chaarawi, herself, was married at the age of thirteen to a man who was thirty years older and who already had a wife," she said. "Hoda was a second wife."

"And you, how did you become a feminist?" I asked her. "My father repudiated my mother and took on another wife. Too poor to support me, my mother gave me to a rich cousin of hers who adopted me and gave me an education abroad. My protectoress died when I was sixteen and I was returned to Egypt, to my father's home, where I was forced to wear the veil. It was terrible. When I first arrived back in Cairo, I was so ashamed of having to wear the veil, I did not leave the house for three months. Then I met Hoda Chaarawi, who was a friend of my adopted mother. She took me under her wing and helped me to adjust to Egyptian society, but she also taught me how to fight for my rights. When we began the movement, I became the editor in chief of the first feminist magazine: *L'Egyptienne*—The Egyptian Woman."

Cessa arranged for me to meet another feminist, a painter who had been jailed for communism by Nasser. The door of her very elegant apartment house in Zamalek was opened by a Nubian. The living room was furnished with French antique objects and Persian rugs. I was led to a glass-enclosed studio with a view of the Nile, and asked to wait. A little later, a very thin, smartly dressed woman entered with a smile of greeting. Every line in her wrinkled face spoke of suffering. After she beckoned me to a chair, I got straight to the point and told her that I had come to see if she would agree to be interviewed for the film. "Who is financing it?" she asked. I was taken aback by the question. "It's a low-budget film and I am directing and scripting," I replied. She looked at me with obvious suspicion and then began to show me her work. "Will your film be shown in America?" she asked suddenly. "I really don't know," I answered before returning to her work. "What is this?" I asked, referring to a painting which was quite different from the rest. "This is a painting I did in jail," she replied. The canvas showed women crouching in a row. "They make the women sit on their haunches like that to humiliate them. I was lucky even to have been allowed to paint." A look of horror must have passed over my face, for she gave me the first friendly smile since I arrived. "I spent five years in the only women's jail in Cairo. There were never more than about three hundred women there, so it goes to show you that crime among women is rare." "What were the women in there for?" I asked. "Killing their husbands' wives, prostitution, drug smuggling, almost invariably for their men, and petty theft," she said with an edge of bitterness in her voice. "How did you survive those years?" I asked. She took a deep breath and lit a cigarette, which she placed in a holder. "It's a cruel experience. One is either broken by it, or one becomes stronger," she replied.

At the door, I asked her whether we could film in her studio and show her collection of prison paintings. "Of course," she said, "but I don't think you should mention on film that I am a communist," she said earnestly. Later as we stood by the elevator door, I turned to her and asked, "Those five years in jail, were they worth it? I mean to go to jail for one's beliefs. Is it worthwhile?" I added falteringly. She looked at me steadily and said, "I had only to sign a document to be released. But I didn't. I wouldn't." Then she added, "Those five years made me appreciate freedom."

One day, just as I was nearing the end of the shooting, I received a phone call from the woman lawyer, inviting me to attend a session at a courthouse which specialized in Family Law. I asked her if I could film the session. She replied that it was not allowed, but that she would intervene on my behalf.

198

We arrived at seven in the morning. The courthouse was already in full swing. The entrance swarmed with poor women, dressed in black and seated on the ground. Screaming, bedraggled children ran everywhere.

The lawyer had managed to get us permission to film, and the crew began to set up the lights. The wooden benches in the courtroom were packed, mostly with women. *"Mahkama,"* shouted the court clerk as the judge entered. Everyone stood up. "Call the first name on the roll," the judge instructed as we all sat down. "Action," I instructed the cameraman, and he began to shoot. A lawyer in a waistcoat came forward and began to speak to the judge. As he turned his head, I gasped. This was the lawyer who had handled my divorce case! Noticing me, he nodded enthusiastically. Then turning to the judge, he said, "My client is requesting a divorce on the grounds of her husband's impotence. I submit a medical report to Your Honor which clearly indicates that my client is still a virgin. A virgin, Your Honor, after one year of marriage!" he declared. The judge peered at the papers before him. "Has the husband been summoned to testify in court?" he asked the lawyer. "Yes, Your Honor, but he has refused to obey the summons," replied the lawyer. "Sentence to be pronounced on February 3, 1978," announced the judge, "and call the next case."

The woman lawyer now approached the bench, also with a client who was petitioning for divorce. The client, a fat woman dressed in a galabiya, her hair covered with a black *tarha* veil hiding half her face, began to speak to the judge. She had been repudiated eighteen years ago by her husband who had since remarried. Nonetheless, he did not divorce her; he had simply told her to go to her father's house. For eighteen years she had been trying to get a legal divorce and child support for her only child. Her husband, she explained, had refused to divorce her legally in order not to pay the child support. Her father had died recently. Her brother was threatening to kick her out of the family apartment, along with her mother, so he could rent the place. Hence the urgency of her plea, she said. She was penniless and she was soon to be homeless as well. The judge asked for some additional documents and ordered a postponement of the case. The lawyer, stony-faced, returned to her client.

I beckoned to the cameraman and told him to stop shooting. This material was strong. The crew turned off the lights. A young woman in a faded pants suit approached the bench. She was carrying a two-year-old boy in her arms, while an older son, about seven, was tagging along, hanging on to her trousers. Accompanying them was a sharia lawyer, dressed in the traditional sheikh's clothing, with floor-length galabiya, a coat, and a skullcap. He addressed the judge in literary Arabic, as is customary with such lawyers: "My client has previously obtained a court order for child support, but it has been annulled at the husband's petition." The woman gazed at her lawyer in incomprehension. I noticed that the cameraman had started to shoot again. "Why?" asked the judge. "The husband claims that these boys are not his. Here are the birth certificates bearing the husband's name." The cameraman was now taking a close-up of the distraught face of the young woman. Suddenly she burst into tears and said, "I don't understand what they're saying. I'm just a poor woman. I'm just a poor woman." The court clerk pushed her back toward the benches, while the lawyer urged her to be silent. The judge looked visibly annoyed and ordered the cameraman to stop shooting. Then he walked out of the courtroom.

"What happened?" I asked the woman lawyer. "The judge was annoyed that this episode was recorded on film. It creates a bad image for our courts," she replied. "But this poor woman— what a case," I exclaimed. "It's one of thousands of such cases which demonstrate how badly we need to change the law," she said. "How?" I asked. "In this case, the husband married a second time, but continued to see and even have marital relations with the woman you saw in court. He had two children by her." "The children we saw in court?" I asked. "Yes, but he was able to claim that they were not his, because at the time she had them, she was divorced," she explained. "And she didn't know she was divorced?" I asked incredulously. "No, which meant she couldn't even obtain child support. The Family Law doesn't even give a woman the right to know if she's still married or not!" she said. "All a man has to do is sign a document which is certified by a religious leader, and that's that."

As we left the courthouse, my cameraman told me how pleased he was that we had gotten such good footage. But all I could see was the woman's distraught face as she listened to her lawyer's jargon in helpless frustration.

We wrapped up our shooting schedule a week later. Meanwhile, I had received an invitation to show the film at a small international festival to be held in New York in the summer of 1978. The idea of showing the film then excited me very much, but in order to meet the deadline, I would have to work day and night on the editing of the film.

To make matters worse, I had a film editor who was no feminist. We quarreled continuously, especially regarding the length of the film. "Nobody, but nobody, wants to see a film about women which is longer than twenty minutes," he would declare. I got eighty minutes.

Six weeks later, we finished the editing and I was able to view the film in its entirety. As I watched the images supersede one another on the Movieola, I felt an extraordinary sense of achievement. My Egyptian women saluted me from the tiny screen and I saluted them. These women had made it in spite of the Family Law. Like Om Abdou, they had made it by standing up for their rights. Cessa, Sonia, Nagwa, the painter, the pharmacist, the flower grower, had survived not because society had stood by them, but because it had tried to thwart them. The frozen tapestry of posturing grief had dissolved into a dynamic collage of battling women.

The film was ready. Two shiny boxes waited for me at the counter of the laboratory, the words WHERE IS MY FREEDOM? neatly written on the lids in red marker. Inside, on the first reel, a dedication: TO MY SISTER ASMA. TO HER ASPIRATIONS AND HER DREAMS.

WHAT WOULD you like to drink?" asked the flight attendant on the jet bound for New York. "Champagne, please," I replied. The champagne was placed before me and I drank it in one go. Champagne was not available in Cairo, so I asked for a second and then a third. Soon, I felt lighthearted. I marveled at being suspended between two continents in midair. The thought of New York in the distance was tantalizing. I lay back and closed my eyes. But there was no peace. Om Abdou loomed before me, her round brown eyes very sad. I wanted to reach out and bury my face in the folds of her wrinkled black dress as I did as a child. "Is anything wrong?" asked the flight attendant gently. I had been weeping. "It's so hot, I can't breathe," I replied in confusion. She adjusted the airjet and the light breeze relieved me temporarily. But soon my thoughts were convulsing again in a frenzied kaleidoscope of sorrow: Asma in her wedding dress, Asma lying silently on the bed, Asma's limp hand in mine. Asma in the box. I rubbed my forehead desperately, hoping to make the images vanish. Asma's favorite waltz, the "Mephisto," clamored in my ears. It was Asma's disheveled hair I was seeing now. Then my father, looking melancholically in the distance.

I reached for a tissue to hide my tears. My brother's expressionless eyes gleamed at me from behind his steel-rimmed glasses. Then I saw Fouad's anxious face: "Laila, you are looking at the world through the eyes of grief."

"Igor, an Israeli?" I asked in amazement. My companion, an expatriate Egyptian, laughed as we sat in a coffeehouse next to the Bleecker Street Cinema in Greenwich Village. Igor and Mona were both organizers of the film festival I had come to show my film at. "You look as if the bottom has dropped out of your world," she said. "We are still at war with them," I answered. "But you are on American soil and this is an American film festival," she reminded me. But she looked worried. "What is it, Mona, are you hiding something from me?" "I should tell you that the Egyptian embassy has withdrawn its films from the festival," she announced with some trepidation. "What?" I gasped. "It's because of the deadlock in the peace talks," she explained. I told her that I had been so preoccupied with my personal affairs that I had lost touch with the political news.

Speaking rapidly, Mona began to fill me in. At a conference in Cairo the previous December, Sadat insisted on Palestinian autonomy in the West Bank. Not only did the Israelis refuse but they insisted on keeping military bases in the Sinai and demanded economic supremacy in Gaza and the West Bank. But Sadat insisted on total withdrawal from the Sinai. As a result, an impasse occurred in talks between Egypt and Israel in January, and Egypt withdrew its delegation. Another meeting took place in March, but that also ended in deadlock.

"But what has this got to do with the film festival?" I asked Mona. "Everything and nothing," she replied.

It became clear from a couple of phone calls to the Egyptian embassy in Washington that my participation in the film festival would be harshly criticized. Mona and I ended up in the same coffeehouse again to talk things over. As we stared gloomily into our cups, a photomontage of my professional life jammed into my mind: the Stoppard play at the American University in Cairo, the accusation of being pro-American; the Chekhov plays at the Soviet Center, the accusation of being pro-Soviet; the 1973 productions for the October war, the accusation of being a propagandist for the Ministry of Culture; *Hassan wa Naima* and *Auction Sale*, the accusation of being pro-Left; and now this. I could feel Mona's eyes on me as I confronted these memories of my political mishaps. But suddenly I came to a decision, perhaps the most difficult one I had made in my entire career. "I'm going ahead, Mona," I said. "I will take the consequences."

People were standing in a long line outside the Bleecker Street Cinema. There was electricity in the air. For this was one of the first film festivals ever to focus on both Arab and Israeli cinema. Igor and Mona, white in the face from fatigue and tension, pushed me into the auditorium. Igor made an introductory speech in which he said that when all else failed, the language of the arts, especially of the cinema, could be the most effective way of maintaining a dialogue between the Arabs and Israel. He also said that the choice of films in the festival was not "representative" of official positions: the filmmakers chosen were those who opposed the establishment viewpoints in their societies.

I made my way to the podium, from which I would be introducing my film and doing a simultaneous translation. I was exhilarated but terribly nervous, like a boxer about to fight the match of his career.

I looked at the audience. They looked at me. I blew into the mike a couple of times and then took a deep breath. "This is a film about the struggle of Egyptian women to realize themselves and to fulfill their professional lives," I began. The lights were dimmed. The credits, the dedication to Asma, and then the first images flashed across the screen. Cessa taking off a veil and speaking shyly to the camera with the words: "I am Cessa Nabarawi, the first Egyptian feminist with Hoda Chaarawi, and the editor and founder of the magazine *L'Egyptienne* from 1925 to 1940." Then as Cessa's narration continued, an image from 1919 of the Egyptian flag, bearing the cross and the crescent, symbols of the unity of Christians and Moslems against the British occupiers, flashed across the screen.

I could not conceal the emotion in my voice as I made the presentation, and I could feel the sympathy of the audience as I spoke.

I had been warned that people walk out of film festivals when they don't like a film. But no one left. They sat through the entire eighty minutes. When it was over, there was a hush, then loud applause. Someone even shouted "bravo." This was more than I had ever hoped for.

Other films were shown that evening, after which we all went to an Italian restaurant where gallons of Verdecchio wine were poured for us. Sitting at my table were Edna, who had made a film which was critical of the treatment of Palestinians in the Is-raeli-occupied territories, Marva from Iran whose film showed the poverty of the peasants under the shah's regime, and Igall, an Israeli who had made a film about the Oriental Jews in Is-rael.

The Israeli caught my gaze as it flitted from one filmmaker to the next. He smiled at me and I averted my gaze, but I could feel him staring. "Who is he?" I whispered to Mona while he spoke to one of the others. "A leftist," she replied. "His film will be shown tomorrow. It's very critical of the Israeli treatment of Oriental Jews." A few minutes later, he got up and sat beside me. I was nervous and pretended to be absorbed in my food. I had never spoken to an Israeli before in my life. "Masaa al-kheir," he said in Arabic. I burst out laughing. "Where did you learn Arabic?" I asked. "In the occupied territories?" "No, in Morocco. I am a Moroccan Jew. My father still speaks Arabic at home," he said, smiling. He was in his thirties, tall with light brown eyes and olive-colored skin. "You must see my film to-morrow," he said. "It will explain a lot of things about me." "Where do you live in Israel?" I asked. "I live in Switzerland now because there is censorship in Israel. My films are not pop-ular there. I allow Palestinians like Raymonda Tawil and Fawzy al-Asmar to speak out. Do you know who they are?" I nodded. They were militant Arabs who lived in Israel and protested against Israeli occupation of Arab lands. "I am against what is happening under the Begin regime," he said, now speaking in French. "The settlement policy, retaliation against the Arabs, military occupation, curfews, arbitrary ar-rests, blowing up of homes—this is not what Israel should be doing to its neighbors." He then told me about the Peace Now movement in Israel, about the artists and intellectuals who believed that the Palestinians should have autonomy and that the occupied territories should be returned to the Arabs. I had never heard of such things before. As the evening progressed I felt myself warming up to him. But still there was something unsettling about talking to an Israeli.

Abruptly I asked him if he had ever killed an Egyptian soldier. At first my question seemed to amuse him, but when he saw the seriousness of my expression he said, "What if I had?" "I would get up and leave this room," I replied. "Laila, believe me I have never killed anyone," he said. I didn't believe him, and yet I remained seated. A waiter shuffled about trying to get our attention. We had been talking for so long we didn't notice that the restaurant had emptied. We paid our bill and walked out into the street, police sirens sounding in the distance. As I got into the bus that would take me back to my hotel, he said, "Please see my film tomorrow." "Of course I will. Ma'a al-salama, go in peace," I replied.

Igall's film showing how Oriental Jews were discriminated against in Israeli society, which treated them as second-class citizens, sparked controversy in the audience. "Disgusting," said a little old lady. "Who the hell does that schmuck think he is? Attacking Israel!" said another woman. The Arabs were not much better. "He's still a Zionist," said a friend. "Wishy-washy," said another Arab, "and they're the most dangerous."

"I never thought I'd see a film by an Israeli which was critical of Israel," I told him when I saw him later. "You have a very low opinion of us," he said mischievously. "Do you think you will find a film distributor here in New York?" I asked, equally mischievously. "I'm trying," he said, "but so far many doors have been shut in my face. There are very bad vibrations from the Israeli consulate, too."

After that we saw a lot of one another, but our conversations were always political. On the last days of the festival, we took a break from the screenings and went to Washington Square, where we sat on a bench munching falafel sandwiches and watching people go by. "We call falafel *tamia* in Egypt," I informed him. "I know," he replied. An acquaintance shouted to Igall from across the road, and Igall answered in Hebrew. Then he turned to me and said, "It's an Israeli friend. You must come to Israel someday, Laila. Just to see what it's like." "I don't want to go to Israel. I know what it's like," I said. "That's a fanatic Arab attitude," he replied. "How can you say that, you who choose to live in a European country rather than be subjected to the bigotry there." "It pains me that I cannot live in Israel, but I need to know it's there. I need to know that the Jews have a homeland." "But Israel," I said, "as it exists today, excluding the Palestinians, discriminating against Oriental Jews, is a racist society. You have shown that in your film. Instead of the Aryan, it is the Jew who is the master race. Besides, Zionism and anti-Semitism are comparable viewpoints: they both assume that it is impossible for Jews and non-Jews to live together." "But, Laila," he said, "you cannot ignore the fact that six million Jews died in concentration camps and that it can happen again." "Must the Arabs pay the price for what the Germans did?" I asked. "And how did you pay the price, Laila?" I felt hurt by his tone of voice which was very cold. But I tried to remain calm as I answered, "My entire life has been influenced by the Arab-Israeli conflict. Because of the wars with Israel, I should say because of the implantation of Israel in our midst, the Arabs have had to fight expensive wars for thirty years. As a consequence, my country has become impoverished and overridden with social problems of such magnitude that they are now insoluble." "The social problems would have existed anyway," he replied. "That's a colonial thing to say," I retorted. "For what is Israel but a colony of the West which seeks to dominate the area?" He was silent and then said, "It was always the Arabs who were attacking Israel."

"Let's look at the historical facts," I said. He fidgeted in his seat. "Please listen. Why doesn't anyone want to listen to the Arab viewpoint?" He smiled. "You are an Oriental Jew, you should at least acknowledge that the whole crux of the problem—the objection to Israel—is not an objection to Judaism (except by fanatics), but to colonialism." "Explain yourself," he said irritably. "In 1919 the Allied powers met in San Remo and literally chopped up the Ottoman Empire, which had fallen during the war: Syria and Lebanon were placed under French mandate—a hypocritical formula for colonization—and Iraq and Palestine (including Transjordan) were to come under British mandate, with a clause inserted providing for the Balfour Declaration. The Arabs had been duped to believe that if they fought on the side of the Allies, against the Turks, they would be given independence. Instead they were further subjugated and the Balfour Declaration made way for the eventual creation of the State of Israel." "I know all that," he said cryptically. "What the world doesn't realize is that the Arab hostility to Israel stems from this historical fact. The Arabs saw and still see in Israel a colonial presence which usurps their land and refuses to allow anyone but Jews to return there." "And that is why the Arabs vow to destroy Israel?" he asked sarcastically. "Igall, for God's sake. From 1948 onward, the Arabs have suffered one humiliating military defeat after another. The Palestinians were driven out of Palestine in 1948 and to this very day are not allowed to return." "But if they had accepted the UN partition and recognized Israel . . ." "Igall, do you forget that at the time of the partition, the Jews made up only thirty percent of the population and owned only eight percent of the land? That is why the Arabs rejected the partition, and besides, by the end of the war, Israel occupied eighty percent of the Palestinian territories." "If the Arabs had accepted the partition . . ." he interjected. "Igall, the Arabs will never accept the colonial amputation of their land." "That is why Arabs looted, murdered, and raped Israelis along the 1948 frontiers?" he asked. "The Palestinians refused to accept the annexation of their land." "I am against annexation," he said. "I know you are, but all you have to do is look at a map of Israel since 1948. Look how it has expanded. It is outrageous. Now it occupies the West Bank, Gaza, the Golan Heights, and even the Sinai, our frontier! This conquest of territory has created a legacy of hatred which can never be undone until Israel relinquishes the occupied territories and allows the millions of Palestinian refugees to have a homeland."

We were silent for a while, then he said, "Why is it that Jews and Arabs always have to have these futile discussions?" "Because the Israelis are intransigent! They want to hang on to those territories. In 1956, after Eisenhower forced them to withdraw from the Sinai, Moshe Dayan vowed to get it back. And he did. Did that bring peace? But Arabs have made concessions down the line: We were forced to accept the creation of the Jewish state, the new borders of 1949, the reopening of the Straits of Tiran to Israeli ships in 1967, the annexation of large chunks of our territories in 1967. And even after all of that, we were prepared to recognize Israel if it returned to the pre-1967 borders. But still the Israelis insist that the Arabs recognize its existence through the use of force. 'Teach the Arabs a good lesson,' they say." "I know, Ben-Gurion said that, but there are Israelis like Uri Avnery who lobby in parliament for the restoration of all Arab territories," Igall reminded me. "But until someone listens to him, the hawks will triumph in your country," I said. "Israelis are paying the price, Laila. The economy is in a mess." "Israel is not a poor country, Igall. Egypt is. Think of all the schools, hospitals, and universities that could have been built if we had not been at war with Israel, while it built more and more settlements." "I understand your feelings about the territories, but we need to secure our frontiers from the attacks of Palestinian terrorists." "Israel's security is in its military superiority, not in its boundaries. Besides, Israel even has a nuclear bomb."

We had been talking for hours. I was exhausted and exasperated. Finally he said, "I am one Israeli who believes in peace. But first, Israel has to be recognized by the Arabs. What could it do to make that happen?" "Concessions. It must give up the territories and talk to the PLO." "And if that doesn't happen?" "More wars. I think an Islamic revolutionary war is brewing in the area. The overthrow of Israel will become one of the primary objectives of these extremists. Unless, of course, Israel makes concessions."

We remained on the bench for a while, painfully aware of everything that remained unresolved between us. "Whatever happens, I want you to know that I've enjoyed meeting you," I said. "You are a fanatic Arab," he said, unable to conceal the smile in his voice. "And you are a Zionist," I replied. "East is east and west is west, and never the twain shall meet?" he asked ironically, alluding to Kipling's colonial poem. "I don't know," I said, shaking my head. "I know we will never meet again, unless there is peace." "Shalom, then," he said, getting up from the bench. "May I at least take you to the bus stop?"

We walked in silence and got to the stop just as the bus was pulling up. "Ma'a al-salama," I said. "Ma'a al-salama," he replied.

L AILA, HOW YOU DOING?" It was Phyllis Chesler on the phone. "Terrible," I replied. "I can only see and think dollars. I want to stay on in New York for a while but I can't afford this hotel." "You can't afford the Tudor?" she said incredulously in her heavy Brooklyn accent. "You Americans take affluence for granted," I said. "What I pay for a day here is a third of my salary as a university professor in Cairo." "Let's see what I can do to help," she said, and the phone clicked.

I had met Chesler just a few days before when she had invited the filmmakers to her home after the festival. It was immediately apparent to both of us that we shared many views on feminist issues, although we differed radically in our perspectives on the Middle East. Phyllis was married to an Israeli, and sounded like even more of a Zionist than he.

A few hours later she rang again. "Have you heard of Gloria Steinem?" she asked. "Of course," I replied. "Well, you're welcome to use her apartment until you find something else," she announced. "That's terrific," I replied. "How did you manage that?" "We feminists have a way," she replied.

The following day Phyllis escorted me to Gloria Steinem's apartment on the Upper East Side. As we entered the apartment, I felt I was walking into a shrine, a feminist shrine. There was a stillness and a faint scent of perfume in the two high-ceilinged rooms, the smell of a place where people come and go but do not stay long. Bookshelves containing hundreds of feminist books lined the walls. Indian fabrics of gold, green, and red draped the sofas, cushions, and the loft bed. A large walnut wardrobe evoking Midwestern America blended in with the soft Oriental background.

Phyllis spoke in muted tones as she showed me around. I followed her about like someone being initiated in a new rite: the feminist religion. For that was the religion worshiped in those two rooms. "Gloria is considered one of the leaders of the movement, you know," Phyllis was saying. "She's almost the symbol of the movement, and to many she *is* the movement," she added. I nodded. I still remembered those images I had of her in the sixties. But I knew so little of that "movement" which had touched the lives of so many American women. I was not a part of it, and I didn't even suspect that it would ever touch my own life. "I don't know anything about feminism in this country," I whispered to Phyllis. She smiled and said, "You soon will." I smiled and nodded. I had already been touched by the spirit of the dweller.

Gloria had welcomed me even though she was not there and I had never met her. I curled up on her soft couch and rested my head on her cushions, leafing through magazines. Feverish thoughts of Asma no longer tormented me.

Gloria arrived a week later, announcing herself on the telephone first. "Laila, it's Gloria," she said, as if we had already met. An hour later she walked into the apartment, carrying a lot of luggage. She seemed taller, thinner, and more beautiful than her pictures. But it was her strength which struck me. She set her luggage down and we sat down beside her large oak desk. She leafed absentmindedly through her mail and began to ask me questions. Was I comfortable? Was everything all right? Did I have any difficulty with the lock on the front door? I was so excited at meeting her that I could only answer in monosyllables.

Then she sat down opposite me and began asking me questions about my film. I fumbled about in my purse and produced an interview with me that had appeared in *The New York Times;*

I handed it to her as if I were presenting my credentials. I watched her as she read it, wondering if she would accept me as a feminist. Was I a feminist? I had never thought of myself as one before, had never located the agonies of my life solely in my sexual identity. But now I found myself wishing I were a feminist—wishing I had the strength and composure of the woman sitting in front of me. When she finished reading she asked me about Egyptian feminism, the role of Mrs. Sadat, and the battle over the Family Law. We talked long into the night. I told her about myself as well, while all the while, she nodded in understanding, as if we had known each other all our lives.

As the weeks went by, I discovered that in New York women formed support networks for one another: an underground of sorts in which they helped each other professionally, politically, and socially. Gloria introduced me to the other feminist leaders who were fighting for the "issues," as they called them: ratification of the ERA, abortion, rape, the gender gap. Women like Bella Abzug, Koryn Horbal, Pat Carbine, Susan Brownmiller, Dorothy Pittman Hughes, Harriet Pilpel, Martha Stuart, and many other statuesque women of marble and bronze resilience. I was awed and inspired by each of them.

Gloria also involved me in the "business" of feminism, as Daviki Jain, the Indian feminist, called it: the encounters, the demonstrations, the lobbying, the fund-raising. So much hard work, I thought as I watched Gloria and the other feminists go about it so tirelessly. They made me see the political side of feminism, for they believed passionately that women needed all the political power they could muster. I was reminded of the underprivileged women of my own country who, though half the population, still did not have the right to choose the men they would marry or whether or not to have a baby.

Returning home to Gloria's apartment after a long New York day, it was peace not loneliness that greeted me. For Gloria had given me much more than a place to stay. She had helped me to recognize that my struggle was the struggle of women of every culture and that all feminists were alienated within their own countries. Only the movement could help women unite and realize their goals. And the movement did not just belong to America. Women could help each other across all frontiers.

In July there were hectic preparations for a rally in Washington in support of the Equal Rights Amendment. One day when I came home, I found a note from Gloria which said, "Contact me when you get to Washington for the rally. Can be reached at this phone number ———. P.S. Wear white."

At Penn Station the next morning, a throng of women clad in white, holding banners, and talking and laughing excitedly filled the platform. As they filled the cars, they began to chant the ERA slogans. I managed to find a seat on the train. Sitting next to me was a man of about thirty-eight who wore a rumpled blazer, flannel pants, a white shirt, and a college tie. He was the only man in sight. I looked at him inquiringly. "Are you going to march, too?" I asked. He smiled. "Oh, yes." He was on his own, which increased my curiosity. Sensing this he turned around to face me and said, "I'm an anarchist and I edit an anarchist paper." He told me about the leftist movement in America, speaking passionately about the poor and the social injustices perpetrated by the American system. The three-hour journey flew by and we arrived in Washington before I knew it. As we stepped off the train, I told him that I did not know where to find the demonstrators. "Follow me," he said. I followed him to the place where the marchers had assembled, right in front of an ancient Egyptian obelisk, or at least that's what it looked like to me. My companion gave me a mock-heroic salute, buttoned his rumpled blazer, and said, "Good luck to the feminists of Egypt," and with that he disappeared into the crowd.

The marchers were coming down the avenue, thousands of them, arm in arm. As they made their way past me, someone pulled me by the arm and suddenly I was a part of this vast collective consciousness, singing at the top of my lungs: "What do we want, what do we want, ERA, ERA." As we passed the Justice Department, the chanting grew louder and angrier. But no one molested us. It was excruciatingly hot, but I felt refreshed at the sight of these thousands of apasionarias chanting their protest right in the heart of government.

Later, speeches were given in an enormous park, as hot and tired protesters sprawled on the lawn. Hearing Bella Abzug toward the end of the day, when even the asphalt was sweating with heat and fatigue, was an unforgettable experience. Like most Arabs, I had always mistrusted the image of the Zionist advocate she projected in the media. But now I saw a woman who transcended Zionism, a gigantic figure who paraded her strength unabashedly and who pounded at women to fight for their rights.

At the end of the day I rang Gloria. "Come over to the Madison Hotel to meet the others," she said. At dinner, to my delight, I was seated next to Bella Abzug. But throughout the meal she ignored me. Finally, when the dessert had been set before us, she turned to me and said, "I've been a Zionist all my life." I was totally taken aback, but still struggled to find an appropriate response. Meanwhile, she had returned to her dessert. "I've been an Arab all my life," I managed to say. Everyone at the table laughed. She turned back to me and smiled.

Also seated at the table was Gloria's boyfriend Stanley Pottinger, whom I had never met before. I was impressed to learn that he, too, had been marching. Such supportive men must only exist in New York, I thought.

I tried to keep in touch with what was going on at home. The peace talks were going badly and by the end of July, Sadat had announced that there was no point in continuing to negotiate with the Begin government. Israel had refused to comply with Sadat's demands that they withdraw their settlements and air bases from the Sinai and restore it to full Egyptian sovereignty. Sadat's demand that the West Bank Palestinians be granted complete autonomy was also rejected.

In September, it was announced that Sadat would be coming to Washington to meet with President Jimmy Carter. Then it was announced that the Israelis were also coming and that a summit conference would take place at Camp David. New York filled up with Egyptian friends who had come with the delegation. "What's going to happen?" I asked. But no one knew. I was invited to a party in Washington, given by an Egyptian diplomat, where diplomats and journalists from Cairo mingled with Israelis as if we had been friends for generations.

On September 16, the papers revealed that the Camp David talks had come to a successful conclusion. Egypt and Israel had arrived at an agreement: Israel would return the Sinai and dismantle the settlements, and diplomatic relations would be established between the two countries after the signing of a peace treaty in March. On September 17, Carter, Sadat, and Begin appeared together on television. Was peace really here? I wondered as I watched them warmly embrace. Only the future would tell. Now it was time to go home.

Fouad, it's me, Laila. I'm back," I said on the phone. "It's wonderful to hear your voice again. When did you get home?" he asked. "Just a couple of days ago," I replied. "What? I can't hear you," he shouted. "It's a bad line," I shouted back. "Can you meet me at the club tomorrow around noon?" "Yes, of course. I'll be there," he replied.

There were deep lines in Fouad's face and his hair seemed whiter than ever before. "How the years have flown by," I said. "It's been eight years since we first met here, after I came back from America." He reached out and pressed my hand into his. "You look wonderful," he said. "New York was good to me, Fouad. I've become a feminist." He gave me a disapproving look, but I went on: "I'm full of hope, I've been renewed." He was silent. "What's been happening at home?" I asked eagerly. He shrugged his shoulders as if to say nothing much. "But, Fouad, Camp David," I said. "What is there to tell you, Laila? Sadat, as usual, was given a hero's welcome upon his return," he said sarcastically. "People," he went on, "think that this so-called peace will bring riches, wealth. That there will be foreign investment, reduced military expenditure, that everything will be fine." "I understand that the Left is opposed to Camp David," I said. "It's a separate peace, Laila. It's Israel's dream to divide the Arab world and to neutralize Egypt in the struggle for Palestinian rights. Sadat has sold out the Palestinians. All this talk about autonomy is meaningless. What the Palestinians want is sovereignty in their own lands," he said angrily. "And how do the Egyptian people feel?" I asked. "The people, my dear, are already welcoming Israeli tourists with 'shaloms.' "

There was now so much to do in Cairo, so much to accomplish. In the ensuing weeks, I spent all my time organizing a women's media group and trying to get screenings for my film. At one of the screenings, arranged for a group of directors and critics, I sat in the small, darkened auditorium almost paralyzed with fear and cursing the day I thought of making the film. I anticipated a considerable amount of negative reaction, but what came forth exceeded my expectations by far. "Was this film made for Egyptian or American audiences?" came the first question. "Who financed the film?" was the next. "These feminists are bourgeois. They do not represent Egyptian women. Did you think they did?" someone said sharply. "Why was your film shown in New York on June 6?" I was then asked. I replied to the critic who asked the question that I did not understand what he meant by June 6. "June sixth was the day of the defeat of the Egyptian army by the Israelis! Was it a coincidence that your Israeli organizers decided to inaugurate their film festival on that date?" he asked, pointing an accusing finger at me. For a few moments I was speechless. The absurdity of this accusation threw me completely. Finally I spoke: "I was not the only one whose film was shown at that festival. One of your colleagues, someone sitting right in this room, also had his film shown there. Why are you not attacking him?" Suddenly a voice from the rear of the auditorium squeaked: "I had no idea my film was shown. It must have been stolen."

A friend who had been helping me organize my women's group called. "Laila, there's a lot of talk going around about you." "What kind of talk?" I asked. "Well, it's not nice talk," she said. "What do you mean?" I asked, my heart pounding. "They say you are a CIA agent and that is why you go to America and the Americans receive you so well." "Do you believe it?" I asked. "I don't know what to believe," she replied. "Goddamn you," I said. "And don't you ever call me again."

The following day I withdrew from the feminist group I had helped to organize. I knew very well that the CIA accusation was an attempt to discredit me and my work. It was no coincidence that the critics who had attacked me at the screening were employed by the state. But I also knew how much energy it would take to discredit the vicious rumors that were being circulated about me. In Cairo, once a rumor is started, it can rarely be stopped.

Nonetheless, I was heartbroken. I had been humiliated and rejected by my own society. I had even been betrayed by my women friends. But a few days later, something happened which saved me from irrevocable despair.

On March 8, 1979, a demonstration against the obligatory wearing of the veil was staged in Iran, and some of the demonstrators were imprisoned or put under house arrest. Urgent pleas for help were sent to Western feminists. Simone de Beauvoir was mobilized as was Gloria Steinem, who called to see if I would join the delegation that was leaving for Teheran from Paris. I did not hesitate to say yes.

"What if you get killed in Iran?" asked my mother as I was preparing to leave. I shrugged my shoulders. "I'm trying to understand," she said with a gesture of helplessness. "But you can't. You never will," I replied, immediately regretting the sharpness of my words but knowing that they were true. Ever since my father's death, the tension between my mother and me had grown. There was now no one to act as a buffer between us. Moreover, her resentment of my life-style had grown so bitter that I feared that she hated me. After Asma's death, any compassion she may have had for me seemed to have disappeared. I was no substitute for Asma and certainly unwilling to become one. Thus the tie between us had virtually ruptured. It was to my brother that my mother now directed her attentions.

"This is the Middle East," she felt it necessary to remind me.

"Women have no rights here. You keep thinking you are still in America. This is still the society of Om Abdou. Om Abdou got everything she wanted without demonstrating and getting into trouble. *She* was patient." I listened to this sermon in silence. Then I said, "If something happens to me, Jean-Pierre will know about it. And if it does, don't be too angry with me," I added. She looked up at me from her sewing and replied calmly, "I can't take any more grief, Laila."

It was a cold, gray day when I arrived in Paris. I took a taxi to the expensive Sixteenth arrondissement, where I would be spending the night in the home of one of the feminists who was to go to Iran.

A maid greeted me and led me through various high-ceilinged tapestried and wood-paneled rooms to a study. The room was strewn with Persian carpets and Louis XIV furniture, and as I waited for my hostess, I cast my eyes over the rows and rows of leather-bound volumes in the long mahogany book-shelves. But soon a slender young woman entered and extended her hand. "I am Jacqueline," she said. "Do you live here?" I asked, for she was dressed in jeans and her manner was not aris-tocratic. "Yes, my grandmother left me this place," she said as she showed me to my bedroom. The bedcovers were satin, the bathroom solid marble. "We will meet the others later," she said as she left.

We met the rest of the delegation in very different surround-ings—a sparsely furnished Left Bank apartment. The women, most of them also in jeans, sat on the floor. After a lot of organi-zational talk, Caroline, the leader, took a square piece of black cloth from a brown package. "These are your chadors," she de-clared. "We will be required to wear them when we set foot on Iranian soil. If we don't," she added gravely, "we may be abused, even killed." Then, "May I please have fifteen francs from each one of you?" I couldn't believe it. I was being given a veil to wear and I had to pay for it!

Progressive feminist movements intervened on behalf of Iranian women, not realizing that sometimes the form and content of their intervention was being used to discredit the Iranian people's struggle against American intervention.

—*Nawal al-Saadawy (feminist)*

ORLY WAS FILLED with reporters and television crews, bulbs flashing everywhere. It was as if our little delegation of women—for we were only about twenty—was about to undertake a voyage to the moon. "Are you the only Arab here?" asked one of the other feminists as we waited to board the plane. I nodded. Considering the implications of this, she extended her hand and said warmly, "I'm Ann Zellensky. I represent Simone de Beauvoir here. Glad to meet you."

The flight was uneventful but there was a tremendous amount of tension in the air. As we prepared to land, Caroline instructed us to put on our chadors. I complied reluctantly but wore it in such a way that my hair showed through so that it could not be considered a veil by Islamic standards.

Posters of Khomeini hung everywhere in Teheran airport. We went through customs quickly. Not a bag was opened, even though we had been warned that we would be thoroughly searched. We were picked up by taxis and taken to the Park Hotel. At one point the traffic stopped to let a string of army vehicles through. They were filled with bayoneted soldiers who waved their arms and chanted, "Khomeini, Khomeini, Khomeini!" The people cheered. Revolution was in the air.

"It is the fever of revolution that you have noticed in the streets. Of course, the real test comes later," said Mehdi Bazargan, the prime minister, as we sat down in his office the next day. Then he added: "I'm sorry to have kept you waiting, but I had the Soviet ambassador here. When he saw how many ladies were waiting to see me, he remarked what a lucky man I was." His words were not appreciated.

"Is the Islamic revolution against women?" asked Alice Schwarzer, a prominent German feminist. "The proper place for women in Islamic society is as wives and mothers," he replied matter-of-factly. "Do you consider women inferior to men?" asked the French feminist Claude Servan-Schreiber. "Nature tells us that there is no equality between the sexes, not in temperament, physical strength, or moral aptitude. That is why in Islam, women are not allowed to act as judges or to lead in prayer," Bazargan replied. "Is it true that your secular Family Law has been abolished and that you are now applying the sharia?" I asked. He nodded, and then asked me in French, "Êtes vous Algerienne?" "Non, je suis Egyptienne," I answered. "Ah," he said in disappointment.

Later we visited the campus of Teheran University, which, oddly enough, was open to everyone. The campus was streaming with bearded young men and chadored women. No one seemed to pay any attention to us. But gradually, imperceptibly, a tight ring of young men shouting "CIA! CIA! CIA!" formed around us. Claude explained that we were from Paris, an explanation which calmed them down because it was in France that Khomeini had lived for a while in exile.

I had brought along a super-8 camera and I looked at the expressions on their faces through the lens. I saw both repression and idealism reflected there. The other feminists began to talk to the students who had now been joined by young women.

All the while, the circle closed tighter and tighter, until all I could see were the young women's eyes masked by their black veils. One of the them was telling us that Iranian women wore the chador so as not to be sex objects, so that men would address themselves to their minds. Meanwhile, the circle had grown so tight that I was hardly able to maneuver the camera. Suddenly one of the women broke away and ran off with her chador in her teeth. Then someone shouted something in Iranian and pointed at me. A militiaman with a bayonet came toward us, shouting at me. "He says you are Iranian," someone volunteered. One of the Frenchwomen began to tell him who we were. "Je suis Egyptienne," I told him angrily. He gave me a threatening look and asked to see my passport. I fumbled for my documents and handed it to him. He looked through it and returned it to me, saying "Sadat" in disgust. We made our way toward the entrance, while he followed behind at a distance.

At dinner I could hardly eat. The other feminists devoured their roasted lamb and rice, but in a few days they would be back in Paris or elsewhere, back to their stable lives, their bistros, their Peugeots, their feminist magazines, their jeans, and their unthreatened lives. In Cairo, I did not know what would greet me. Women there had already started to wear the veil.

The following day I was one of four feminists selected to meet the leaders of the March 8 demonstration against the chador. We were picked up at the hotel by a young man who constantly looked furtively about. We headed toward the outskirts of town. The car stopped in front of a two-story limestone house. The room we entered was small and sparsely furnished. After a few minutes, three young Iranian women walked in. All of them wore jeans. One of them, "K," as she cautioned us to call her, was a friend of Kate Millett's. She had been a student in the United States and had returned to Iran after the revolution. "They accused me of importing Western ideas," she said. Her words had a familiar ring. "All we wanted to do," said "F," the second woman, "was organize women, trade-unionize professionals, and fight for women's rights, of course. We were all in favor of Khomeini's revolution. But during the antichador demonstrations, we were accused of being counterrevolutionaries, CIA agents." I looked at her compassionately. She must have been about twenty-six. She had short black hair and large, almond-shaped eyes. Her chin protruded with strength and determination. They will destroy her, I thought. "We have been isolated, we dare not leave our homes. We have no contact with the outside world. We would like you to keep in touch with us," said "N," the third woman.

It was clear that these women were in very real danger. Later, as we made our way to the waiting car, I asked my companions if we would be able to contact them again, to make sure they were safe. The European feminists shrugged their shoulders. Who knows? they said. Where are you now, "K," "F," and "N"? I still wonder.

On our way back to the hotel, I noticed that the facades of all the buildings were scrawled with red and green revolutionary slogans. Khomeini's face was everywhere. His eyes followed us through the winding streets. His fingers pointed at us in accusation.

"We have been granted an interview with the ayatollah," declared one of the French feminists triumphantly. "This will be the first time that he will meet with Western women," she added. It amused me that Caroline always seemed to forget that she had an Arab in the group. "Tomorrow at dawn, we leave for Qom. And by the way, you will all have to wear chadors. That was a condition. I'm sorry." I looked at her, took a deep breath and said as calmly as I could, "I'm sorry, too, because I will not be able to join you. I refuse to wear a chador." Everyone turned and stared at me as if I were Oliver Twist asking for another helping. "Why not, for heaven's sake," asked one of the women. "We came here to protest the chador, not to wear it," I reminded them. "You wear the veil to see the pope," someone snapped. "You do. I don't!" I replied. "Bravo," said Ann Zellensky quietly. Then Alice Schwarzer got up and declared that she felt the same way: "I'm going to try to place a call to Paris, to find out what Simone de Beauvoir has to say." "Is it because the chador is an Islamic veil and you are a Copt?" one of the others asked. "It's not even purely Islamic," I replied. "It's a *shi'ia* form of dress, which springs from the ethnic culture of Iran. Besides, the veil was advocated by Saint Paul and worn in ancient Greece and Byzantium long before it was worn by Moslem women." "Then it's just a symbol," said a feminist who was also a journalist. "For you it's a symbol, because you don't have to wear it. And if you wear it to see Khomeini, to get your scoop, it becomes a fancy-dress costume. You can take it off when the

party is over. For Arab women, it is the *condition* of segregation,"
I said angrily. "Take it easy, Laila," said Ann. Meanwhile, Alice
Schwarzer had reentered the room: "Simone de Beauvoir says to
you all, 'What the hell do you want to see the ayatollah for?'

The following day, only four of the twenty women went to
Qom. The audience with the ayatollah lasted three minutes,
during which he did not utter a single word.

As soon as I returned to Cairo I contacted the major newspapers and gave them a complete account of my visit to Iran. I thought that this might avert rumors of a "secret mission" or any such thing. At first the story brought a very positive response. I received many laudatory phone calls and people stopped me wherever I went to say "bravo." Jean-Pierre, the French journalist and family friend, made the whole thing a cause célèbre by writing a long article in *Le Monde,* which he called "No Veil for the Ayatollah's Pleasure." Then, without warning, the tide changed, and I found myself at the mercy of the political hurricane that was sweeping Egypt in the aftermath of Camp David.

Practically every country in the Arab world had condemned Camp David. A summit meeting was held in Baghdad to urge Sadat not to sign a peace treaty with Israel. Two and half billion dollars were to serve as an incentive. Sadat responded angrily, "Not a thousand million, not two thousand, or hundreds of thousands of millions of dollars can buy the will of Egypt!"

At the end of March representatives of the Arab countries met again in Baghdad and a decision was made to cut all political and economic ties with Egypt. Moreover, Egypt was expelled from the Arab League and from OPEC. A few weeks later, Saudi Arabia broke off diplomatic relations with Egypt. Furious, Sadat decided to take a national referendum on the peace treaty. Egyptians were asked to say yes or no to it. Ninety percent of the electorate said yes.

But the trouble had not come to an end. At Assiut University, a large campus in the south of Egypt, violent and bloody student demonstrations were triggered off by the presence of the shah of Iran in Egypt. The demonstrations were organized by Islamic student groups, who, among other things, denounced the peace treaty with Israel because they claimed it was opposed to Islamic beliefs.

In another angry speech, given this time at Ain Shams University, the second largest university in Cairo, Sadat alluded to these demonstrations by saying: "Nothing is easier than to create a revolution through tribunals which daily send people to their deaths. The real challenge is to rebuild the country. These people in Iran have digressed from the real path of Islam. Islam which favors equality between men and women. Do *they* wish us to be like them and have our women wear veils which make them look like walking tents?" he said in an allusion to the Islamic fundamentalists who had organized the riots at Assiut University.

Sadat's speech heartened me. I even imagined that the president approved of my trip to Iran.

In April, that year, was Sham al-Nessim, an ancient feast day on which the Copts and Moslems alike usher in the beginning of spring. Families flock to the shores of the great river, while young girls in their new cotton frocks dot the banks with pink and blue and green.

Before leaving the house, my family would prepare a picnic basket with boiled eggs, baladi bread, spring onions, and *feseekh,* salted fish. My father would buy the fish himself, setting it on the kitchen table the night before and squeezing lemons, many lemons, on it. He also bought the onions, handpicked from the basket of an old woman on the street corner. My father loved onions, and the woman would always save the best ones for him. My father would proudly display their long green stalks and white bulbs. Sham al-Nessim was not Sham al-Nessim without the salted fish and the onions.

We were awakened at dawn and, after dressing, were bundled into the shiny red Packard, my father driving, of course. The road to the barrages, which was narrow, dusty, and unpaved, wound past tiny villages of mud huts. Villagers with their water buffaloes sauntering behind them, children playing in the mud, women carrying water jugs, passed next to the red car. But the sight of the peasants did not disturb me—for in those days, I gazed on rural Egypt with innocent eyes.

It would be misty as we reached the barrages. The sun was already beginning to penetrate the dewy gray clouds. The iron bridge thundered below us as we crossed the river. Mohammed Ali, the nineteenth-century dictator of Egypt, had built the barrages, this intricate system of locks at the delta. He knew that whoever controls the water supply of a desert country controls the country.

The grounds around the barrages consisted of sloping lawns interspersed with flower beds of pansies, dahlias, and roses. Acacia trees lined the edges of the trimmed lawns. A vendor selling cotton candy would call out "Ghazzal al-banat" for all to hear; the balloon seller would meander with his wares in the midst of the shrill cries of children reaching out to touch his wares, while the bagel or *semeet* peddler seated beside his basket would call out "Semeet, semeet."

We would all walk down to the banks of the waterway waiting to board a felucca. After a little haggling with the boatman, we would step onto the gently rocking sailboat. The family would sit on the narrow benches encircling the boat as one boatman lifted the oars and the other unfolded the sails. A slight breeze and we would be on our way.

As we glided along the Nile, the sun would struggle to break through the mist. Soon the basket would be opened and my father would hand out the boiled eggs and onions, while my mother would place the fish in the baladi loaves. We would eat hungrily and drink sugared tea from a thermos flask. The sound of the water trippling against the oars would be broken by the boatmen's voices joined in a sad, nasal lament. Gazing at the horizon, my father would hum along. Suddenly a commotion would be heard from the shores: "Al walad ghere'e fil bahr"—a child has fallen into the river. Then "Khalass, anquazouh"—he has been saved. "Il hamd lil 'Lah," my father would say—God be praised.

On Sham al-Nessim in 1979, I had been invited to spend the day at the *ezba* or farm of some friends, but I decided against it, preferring to spend the day alone. It was an opportunity to read and rest. Leafing through a magazine which was published by the government, I came across an article called "The Islamic Revolution and the Witches of Freedom." It was written by my former collaborator, the actor-dramatist Mr. Helw, who was said to be close to Sadat. I wondered what he meant by witches and I began to read:

> I stand neither with the Ayatollah Khomeini nor with the advocates of the shah. I stand with Allah, and all those who abide by his teachings. But my dear friend, Dr. Laila Said, and her companion witches have another viewpoint which they call "women's liberation" . . .

My God, he was writing about me! I was a witch! Too funny. I read on:

> My dear friend Dr. Laila obtained her doctorate on the actor Najib al-Rihani, and not on the Ayatollah Khomeini, and this is maybe why she erred so spectacularly when she declared in the pages of our newspapers that the wearing of the veil by Middle Eastern women is reactionary, uncivilized, and a threat to the progress of women. Surely, Dr. Laila's meddling in matters relating to Islamic law is a delicate affair. It may even appear to some that she is stirring sectarian strife. But I am not of this opinion. For I know Dr. Laila: she is an artist, even though her mind is made in the U.S.A.

This was outrageous. First I was accused of being an agent of the CIA and now this—to be accused of creating strife between the Copts and Moslems of Egypt was just too much. It was practically an accusation of treason. I read on with a sense of dread and revulsion:

> Undoubtedly, Dr. Laila, whose family is from the south, knows our traditions only too well. She must know that women in the sa'id of Egypt wear the tarha to cover their heads, and bishas to hide their faces, so that even the devil cannot set eyes on them. And no one can claim that these women have no rights. I fail to understand what satanic conceptions led Dr. Laila to associate the freedom and progress of women with Western dress, cocktail parties, drunken dancing, hysterical music, and the provocative display of bodies. Neither do I comprehend the real purpose of this so-called International Committee for the Rights of Women which Dr. Laila champions in the name of Arab women . . .

The CIA accusation again, very dangerously phrased. I forced myself to go on reading:

> Moreover, as we have been told by Dr. Laila, Simone de Beauvoir heads this organization and we all know who she is: an adulteress who lives out of wedlock with the boy of her dreams. And this is the model for emancipation with Dr. Laila holds up for our women: this violator of religious customs and traditions. What seems to have eluded Dr. Laila is that the Iranian revolution springs up under the banner of an Islamic revolution and not under the slogans of Kate Millett or Simone de Beauvoir: exponents of wantonness and drug taking and ungodliness. I do not profess to be a sheikh, but I am able to say that women's virtue lies in their adherence to the dress prescribed by the sharia and by the teachings of Islam. You neurotic, hysterical doctor. You have desecrated a domain which is not

yours to invade or to sully with your sinful practices. For we, dear friend, respect religion and we respect the commitments of others to the teachings of their religions . . .

I set the paper down, unable to read any further, and rushed to the bathroom where I began to vomit.

"You have been used as a whipping boy, if you'll pardon that phrase," said Jean-Pierre when I phoned to tell him what I had read. "But why?" I asked. "Because a lot of people were angered by your antichador campaign. The government cannot afford to support people like you. Sadat has enough on his hands," he added. "But this is preposterous," I lamented. "I know," he said quietly. "What shall I do, Jean-Pierre?" I asked. "Write a rebuttal. They are under obligation to publish it."

I wrote a long letter to the editor, but it was never published or answered. Then I tried to get the support of my women friends. But no one wanted to get involved. Finally, I decided to see my lawyer. "You can sue for libel," he said. "You have been smeared. You have been called a promiscuous woman, a foreign agent, and an instigator of sectarian strife." "The whole list," I said wearily. "Cheer up. We'll fight them. But you realize, of course, that we will be suing one of the most powerful magazine editors in the country and a close friend of Sadat's, for we have to sue the editor for allowing this piece to be printed." I nodded. "Please, please, go ahead," I said.

A few days later, I visited Cessa Nabarawi, the eighty-two-year-old feminist who had been in my film. "Please come to court with me," I pleaded, fully expecting her to say she was too old. "Of course I will," she said without hesitation.

The courtroom was packed, mostly with women carrying babies and surrounded by children. Cessa and I sat down on one of the wooden benches which spanned the overcrowded room. Scores of other women were now overflowing into the passageways and looking curiously in our direction, for we were the only women in Western dress. A hush fell over the courtroom as the clerk shouted *"Mahkama."* Everyone got to their feet as the judge and two magistrates walked in. "Be brave, " said Cessa as I went to the stand before the judge.

Declaiming loudly, my lawyer began to read the magazine article; the courtroom echoed with indifference, and one of the magistrates stared at me with contempt. My lawyer, who had now stopped reading, was saying, "The five commandments of Islam do not stipulate that a Moslem woman must wear the veil!" His voice rose higher with indignation: "Sitting in this courtroom is Cessa Nabarawi, one of the pioneers of the movement for the emancipation of women and one of the first women to remove the veil in our times. And that was in 1923!" he said triumphantly. "My client is a respectable professor, an artist, not a, a, . . . as Mr. Helw says. And President Sadat himself recently denounced the chador in his speech at Ain Shams University," he shouted with synthetic rage. The magistrate on the left was still staring at me. "Sentence will be heard May 30," the judge said.

Cessa and I walked silently into the glaring sunlight. We did not speak until I helped her out of my car. I thanked her and apologized for subjecting her to this petty trial and the sordid courtroom. She stopped me in midsentence. "Keep fighting," she said as she made her way slowly up the stairs to her apartment.

After leaving Cessa I drove back into the business section of the city. I had an appointment to see the editor of one of the major papers. He was a friend, and I was hoping to enlist his support. When I reached his office, his secretary asked me to wait for a few minutes because he was praying.

Hassan Bey welcomed me as he usually did, with a big smile. He was one of the most elegant men in Cairo, with silver hair, an aquiline nose, and an almost ascetic face. As I sat opposite him he rang for lemonade which was promptly brought in on a silver tray. I came straight to the point. "All I want is for you to publish in your newspaper that I am suing the magazine for libel," I said. As he leaned forward I found myself staring at his polka-dotted, initialed silk tie. Noticing this he brandished it and said, "Pierre Cardin." I smiled. "Will you help me?" I asked. "I'm afraid I cannot publish anything about this matter. The editor of the magazine you are suing is a colleague. It would be unethical."

During these difficult days I often found myself ending up in my mother's apartment. It was preferable to being alone with my torments. We often had lunch or dinner together. One evening, as she was putting a grilled fish on my plate, she suddenly informed me, very quietly, that I was being attacked in the sermons at the mosques. "What?" I asked in disbelief, almost swallowing a fishbone. "One of your aunts called to tell me," replied my mother. "You should get out of town. You may get killed," she said. "Goddamnit," I exclaimed. "What?" asked my mother, uncomprehending. "Oh, its just an expression I learned in America," I replied.

Jean-Pierre kept in very close touch, and one day he phoned very excitedly to say that Simone de Beauvoir had sent a cable to President Sadat on my behalf. A French feminist magazine, *F,* had also written a supportive piece. "Meanwhile, I'm being attacked in the mosques," I told him despondently. A week later, he sent me his latest article on my predicament, "The Revenge of the Mullahs!"

Despite Jean-Pierre's support and the support of the feminists in France and the United States, I was filled with despair. I wondered if I would ever be allowed to work in the theater again. Was this the time of reckoning? I had surrendered to my work as I had never surrendered to a man, and now I might lose it, too.

It was useless, all this fighting, I thought one night as I sat in my apartment. I went to the bathroom to splash my face with cold water, thinking this would make me feel better. Then I caught sight of myself in the mirror. There were lines around my eyes and my mouth which I had never noticed before. I'm going to seed, I thought as I popped out my contact lenses. I went into the kitchen and groped blindly for the wine bottle in the refrigerator. After pouring myself a glass I went into the living room and put on a record. The music filled the room and a few moments later, I was already feeling better. I *would* go on fighting. There was no need for self-pity. Besides, I enjoyed fighting, and maybe I would even win. The important thing was not to lose heart. I looked at the picture of my father on a nearby table. He smiled at me.

There was a slight breeze blowing in from the balcony. The Nile glistened in the darkness. Suddenly a brightly lit tourist yacht floated gaudily by, illuminating the water around it. Then it disappeared into the night like an apparition.

M AY IS the dusty month in Cairo. The desert winds, *khamseen,* blow over the city, covering everything with a very thick dust. Khamseen means fifty, and for fifty days Cairo lives under an oppressive, yellow dust that overlays the skyscrapers, bridges, buses, cars, trams, and even the river. The gusts are sometimes so strong that people stay home for shelter or seek refuge in the alleys between the tenements. The smell of burning refuse, piled high in the streets, mingles with the dust.

At the beginning of May, I began to prepare for my forthcoming season at the wekala. To reach the wekala, I took a highway which runs north past the City of the Dead, Cairo's vast cemetery, a city within a city of streets and avenues lined with myriad mausoleums. It is also a city of the living, for hundreds, even thousands, of homeless families squat in its midst. On the opposite side of the road, the thirteenth-century fortress of Saladin rises on a little spur of the Mukattam Hills, a limestone range which runs across Asia as far east as China. Not far away from this spot was a place called Yeshkur where Moses was supposed to have had conversations with God. Surrounding the Citadel on all sides are the famous medieval mosques of al-Azhar, Qalaun, and Mu'ayid, their numerous minarets crowding the horizon.

I parked my car as close as I could to the caravanserai, and then made my way through the vegetable market to the courtyard. The troupe was waiting for me inside, but it had dwindled because the actors knew there would be no budget from the Ministry of Culture that year and they would not get paid. Or else, like Adel, they had deserted the theater for television. I was very grateful for the loyalty of those who remained. "I have good news," I said to them, trying to sound cheerful. "The censors have okayed the Sanoua plays, so we can start rehearsing at once." I showed them the stamped scripts. "These plays don't require a budget. You can all double up and we'll use modern dress." "Don't worry, doctora, we'll manage," they laughed.

"Let's start reading the *Two Wives,*" I suggested. "It's a skit against polygamy." "Doctora, you're incorrigible," one of the actors said teasingly. "Have you been around the City of the Dead lately? It's mostly repudiated wives who live there with their children," I replied. "Why has it never been produced before?" asked an actress. "I don't think the establishment is interested in criticizing polygamy. Anyway," I continued, "it's an innocent little farce about an old man who marries a young girl and brings her home as his second wife to live with his old and ugly first wife." "What a riot," said one of the actors. "It happens all the time," said an actress. "The two wives start to fight and the husband gets caught in the cross fire." Laughter from the group. "The piece depends a lot on physical comedy and I can see that most of you are out of shape," I observed. "You're not going to have us swinging from ropes again?" asked a cheeky actor. "Let me continue, please," I said. "You can imagine that lecherous old man—it won't be easy playing him when you're all in your twenties," I added. "I'm very good at old men," chirped someone. "Anyway, what I am trying to say is that the comedy lies in the situations, but it is only through your acting skill that these situations can be really funny. This is like a *commedia* skit. You have the scenario, but you must flesh it out, bring it to life with your physical movements and body language." They were silent. "What happens after that?" asked someone. "Well, the old man brings home this young thing, introducing her to his wife and saying, here, this will be my second wife. I'll leave the two of you to get to know each other." Everyone laughed. "The two women glare at one another from across the stage, hating each other's guts, but smiling in pretense. The trouble starts when the older wife informs the younger one that she will have to do the cooking and cleaning. Naturally they begin to quarrel. 'I was brought here to be beautiful,' says the new wife. 'Were you now?' says the first wife, taking off her slipper and beating the younger one with it. The young wife goes at the older one with a pot. When the husband tries to intervene, he gets both the pot and the slipper on his head . . ."

"This is going to be fun," said one of the actresses, already seeing herself in the part of the young wife. "What about the other two skits?" asked someone else. "They are also commedia-like. One of them pokes fun at the new Europeanized bourgeoisie of Cairo in the 1870s, and the other is a satire on theatrical censorship in those days," I replied. "In those days, ha, ha," they laughed. And so, in the midst of this merriment, we sat down and began our first rehearsal.

The next weeks were filled with the gaiety of Sanoua's pieces and the extraordinary creativity which they provoked in the actors. We experimented with new improvisations every day, until the right physical movement or verbal inflection was found. Scenes were blocked and reblocked to extract the maximum humor from them. The actors were encouraged to play out their characterizations as broadly as possible, in order to stay close to their popular inspirations. For the dramatis personae of Sanoua's skits were drawn from the quarters of the city like the Ghouria or Khan Khalili—just outside the wekala.

As the rehearsals progressed, I found myself yielding once more to the miraculous catharsis of the theater. The events of the past months were completely overshadowed by the feverish preparations for our opening. Then one night when I left the theater, I found a parking ticket on my car. It made me angry. The policemen all knew the car and got their baksheesh on time. This was my eighth year at the wekala.

As soon as I arrived at the wekala the next day, I knew something was wrong. I knew it the moment I stepped into the alley. The garlic vendor who had always welcomed me effusively now averted his eyes. I walked to the entrance of the building and found the doors locked. I looked up at the windows which open onto the alley in the hope of catching someone's attention. They too were closed. Suddenly the wood creaked and one of the windows flew open. An angry, bearded face stared down at me. I opened my mouth to ask for help, but before I had a chance to speak, the window was shut with a bang. "They don't want you in there," someone in the alley volunteered.

The actors arrived and stood for a long time in the alley, hoping the porter would turn up and let us in. But no one came.

Samy Wahabi stared at me from across his large mahogany desk at the confiscated villa which housed the Ministry of Culture in Zamalek. Paintings by postrevolutionary Egyptian artists hung on the walls. The undersecretary was about fifty-five, with a pockmarked face and Mongolian features. His face always bore a sly expression. As I sat before him, I remembered another encounter we had had almost fourteen years before, when he headed the "Culture for the Masses" program under Nasser. "You used to be such an innocent little kitten," he said, obviously alluding to that encounter. "I was never a kitten," I said, trying to control my tone. He ignored my comment and began to shuffle the voluminous papers on his desk. "Why Sanoua now?" he said, still shuffling. "Why not?" I replied. "Sanoua is the founder of the popular, vernacular comedy of Egypt." "I know all that. But why *now*," he persisted, finally putting the papers down. "I don't understand," I replied. "Of course you do," he said. "We are simply not ready for the normalization of relations with Israel yet." I looked at him in disbelief. "Jacob Sanoua was an Egyptian Jew, true, but what does that have to do with Israel?" He gave me a long hard stare. "You are not fooling me, Dr. Laila," he replied. After a few seconds I said, "Jews have lived in Egypt since the third century B.C. We cannot assume that they were all linked to Zionism. Besides, hearsay has it that Sanoua converted to Islam." Wahabi smiled cunningly. I moved nervously in my chair and said, "Please, these farces have nothing to do with Camp David or the political situation now. They are period pieces."

Someone entered the room, and for several minutes I was ignored. I spent the time wracking my brains in order to recall the latest political events: Begin had just visited Cairo but I didn't have the faintest idea of the result. Then, oh, yes, there was this bill in the Knesset for the annexation of Jerusalem. That must be it.

As soon as we were alone again, I said, "Look, Wahabi Bey, you've known me for a long time. You know I am a hardworking stage director. I chose Sanoua because I had no budget and I felt that I could stage his plays on very little money, money which I am putting up myself." He received my words in silence. "Besides, we have censorship approval," I said. Another silence. "Censorship has nothing to do with this," he said, speaking slowly. "We are forbidding these productions for reasons of security. The Moslem Brotherhood has its centers all over the area. If there were trouble, the ministry would be held responsible." "But I've been working there for eight years!" I protested. My throat was dry and I asked for a glass of water. Once again I was treated to lemonade, this time in a crystal goblet. Wahabi watched me closely as I gulped it down. "Why did you close the theater in my face," I said, setting the glass down. "Why humiliate me like that in front of my actors?" I asked, my voice barely concealing my rage. "We have other plans for the wekala. We are planning to have a performance of religious songs there. Islamic songs," he added by way of explanation. Then leaning back in his chair he said again but almost inaudibly this time: "You used to be such an innocent kitten." "Please let me have the wekala back," I pleaded. "No," he said, his eyes gleaming.

"We'll get the wekala back," I told my actors, who had gathered at Fishawi's café. "Just give me time." "Doctora, don't worry, we all know Wahabi is harassing you," someone said. I smiled gratefully and said, "We'll carry on the rehearsals in my apartment." I looked at their despondent young faces. "Please keep your spirits up."

I lobbied constantly with everyone I knew in any kind of position of power and was beginning to despair when I heard that

Enayat, a friend of Asma's, had returned to Cairo from Washington in order to marry a powerful politician. I called her at once.

"Enayat, it's Laila. Do you remember me?" I asked. "Of course, we met in Washington when you were showing your film," she replied. "I have a bit of a problem I would like to see you about. Pardon me for talking business right away, American style! But I need your husband's help. He's a powerful man in our Ministry of Culture, you know," I added. "Why don't you come over for coffee, tomorrow, around eleven," she said. "Fine, perfect. I'll be there."

Enayat sat on her velvet couch draped in a Moroccan caftan which enhanced her Turkish beauty. She was one of the most beautiful women I had ever seen, with a kind of quiet sensuality. Yet it was intelligence, not sensuousness, that radiated from her dark, almond-shaped eyes. She was tall and extremely thin and wore her hair tied neatly at the nape of her neck.

"Cairo is festering, I can feel it all around me," she said, snuffing out a Kent cigarette. "I only came back here because of him." She was referring to her husband, who was said to be Sadat's closest confidant. "If I were single, I would not live here," she continued, looking into my eyes. Then suddenly, "I've been meaning to tell you how sorry I was to hear about Asma." The mention of Asma's name made my throat tighten and all the tensions of the past days erupted. Enayat watched me weep in silence. As soon as I was able I asked her to help me get my theater back. "Look," I said, handing her a small paperback volume of a history of comedy, "here is a chapter about Sanoua. Sanoua is an Egyptian. He's mentioned in all theater histories of the period . . ." She smiled compassionately as she took the volume. "I'll show this to my husband," she said reassuringly. "Help me get my theater back," I said. "I'll do my best," she promised.

At the door of her elegant apartment, she said, "I know it's unfair. They don't understand you. Besides, there is a strange atmosphere in the country these days," she added. "Do you mean this religious thing?" I asked. She lowered her eyes before replying: "Of course, you made things worse by going to Teheran. How do you expect them to feel when you protest the veil in the company of Western women?" "You have a point," I said wearily. Enayat puffed impatiently at another cigarette, but her eyes were full of warmth. I looked at her, marveling at the fact that she had relinquished her teaching job in America, relinquished her freedom, in order to get married. "I know what you are thinking," she said. "But you see, I love him. And for you I will talk to him," she promised.

I anxiously awaited her call. It came two days later. "Laila, you will get your theater back. There is one condition, though: no Sanoua." "All right," I said quietly. "Sanoua is not as important as the wekala," I added. "What will you replace him with?" she asked. I proposed *Chafeeka wa Metwalli*. "Do you have censorship approval?" she asked. "Of course. I staged it in 1975." "Fine," she replied. "Could you come by and pick up my husband's letter to Samy Wahabi? I thought you might want to give it to him yourself," she said mischievously. "I'll be right over," I replied, wondering how I could possibly thank her.

I returned to Samy Wahabi's office with the letter. "I would like to have this authorization to use the wekala undersigned by the legal department of the ministry. I was advised that this was the only guarantee that it would not be taken away from me again," I said. His face turned yellow. There was no offer of lemonade. He rang for the legal administrator of the ministry, who appeared within minutes, to sign. Meanwhile, I lit a cigarette, enshrouding Wahabi in a cloud of smoke.

After notifying my troupe we gathered in the courtyard of the wekala. The doors had been flung open in welcome. Upon looking again at the beloved stones, I recalled a scene I had once witnessed in an ancient, little Coptic church in Fustat, the oldest quarter of the city—a man upon reaching the altar flung himself facedown on the ground in an expression of pure reverence. At that moment, I, too, wanted to throw myself down and kiss the stones.

●

Not long after the rehearsals of *Chafeeka* began, one of the actresses came rushing to tell me that the ladies' room had been padlocked. A few days later, the water and electricity were turned off. At the last minute, the musicians disappeared. Was this the work of Wahabi? I wondered. Nonetheless, we managed to find replacements for the musicians, and to overcome the other exasperating obstacles.

Just before our first performance, Hamdi, a well-known Islamic scholar, appeared at the wekala. He carried a large thermos containing apricot juice. "I'm here to help," he declared. This surprised me because his politics were antithetical to mine. "Well," I replied, trying to recover from my astonishment, "I haven't got anyone for the box office. Will you sell tickets for me?" He nodded and smiled as if I had offered him the leading role in the play. As I was leaving, after explaining his duties to him, he said, "I was in Iran when you were there." "Protesting the veil?" I asked. "Of course not," he said impatiently. "I am a supporter of Khomeini and that's what I would like to discuss with you." "Look, Hamdi," I replied, "let me say this in plain American vernacular: the ayatollah pisses me off and I have better things to do than to discuss him at this moment. Now if that's all you came for, please go. But leave the apricot juice, the actors will appreciate it." "Calm down, doctora" he said quietly, "I really want to help you."

Hamdi was an Islamic fundamentalist, hardly the sort of companion I would have sought out during those stressful days. With his short-cropped hair and his habit of squinting behind his thick glasses, he was not a handsome man, yet he was very kind and because of this a sympathetic bond developed between us.

One day as we were hand-scrawling posters for the show, he began to talk about the political problems I'd been having. "The Sadat regime has encouraged the right-wing militant groups," he said. "I've even heard that the regime is providing them with money and facilities." "How is it that you speak this way?" I asked, taken aback. "You thought I was one of them?" he said, leaning over and looking into my eyes. "I am of the Islamic Left," he explained. "To them I am a radical because I maintain that Islam can be used politically, to radicalize people. In the spirit of Islam you will find tolerance and justice and all the elements of a classless society. In the real Islam, the ruler and the beggar kneel side by side to worship Allah and in this very act—of prayer—lies the essence of the social message of Islam. In Allah's eyes, we are all one." I looked at him in admiration. I have always admired idealists. "And how will you bring about this social revolution?" I asked. "In the schoolroom and the university lecture hall. That is why I have been suspended from teaching my classes at Cairo University." "Yes, I heard about that," I murmured. "It is Sadat who has done this to me. Because Sadat doesn't care about the lot of the people. All he cares about, and in this he is no different from Nasser, is to stay in power. Laila, you should realize that you are being persecuted by the very regime you uphold. It is Sadat who is behind the attacks on you." I reminded him that it was someone close to Sadat who made it possible for me to get the wekala back. "Sadat doesn't like leftists, liberals, Marxists, or feminists," he continued. "But the regime supports women's rights," I insisted. "Maybe," he said, "but the regime is right wing. To Sadat, Allah is American!" "So, even the CIA is against me," I mused sarcastically.

A week before we were due to close the show, a mysterious person walked into the wekala, picked a fight with the cast, and beat up two of the actors. The police were called and I was asked to come to the station to file a complaint. Hamdi and some of the actors came along. The performance was canceled.

The police station was located in a confiscated villa on a street that overflowed with sewage water and rubbish. The area surrounding it had seen better days. Mud-brick tenements were tightly squeezed between other crumbling villas. Children played in the street even though it was after midnight, and the only light came from the kerosene lamps of street vendors who kept vigil by their fruits and vegetables, hoping to sell another kilo of tomatoes or onions through the night.

As we walked into the police station, Hamdi said with emotion, "This used to be a meeting place for the Moslem Brotherhood party." "When?" I asked. "In the Nasser days. But in 1954, when they tried to assassinate him, Nasser had it confiscated. And now it is a police station," he said dryly. I laughed and said, "The conversion of right-wing outposts into outposts of the right wing."

The parquet floor of the station was laden with dirt. The rooms were bare but for a few benches and aluminum desks a few on-duty officers sat behind. Seated on the benches were haggard-looking people, their faces yellow in the light projected from a single bulb overhead. Hamdi, the actors, and I took our places beside them.

It was three in the morning, but we had to wait an hour for our turn to come. While we waited I kept my eyes on the bulb swaying ever so slightly from the threadbare cord. Occasionally, I glanced at the faces of the policemen who passed the time drinking tea, telling callous jokes, and interrogating people. "You look tired," Hamdi said, tapping me lightly on the knee. I looked at the sooty walls. Even the dirt seemed impenetrable.

When our turn came, we were interrogated about the occurrence in the wekala, while a nearby soldier yawned as he wrote down everything we said. Then we were told that the matter would be investigated and we would be notified.

A couple of days later, the show closed. On the final night, the wekala looked like an abandoned lover; its few, isolated projectors hung on precariously to their gelatins, which blew indifferently in the evening breeze.

I had the strangest feeling that I would never see it again. Enayat had said that I had won my battle "hands down," but as I drove past the dark mausoleums of the City of the Dead that night I no longer believed it.

That summer Mrs. Sadat's Family Law amendment was passed. The new law was criticized by many feminists who found it tame, but I saw it as a great step forward, a victory. "Mrs. Sadat's law," as it became known, made it illegal and punishable by law for a man to divorce his wife without her knowledge. It also made it illegal for him to turn out the wife from the matrimonial home if there were children. Now a man would have to think twice before divorcing his wife, in order to keep from making himself homeless. In addition, child custody by the mother was extended to fifteen for a boy and twenty-one for a girl. A woman could no longer be forced to return to her husband by the police, and she no longer required male authorization to travel. Polygamy, however, was still legal, provided a wife acquiesced.

Mild as these reforms may seem, they angered many men, and Mrs. Sadat was severely criticized for defying the sharia or Islamic law.

In 1980, statistics showed that only 23.5 percent of women in Egypt practiced birth control, and one out of every four marriages ended in divorce. The husband invariably remarried and had more children.

"Laila, I've been trying to reach you for days," said my lawyer frantically. "I even left a message with your mother." "My mother seldom gives me messages," I replied. "She says she's not my secretary! Anyway, what's going on?" "Well, I'm phoning to tell you the outcome of the case," he said. "Oh?" I replied in trepidation. "You won," he declared. "I don't believe it," I said jubilantly. "Now don't get so excited. It's complicated. The editor and the writer of the article have been sentenced to six months in jail." "Hurrah," I shouted. "But they have the right to appeal and they will." "On what grounds?" I asked. "Well, strictly speaking, as journalists they can only be prosecuted by the Socialist Prosecutor." "But Helw is not a state-employed journalist; it's unfair," I cried. "I know," he answered. "Do you think they'll win?" I asked. "They might. Don't forget the editor is a big shot and he *is* a state-employed journalist. But it's an unprecedented victory for you. It's the first time, to my knowledge, that an Egyptian court has ruled in favor of a case on feminist principles."

For a while, I was ecstatic. Then I got another telephone call from my lawyer. "They won the appeal," he said.

Press," said Jean-Pierre, flashing his card in the face of the police officer who was guarding the entrance to the courtroom. I remained as close as I could to my journalist friend. We were there to hear the outcome of the 1977 food riots trial, in which hundreds of students had been arrested and detained for demonstrating against the lifting of food subsidies. The place was packed with civil employees and workers in beige denims. Here and there older women in galabiyas, covered with veils, dotted the room. Surrounding the courtroom were several policemen, their revolvers strapped into leather belts.

As we let ourselves down on one of the wooden benches as the trial preceding the one we had come to hear finished, I noticed a large iron cage packed with bearded young men in white prison uniforms. "Who are those men?" I whispered to Jean-Pierre. "Communists," he replied. "What are they being held for?" "For trying to reestablish the banned Communist party of Egypt," he whispered back. After the judge spoke, a din arose in the courtroom. The judge banged the podium angrily and walked out. The sound of shuffling feet and shouting voices began to fill the room. The young men in the cage were being escorted out by the police. As they passed us they chanted in unison: "Communists till death, communists till death." Some of the older women began to weep, others to wail rhythmically, as in funerals. "The mothers," said Jean-Pierre, leaning toward me. The young men ignored their families and walked out passionately, singing their refrain. A few minutes later, the court-room was empty.

Jean-Pierre and I remained in our seats. "Why don't you go and ask when they will be hearing the food riots trial," he suggested. I went up to the judge's chamber and banged on the door. A court clerk opened it angrily. "What is it?" he said. "I'm sorry to disturb you but I have a relative who was involved in the food riots case and I wanted to know what time the case will be heard," I said. Actually, a young student journalist whom I liked very much had been jailed. "The judges are deliberating at this very moment. If you wait a few minutes, I'll have a list of the names and sentences," he informed me. I told Jean-Pierre and took my seat next to him again. By this time the courtroom had once again filled up.

The court clerk emerged and everyone rushed forward to see the lists. "Is your friend there?" asked Jean-Pierre, who had come up to me as I scrutinized the list. "They've all been pardoned with the exception of twenty," I told him, still looking for my young friend's name. "What did they get, those twenty?" "One to three years in jail. There are three women among them. One of them is Coptic. Isn't that something?" I said proudly. "Is your friend there?" he persisted "Yes," I replied, sighting his name. "He's one of the twenty."

As we left the courtroom Jean-Pierre tried to console me: "Even those twenty will remain free until Sadat endorses their sentences. Or until he pardons them. After all, their only crime was the distribution of pamphlets against the regime in work-ing-class areas." "And for this they get one to three years in jail," I said bitterly. "This is not America, Laila. These are le-nient measures. Under Nasser, they would have gotten life."

Sadat did not endorse the sentences and the students were not jailed. This was 1980 and the president was still trying to con-tain the opposition which had grown since Camp David—not an easy task, for the rais had promised that in 1980 all our problems would be solved. There were still bread shortages though, and an inflation of 30 percent at the beginning of the

247

year. The housing situation continued to be very bleak. It was estimated that an additional 650,000 units per year would not even meet the demand for housing. Corruption was rampant. Tax evasion for the fiscal year was estimated at 500 million Egyptian pounds. "It is the middlemen who are cheating the people," said Sadat in one of his many speeches. Sadat then promised that he would punish the profiteers and that we would embark on a national "battle for prosperity." A difficult task, for in 1980 the gap between the rich and the poor had grown so wide that only 9 percent of the population was estimated to be living above the poverty level.

In spite of all the problems, we were told that Egypt's overall economic standing had improved in 1980. Millions of dollars were coming in from tourism, the revenues of the reopened Suez Canal, and foreign economic assistance, especially from Western Europe and the United States.

The real thrust of the opposition against Sadat was political. One year after the signing of the peace treaty with Egypt, Israel was adding new settlements on the West Bank. The Palestinian autonomy talks were suspended as a result. "We appeal to the Egyptian people to boycott the Israeli presence in Egypt" was the title of a document signed by forty noted intellectuals, two of whom had been Sadat's colleagues in the Free Officers' movement, the military group that had made Egypt a republic when they ousted King Farouk in 1952.

Opposition to the peace treaty with Israel came from other directions as well. And as later events were to demonstrate, the peace wth Israel was one of the main causes of Sadat's downfall. The Moslem fundamentalists, even the more moderate ones, reinforced their objections to the treaty by outlining the continuing resettling of the West Bank by Israelis, the annexation of Jerusalem, and the blowing up of the Iraqi nuclear power plant.

Sadat, however, seemed to feel that this opposition could be contained and appeased. He firmly believed that the real threat came from the communist sympathizers within his regime. He sympathized and identified with the Moslem organizations, of which he had once been a member, and he continued to have dialogues with them. As part of the appeasement campaign, they were allowed to publish weekly magazines, openly voicing their opposition to Camp David. Moreover, at the beginning of 1980, 250 million pounds were authorized by Sadat for the construction of a thousand new mosques. "This in a country where people are short of food and housing," lamented Jean-Pierre in one of the articles that were starting to anger the establishment because Moslem fundamentalism was considered a "nonissue." But Jean-Pierre would not be deterred from writing his pieces. "This year," he warned in another article, "will see the beginning of religious strife in Egypt. There exists now on Egyptian university campuses, militant Islamic student organizations, financed by Egypt's enemies, that is, Qaddafi. These young men and women who are caught at the mercy of a devastating economic situation are searching for an ideal. Islam is their answer. Sadat's peace has only inflamed them against the regime. Today they have become a force, the only force to be reckoned with (with the exception of the army) in Egypt."

Only a few days after this article was written, students at Al-Azhar University, the Islamic university of Cairo, staged a sit-in and signed a petition demanding an end to all relations with Israel, the declaration of a holy war in favor of the Afghan rebels, and the application of sharia or Islamic law to all aspects of Egyptian life, particularly to personal conduct, family life, the status of women, and criminal conduct. The students also insisted upon the banning of Franco Zeffirelli's film *Jesus of Nazareth*, which they considered sacrilegious. In the eyes of the Islamic militants, Jews and Christians should be treated alike, as *dhimmis,* or people of the covenant. They would be tolerated because they paid a *jizia* or taxes, but they would not be allowed to enter the military, thus keeping them in the lower echelons of society, second-class citizens, as they had been in the religio-military hierarchy of the early days of Islam.

Next, ten members of an extremist group which called itself Al-Jihad, or Holy War, were arrested in Alexandria after attempting to bomb two Coptic churches there. Meanwhile, on the campus of Cairo University, extremist Islamic students agitated against the scheduled appearance of a pop group on the grounds that its leader was a Copt and because they considered Western music a "manifestation of the decomposition of society."

The Copts, too, were opposing Sadat. On March 21, the president had called for a plebiscite to make changes in the Egyptian constitution. Among these changes were: an amendment that would make him president for life; one that would make sharia law the basis for legislation; and another that would make Islam the religion of the state. "Islam is being made into a form of nationalism," protested the Coptic patriarch, Shenoudah.

Then, in April, when Sadat went to Washington to discuss the stalemate in the Palestinian autonomy talks, a group of expatriate Copts booed and jeered him from outside the gates of the White House. They also took out advertising space in the *Washington Post* and *The New York Times* condemning Sadat for making peace with the Jews before he had made peace with the Copts of Egypt. Bishop Samuel, who acted as a kind of liaison between the Coptic community and the regime, tried to convince the president that the Copts of Egypt had nothing to do with the disturbances created by the expatriates, but it was no use. Sadat was furious.

To make matters worse, in April, religious strife broke out on the provincial campuses of Assiut and Minieh. Coptic and Moslem student factions had clashed again. This time the incidents were triggered off when a Moslem was caught holding hands with a Coptic girl. In 1979, there had also been outbursts on these campuses when Islamic extremists tried to impose segregation of the sexes in the classrooms and to keep Coptic students from attending classes.

In 1980, just before the outbreak of violence on the campuses, the words "sin shop" were often seen scrawled on shop windows of hairdressers, photography stores, and liquor shops. In addition, there were rampant rumors spread by Moslems of a Coptic conspiracy with the Zionist state against Islam.

In May, Sadat, calling himself a "Moslem president of an Islamic state," gave a speech in which he warned the Copts "not to play with politics." He was referring to the disturbances caused by the expatriates, as well as an alleged plot by Pope Shenoudah to set up a separatist Coptic state with its capital at Assiut. The Coptic community was outraged, and turned against Sadat. "The fundamentalists are being spawned by the regime," a prominent Copt told Jean-Pierre.

Then, in yet another televised speech, Sadat asked the twelve million voters of the country to say yes or no to a referendum which would make sharia or Islamic law the *only* basis for Egyptian law. Ninety percent of the voters said yes. To the Copts, this was the last straw.

The application of sharia was one of the ways in which Sadat sought to appease the fundamentalists, who believe that God's will can only be done if sharia is implemented to regulate the conduct and behavior of devout Moslems. He also created a radio station, the Koran station, to broadcast nothing but readings from the Holy Book all day long. Other programs on radio and television now had to be interrupted for the call to prayer five times a day, and Sadat often showed himself on TV, praying in a mosque. Moreover, the growing fundamentalist movement was permitted to publish a magazine, *Al-Da'wa,* The Call, and to organize large prayer rallies in public places. At one such rally, which was staged right in front of Abdine, the presidential palace, 400,000 extremists were present. They were also allowed to sponsor student elections on the various campuses of the Egyptian University. The Moslem Brotherhood Organization, although never legitimized, was permitted to function from a refurbished office in downtown Cairo, which bore the emblem of its name—"Al Ikhwan al-Muslimun"—a Koran with crossed swords—on its door. This emblem had been introduced by the founder of the organization, Hassan al-Banna, in the twenties.

But Sadat did try to contain the movement in certain ways; in particular by not allowing them to lobby through overt political campaigns. But they still managed to make their voices heard in parliament, where conservative religious members represented them. Gradually, their political power increased, their magazines proliferated, their daily sermons grew louder in the tax-exempt mosques which were mushrooming all over the city, and their youth began to tighten their control over campus life.

Around 1980, the brotherhood aligned itself with extreme factions such as Al-Jihad in its loud opposition to the peace with Israel. If Islam was the state religion, they asked, then why was there an alliance with the United States, peace with the Jews, and fraternization with the Copts? Although the Christians and the Jews were referred to as "Ahl al-Kitab," the People of the Book, in the Koran, they were generally considered infidels because they had rejected Mohammed as the new apostle of God. Their opposition to Israel was based on the grounds that the Zionists had usurped Islamic territory. Jihad, Holy War, would have to be waged until this land was returned. Moreover, they were deeply grieved by the estrangement of Egypt from the Islamic world, because of its peace with Israel.

They also made domestic demands which would have transformed Egypt into an orthodox Islamic state: the abolition of secular and scientific education; of movies, TV, and Western music; and the establishment of religious courts, such as those currently in existence in Iran. Sadat turned a deaf ear to these demands.

The opposition he did take seriously was from the Left, particularly the increasingly vocal criticism of Camp David. In May 1980, Sadat promulgated a law intended to silence the Left. It was labeled the "Qanoun al'Aib," the Law of Shame. Among the crimes to be punished by this law was "the publication of misleading news or information which would inflame public opinion, generate envy or hatred, or threaten national unity and peace." Other crimes included "the undermining of the dignity of the state, the endangering of public property , the squandering of public funds, the abuse of power, influencing the prices of public commodities and the accepting of bribes." Finally, in order to further pacify the fundamentalists, Sadat's law made it punishable by death to "advocate any doctrine which implies the negation of divine teachings or allows youth to go astray by the advocation or repudiation of accepted religious, moral, or national values."

Things began to come to a head in July and dramatized, more effectively than anything before it had, the case against the peace treaty with Israel. The Knesset voted to annex Jerusalem. As a result, Saudi Arabia called for a Holy War, a call that thundered through the Islamic world. Meanwhile, Israel continued to build new settlements on the West Bank—another slap in the face of peace and of course, Sadat. The appeasement of the Islamic fundamentalists was becoming more and more difficult. But Sadat continued to permit their activities, as long as violence did not erupt.

Meanwhile, other forces against him were mobilizing. In September, the Iran-Iraq war broke out. "Fifteen months ago," declared Sadat, "these countries formed a unified rejectionist front against Egypt. Today, Iraqis and Iranians are killing each other. Baghdad has broken with Damascus, and Tripoli and Saudi Arabia have broken off with Qaddafi. Which of them can sit down with the other?" Sadat still entertained hopes of winning some of his Arab allies back. He made friendly noises to Saudi Arabia. Saudi Arabia turned its back on him.

At this point, Sadat turned to the United States, which increased its aid to Egypt and also allowed us to buy the much coveted F-16s. In exchange, the United States was granted air bases at Ras Banas by the Red Sea. "Sadat has allowed Egypt to become a colony of the U.S.A.," cried the fundamentalists and Sadat's leftist opposition both. Angrily, he replied: "Although the U.S. has big bases in Britain we never read in the newspapers that America is occupying Britain. . . . Today we can hold up our heads with England and America, with all the Western democracies, because we are a democracy—only seven thousand years old."

But though we were not a democracy, we *were* seven thousand years old, and it was through faith in our ancient civilization that Sadat was able to strike a deep chord in many Egyptian hearts. In spite of the snowballing opposition to him, most of us were still willing to go along with Sadat. For most Egyptians were not leftist or fundamentalist but nationalist, and Sadat was promising us the liberation of our land, the Sinai, from Israel. The day of its return was drawing close. But would the extremists wait for it?

By the beginning of 1981, however, the opposition to Camp David had hardened. At the end of February, an influential group of intellectuals—Marxists, Nasserists, left-wingers and right-wingers—issued a declaration through a member of parliament, urging Sadat to renounce his peace treaty with Israel because it brought neither "peace nor prosperity" for Egypt. It had merely increased the military budget and led to the installation of foreign bases in Egypt.

Simultaneously, another relatively moderate opposition group, "Hisb al-Amal," the Action party, declared in its paper, *Al-Chaab,* The People, that it would withdraw the support it had previously given Camp David because of the annexation of Jerusalem. "No for Camp David—No for Normalization," read its captions. Meanwhile, the Egyptian Socialist party, the National Progressive Union, publicly condemned the Camp David peace process in its paper, *Al-Ahali,* The Masses. "No to a Separate Peace with Israel" became their slogan.

Opposition to Camp David also manifested itself in the professional syndicates of Cairo. A group of attorneys at the Lawyers Syndicate burned the Israeli flag and hoisted the Palestinian one at Sadat's suggestion of professional exchanges with the Israelis. Normalization was also rejected by the Medical Syndicate. When one of Sadat's doctors visited Jerusalem on a professional visit, he was severely chastised by his syndicate. Sadat gave him a medal. But the message was clear: no normalization. Moreover, there were frightening rumors of a group of army officers who had been arrested for having formed a secret coalition with the Moslem Brotherhood.

Besieged on all sides, Sadat was now like a man on the run. His personal security was intensified. Whenever he appeared in public he was guarded by a special brigade, equipped with armored cars with computerized communications systems. A battalion of security men followed him everywhere: to his home in Giza, his rest house in the barrages, his village at Mit Abou al-Kom, and his holiday villa in Alexandria. When he traveled by helicopter, he was always accompanied by at least two look-alikes, to confuse potential assassins.

His entourage became limited to a few trusted friends, and his wife Jihan.

"Copts and Moslems are killing each other right in the heart of Cairo," everyone was saying one hot day in July 1981. I was rehearsing a production of Brecht's *Mother Courage*, which was to be staged in the open air at the thirteenth-century Citadel of Saladin. When I got home in the evening, I called Jean-Pierre. "What's happening?" I asked. "Exactly what I had foreseen," he said calmly, "sectarian strife." "But who provoked it?" I persisted. "It's in the papers, read the papers," he said in a strange voice. "Jean-Pierre, are you all right?" I asked, "Yes," he said wearily, and added, "À bientôt." Then the phone clicked—twice.

I obtained a copy of *Le Monde* and read Jean-Pierre's account. It had all started in Alexandria a couple of months earlier, in an impoverished area called Omrozo. A Coptic baker and his Moslem assistant had a fight. The assistant was thrown to the floor, struck his head, and died. A riot rose in the quarter and slogans about how Copts were killing Moslems were circulated. More violence and bloodshed occurred. Eventually, the police restored order. Then, right here in Cairo, in a very poor district called al-Zawya al-Hamra, Copts and Moslems began to kill one another in broad daylight. (The Copts had tried to build a church in the area without the necessary permits, and the Moslems had tried to stop it. The Copts attacked and killed some of them.) At first the police did not intervene, but simply encircled the area and watched. Jean-Pierre deduced that the Ministry of the Interior allowed these events to play themselves out in order to take the limelight off the storm around Camp David. By the time they had decided to intervene, a bloodbath had taken place.

"I've been given one week to leave the country," said Jean-Pierre on the phone a week later. I dropped everything and went over to his apartment. His face was almost yellow and he paced about frenetically. "You shouldn't have come; you know I've been put under surveillance," he said sternly. "I don't care," I replied. "Tell me about it; why are you being kicked out?" "Here, read this," he said, thrusting a copy of Cairo's English paper, *The Egyptian Gazette,* at me. The story had made the front page: "Foreign Correspondent Asked to Leave," read the caption. "The State Information Chairman told the press that he had been advising the French correspondent to stick to true and factual information about Egypt and to avoid subjective handling of topics that distorted the country's image abroad."

"I'm going to miss you, Jean-Pierre," I said sadly as I set the paper down. "I'll miss you too, and I'll miss Egypt," he replied. "Part of me wishes you had never written the pieces on Islamic fundamentalism, sectarian strife . . ." "But the fundamentalist problem is very grave, Laila," he said, interrupting me. "The Islamic brotherhoods have consolidated their power with the students and the rural bourgeoisie, and have infiltrated all the principal institutions of the country. All that's left for them to infiltrate is the army," he said. "None of this would have happened if the Israelis had made concessions on the issue of Palestinian autonomy," I said angrily. "You're partly right," he said, "and of course the Israelis haven't made things better by annexing Jerusalem and bombing the Iraqi reactor just three days after Begin and Sadat met at Sharm al-Sheikh. Yes, Israel is making it very difficult for Sadat and for Egypt."

Mother Courage opened to very favorable reviews. After Jean-Pierre's departure, I threw myself even more avidly into my work. The actress playing the lead had walked out and I had to do the part as well. I was thankful for it, because it kept my mind off the tensions around me. I did not fail to notice that the grounds were heavily patrolled, and at night, as the show was ending, jeeps would come to a screeching halt in front of the Citadel

Prison—the oldest political jail in Egypt, built by the British. The prison stood about a hundred feet from where we had set our scaffolding for Brecht's antiwar play.

The show ran until August 30. On August 31, I went over to the citadel to meet with the cast, in order to strike the set. I was stopped at the bottom of the hill by several units of military police. "You can't go up there," they declared. "For Allah's sake, why not? I've been going up there for two months. I am Mother Courage," I said, trying to sound lighthearted. "Mamno'u, doctora," they said firmly: forbidden. Meanwhile, the actors had arrived and had gathered at the bottom of the hill. "What's happening?" I asked them as we stood next to my car. "They've been arresting people," said one of them. "How do you know?" I asked. "Everybody knows when people get arrested. Besides, they're bringing them right up there," said someone pointing to the citadel on the hill. "Up there?" I asked. "To the prison," said another actor. "But I thought it was no longer in use," I said incredulously. "Come on, doctora, what did you think all these jeeps were doing?" "Why didn't they tell us this was happening?" I asked. "Really, doctora," said another of my students, "do you expect them to tell us that they are arresting people and bringing them to this prison, right under our noses?" The others began to laugh nervously. "Well, we closed just in time," I said, pretending to joke as well.

In the ensuing days, people talked of nothing but the arrests, which were also reported by the foreign press and the radio services. There were new rumors and new names, every single day. At night, I locked my apartment, and waited for the dreaded mukhabarat to come. I had heard that they had arrested many dissidents, artists, and writers.

On September 3, I walked into my mother's apartment after another sleepless night. She was poring over a newspaper. She lifted her head. "I didn't think I'd see you for a long time," she said cryptically. "Why not?" I asked. "Haven't you read the papers?" "No, I just woke up. I only got a couple of hours' sleep last night," I answered. She nodded in commiseration and handed me the paper. "They've published the names of the one thousand five hundred dissidents who have been arrested. I was searching for your name among them." Remarkably, my name was not on the list.

Sadat had cracked down on all the leaders of the opposition to his regime and to his peace with Israel. I recognized names of journalists, writers, feminists, priests, sheikhs, politicians, lawyers, editors, and doctors. There were people on that list like the leader of the Wafd, the Nationalist party, a man in his seventies, half the members of the central committee of the Socialist party, all the leading members of the Lawyers Syndicate, members of the Press Syndicate, the Medical Syndicate, prominent judges, labor leaders, and 170 bishops and priests.

On September 5, Sadat reported that Pope Shenoudah had been suspended as spiritual head of the Coptic Church. He was replaced by a committee of five bishops, of which Bishop Samuel was the most prominent.

A few nights later, I walked into my mother's apartment at midnight. I was frightened. They were still making arrests. "I would like to spend the night here," I said. "I don't want to be alone in the apartment if they come knocking in the middle of the night." At this point my brother emerged sleepily from his room. "What's the matter?" he said, rubbing his eyes. "Your sister is scared. She thinks they're going to arrest her," said my mother. "Look, Laila, if you're guilty, why don't you give yourself up? There are many rumors that you are a communist." I stared at my brother in disbelief. He stared back. "I'll get you a Valium," said my mother. "I'm not guilty," I replied when I could get my voice back. "I have done nothing to hurt Egypt."

On September 6, Jean-Pierre wrote an article from Paris in which he said: "In effect, everyone knows that the only opposition which could be dangerous for the regime is that of Islamic fundamentalism whose recently discovered infiltration of the army was perhaps the decisive element that has incited the rais [Sadat] to take on the Moslem Brothers, as before him Farouk and Nasser were obliged to do."

On September 22, it was announced that all the Moslem Brotherhood organizations were banned, their activities prohibited under any circumstances.

On September 23, Sadat gave an interview to an American TV station. He was asked why he had arrested his political opponents, as well as Moslem fundamentalists. "Because of religious strife," he said. "These politicians I have arrested joined the religious elements, and would have exploited my arrest of the fundamentalists."

What Sadat didn't tell the American press was that since the beginning of 1981, word had been circulated among the militant Islamic brotherhoods that Sadat had been condemned to death.

"Sadat has been shot!" shouted my brother as he rushed into my mother's house. Sadat, shot? Impossible! "That's why they stopped the military parade on television." I ran to the TV. Sure enough, they were showing a documentary on Coptic art. I went to the balcony to have a look at the street. Everything seemed normal. I rushed back to the TV. Still the documentary. My brother was now on the phone. "It's only a slight injury to the hand," he was saying loud enough for all of us to hear. I turned the other channel on. Nothing. Too bad I hadn't watched the parade. But I had stopped watching them years ago. Every year since the October war, we had impressive parades on TV. The army was shown off. Nasser loved parades. Sadat loved them even more. He even had special clothes made for them.

An hour passed and no one seemed to know what had happened. I called Enayat, who said she'd heard nothing. Her husband was one of the closest people to Sadat and she had heard nothing? I phoned another friend, a journalist. Yes, he had heard it on the BBC. Sadat had been shot. "But be calm," he urged. I called to cancel my dinner plans though the others had decided to meet anyway. "But Sadat has been shot!" I said. "We are not sure," was the reply. "Only God knows, only God decides." I put the receiver down angrily and went back to the television. Still the documentary. My brother, who had been on the phone the whole time, rushed back into the room with more news. Sadat had been taken to the Maadi hospital. Mubarak had also been shot but no one had been killed. I called up another friend—a businessman with connections. "Don't show any spirit of grief," he said. "And don't repeat the news of the shooting. You may be accused of spreading malicious rumors."

I collapsed in front of the TV, my mother beside me. We stared at the screen like zombies. My brother shouted from the phone: "He's still alive!" But suddenly the screen went blank except for an inscription from the Koran:

Nothing will befall us except what Allah has ordained. He is our Guardian. In Allah let the faithful put their trust.

The meaning of those lines was clear. It was over. Sadat was dead. At about 7:00 P.M. Hosni Mubarak appeared to make the official announcement. His hand was bandaged, his face expressionless.

The Voice of America played Chopin's funeral march and periodically announced in Arabic that Mohammed Anwar al-Sadat had died.

"Al bakia fi hayatek," I told my mother in condolence. She was weeping and saying, "Poor Sadat, poor Sadat." I sank down next to her on the couch and the two of us wept unrestrained tears.

It was October 8, the tenth anniversary of the 1973 war, and the ubur, our victorious crossing of the canal. It was the anniversary of the destruction of the Bar-Lev line, symbol of the Israeli occupation of Egypt. It was also Id-al-Adha, the Feast of the Sacrifice.

In the ensuing days everyone stayed behind locked doors. A power struggle was said to be taking place between the Islamic fundamentalists and the regime. The rumors were that there had been an attempt to take over the state-owned radio station in order to mobilize the masses to rise in the name of Islam. There were rumors that one of the assassins had fled and escaped to Assiut. There were rumors that the fundamentalists had taken over the campus at Assiut and were killing all who stood in their way. If they took Cairo, who would they kill first? The artists, someone said. No, the Copts, said someone else.

There were rumors that a battle was being fought in Assiut between the police and the fundamentalists. A couple of days later, the papers were full of the arrests of the Assiut conspirators. They had all been rounded up and jailed. Their uprising had not succeeded in mobilizing the masses.

But martial law was imposed and the streets immediately filled with army vehicles and bayoneted soldiers. There were policemen at every street corner and everyone stayed home to watch the funeral on television. It was dangerous to be out on the streets. Besides, you needed a special permit to go to the funeral. Security for the funeral, which was attended by kings, prime ministers, foreign ministers, and three former U.S. presidents, was very tight.

The day before Sadat's funeral, another funeral was taking place. It was Bishop Samuel's. He had been asked to sit close to the president and the sheik of Al-Azhar during the parade in a symbolic gesture of unity. Bishop Samuel was one of the twenty-eight people who were killed on October 6 with Sadat.

I watched Sadat's funeral the next day with my mother. But first, there was a hastily prepared documentary on Sadat's visit to Jerusalem: Sadat boarding the plane, Sadat reaching Jerusalem, Sadat waving at the Israelis from the entrance of his jet, Sadat descending the steps slowly, Sadat embracing Begin.

Two days later, my mother, brother, and I drove to the site where Sadat had been buried. It was just across from the reviewing stand where he was assassinated. The burial ground was surrounded by military police and the sand dunes around it were patrolled by soldiers on horseback and on foot. The chair on which the twenty-four-year-old officer, member of Al-Jihad, had stood while he put thirty-four bullets into Sadat's body remained in place.

I
T WAS ANOTHER ONE of those Cairo traffic jams. The road to
the institute was blocked. The cars stood bumper to bumper in
the stifling heat. As I sat in my car, wondering if the traffic
would ever move, I noticed a familiar car ahead. It was Fouad's.
I had not seen him for more than a year. I shouted and he
turned his head in my direction, beckoning me to get out and
join him. "Fouad, how are you?" I said breathlessly as I got into
his car. "I was abroad, teaching," he said, squeezing my hand.
"And whatever brought you back?" I asked sarcastically.
Shrugging, he asked me about myself. "I'm tired, so tired . . .
But aren't we all?" I went on. Since I was already too late for my
appointment, I suggested that we have a cup of coffee.

"There are twelve million people in Cairo," Fouad said as we
walked past the deadlocked traffic. "Yes, I know. I read somewhere that two hundred fifty thousand people live in one square
mile in Cairo, as compared to twenty-five thousand in New
York," I added. He took my arm as we crossed the road to a
Wimpy restaurant. It was quiet inside. I sighed with relief.
Fouad looked about him in disapproval. We sat down and ordered coffee and cold water.

"Fouad, it's so good to see you," I said, looking at him long-
ingly across the table. "I've missed you," he said in a voice filled
with emotion. We smiled at one another. "And by the way, I
heard your production of *Mother Courage* was a great success.
Very shrewd of you to stage it at the citadel." "Yes, wasn't it?

After all, the citadel is the symbol of military occupation in Egypt. Saladin built it with stolen stones from a pyramid in Giza and it became the fortress of all subsequent conquerors, Mohammed Ali, Napoleon, the British." "But I heard rumors that your production was apropos of Camp David," he said. I laughed and answered: "Rumors. I was accused of everything. My motives have never been so thoroughly questioned!" "But it was relevant to the peace?" he persisted. "Inasmuch as it is an antiwar play, yes." He looked at me questioningly. "Brecht attacks the use of religion as justification for war. For instance, the Thirty Years' War in Germany between the Protestants and the Catholics. We also have a thirty years' war—between the Arabs and Israel. And who is paying the price? The people. At last we get a Saladin; Sadat loved to be identified with him-who-makes-peace . . ." "Not before he had liberated Palestine from the Crusaders," interjected Fouad. "Absolutely. But he did sit down and negotiate with his enemies." "And what else?" asked Fouad, obviously amused. "I thought the fun poked at religion was very relevant to the sectarian strife that's been going on. The Copts are accused of being disloyal. Did you know that in the twelfth century the Copts sided with Saladin against the Crusaders?" I asked. "But do you think your audience understood all these nuances?" he asked.

The waiter had brought the water and set it before us. I drank thirstily. "The leftist critics attacked me. They said it was a disguised endorsement of Camp David. One actress, leftist of course, turned down the main role because she said she could not act in anything that was pro peace, so I stepped in." Fouad threw back his head and laughed again. "Well, I didn't think it was very funny," I said. "But you'll roar when you hear this. The Copts were upset by the play. So upset that the censors came in one night and deleted the word 'pope' from Brecht's text. They said I was making fun of the Patriarch! The Copts had complained because it was an anti-Christian play, and a Coptic security man came up to me one day and asked why I was making fun of the Christians." "What did you say?" asked Fouad. "I said it was Brecht, not me! But it was such a hassle."

The waiter brought our coffee but it was American coffee, not the Turkish coffee we had ordered. Fouad protested, but the waiter shrugged and informed us that they only served American coffee at the Wimpy. "You do the most extraordinary things and you don't expect a hassle?" said Fouad, pushing aside his cup impatiently. "What do you mean?" I asked, bewildered. "You stage an antireligious play during Ramadan, the holy month of Islam, you stage it almost defiantly in the densest mosque area of Cairo, and you ridicule religion at the worst times of sectarian strife, and you don't expect a hassle?" he asked incredulously. "Fouad, I'm an artist," I replied in despair. But Fouad continued: "You stage an antimilitary play in a military society par excellence, and you stage it right in the middle of an army barracks—the citadel is a military zone, you know—and you expect the government to bring you flowers?" "You are saying then, Fouad, that I should not function as an artist for fear of being suspected of political subversiveness?" "Not at all," he said, "but everything you do seems Western, Western motivated." "I thought you once said that I was an Egyptian and that that was enough. But it isn't, is it? You know how loyal to Egypt I am. Why then am I being made to feel like a foreigner?"

Fouad looked at me with a hint of admiration in his eyes. "You're a fighter, Laila, and this is not a society which admires aggressive women. But there's still so much for you to do here. Don't give up." "It's just that I am so tired. It's been ten years of fighting. Do you know, during the final performance of *Courage,* I was pulling the wagon round and round in a circle, when I suddenly fell down. I just lay there. I was too tired to get up. Thank God, my young assistant, who kept a motherly eye on me, made me get up and continue with the scene before the audience knew what had happened. But I'll never forget it."

The conversation had come to a halt but it was not resolved. I suddenly felt hungry and asked for a hamburger. Fouad beckoned to the waiter and ordered for us. "Now that Sadat is dead, I think this country is going to close up again. I think it's time I should leave," I said, trying to break the silence. "You should not regret Sadat's death," he said. "But I do, I do. Thanks to him we have the Sinai, we have peace. I don't blame Sadat for everything, like all you other intellectuals." "Egypt was never more corrupt than under his regime. You could make three hundred million dollars in eight years of infitah, when before you had a salary of thirty piasters a day," he said scornfully. "You are referring to Oman, a drug peddler. They make money everywhere," I said. "There can be no peace without the resolution of the Palestinian question," he declared. "Of course, but Egypt *does* have peace. And that's important. Egypt is out of this mess," I replied. "Alienated from its Arab neighbors, deprived of its position of leadership, ignored by the Islamic world." "I'm so tired of hearing this," I said. "We have so many internal problems we need to resolve: the population explosion, the rise of fundamentalism," I said. "You think you are really threatened by this?" he asked. "You're not?" "As I see it, these young militants are using Islam as an escape." "From what?" I asked. "From the dead end they meet in Egypt. There are no economic opportunities for them and no political ideologies to engage them. Islam fills the vacuum. It gives them an ideology and a life-style, a life-style which to them is authentic and in keeping with Islam. Sadat's infitah and the gadgets of the consumer society have turned them even more against the West than their ideology dictates."

I was silent for a minute and then said, "Are you becoming anti-Western as well?" "I am not exactly a fundamentalist, Laila, but Sadat's policies have generated this anti-Western feeling. In the name of development, we are being used as dump heaps for the industrial and agricultural waste of the Western world. We have become the victims of their multinational corporations." "How?" I asked. "They force us to buy not what we need but what they need to sell, the way Vasco da Gama and Captain Cook sold the savages beads and baubles. Only today the trinkets we are being sold are deadly weapons." "But I thought we needed weapons," I said. "What for? To fight Libya? Do you know that Egypt has bought six hundred million dollars' worth of weapons from the West since 1975?" I shook my head. "You don't realize that the weapons industry has become the fastest-growing industry in the Western world and the Soviet Union. The nuclear war will start here because we are their testing ground."

"Ah, the hamburger, at last," I said. "And this is supposed to be a fast-food place," I added as the waiter placed our plates before us. "Even that hamburger is a symbol of the consumer society Sadat has imposed," said Fouad sarcastically. "Fouad, please, don't ruin my meal for me," I said. "To go back to what we were saying—I agree with you on the nuclear war business, but I want to say that the Arab-Israeli conflict is the way the superpowers are perpetuating their control here. But what if there were no Arab-Israeli conflict and we all made peace with the Israelis?" "The superpowers would create a conflict," he said with an edge in his voice. "But enough of politics, tell me about yourself," he added, reaching out for my hand.

I put my sandwich down, and searched for words. "There is no one in my life. Nobody." "Regrets?" he asked. "Of course not. I have no regrets about my life. I have become a person, whereas before I was a lump of flesh. I'm free. I can come and go as I wish. I can choose. Can you understand the value of all this?" He nodded. "But freedom often implies loneliness," he said. "Yes. I am lonely. Lonely for an understanding and loving human being. I doubt I will ever find him. What saddens me, though, is not that, but that it is becoming difficult for me to work here." "Why?" "I don't know. I must have committed some crime because they will not give me back the wekala and the wekala *is* my professional life here. If they had torn out my nails one by one, it would not have hurt more. Anyway, I don't know what the future holds. Sometimes when I think about it, I am filled with terror." "Laila . . ." he said compassionately. "Enough of Laila, tell me about yourself," I said.

He beckoned to the waiter for the check and then said, "I'm married now. She's very different from you," he added, lowering his eyes, "but I couldn't face the idea of growing old alone." What seemed like hours went by. "Shall we go?" he asked, getting up. The street noises and the carbon monoxide from the cars enveloped us again. The traffic was moving a little better now. We braced ourselves in anticipation of the exhausting day ahead. Fouad reached his car and started his engine. "You must promise to take care of yourself," he said. "I'll be all right, it's Egypt I'm worried about."

"Egypt will survive, even our joie de vivre has survived worse times. As Tewfik al-Hakim says, can you really believe that the thousands of years that have made up Egypt's past have vanished like a dream?"

My land, my land,
To you I give my love and heart.
Egypt, mother of the universe,
You are my goal, my hope.

—*Patriotic song*

AT THE INSTITUTE the academic year was coming to an end and I had no theater, or plans for a summer production. I went around to see my old friends at the ministry. There were many new faces after the assassination of Sadat. An English teacher I used to know when I was teaching at Cairo University had been appointed undersecretary of the ministry. I decided to ask him for the wekala. "Laila, this year we are celebrating the thousandth anniversary of Al-Azhar, and we have decided to stage a play for that occasion," he said very politely. "You mean a religious play?" I said. "A historical play." "I'd be happy to stage a historical play for that occasion," I volunteered. He coughed uneasily and said, "The esteemed director Said Adham is back in town and has asked for the use of the wekala. We have decided to give it to him." "But he's a friend, he'll find somewhere else for his plays," I answered. "He has already been selected to do the Azhar commemoration play at Wekalat al-Ghouri," came the reply. Seeing my disappointment, he said, "Maybe you would like to do something in another theater?" "Yes, why not?" I replied. "I'll be in touch with you," he said.

But he never called and I was never offered another theater. "The Americans and the West are no longer fashionable," said a journalist friend. "Mubarak is interested in mending his fences with the Arab and Islamic world. Besides, all your contacts in the ministry have been replaced." I nodded. Even Enayat's husband had resigned. "I don't think the ministry is going to back you these days," he added.

I would find work in spite of the ministry, I told myself, as I paced up and down in my apartment. They couldn't stop me from making another documentary. Maybe that's exactly what I should do. I had always wanted to make a film on village women as a sequel to my first film. But permits to film in villages were very hard to obtain. And what village should I use for my location? Then it occurred to me—Om Abdou's village. I was sure to be welcomed there.

In the kitchen, where my mother was warming my brother's meal, I asked her if she thought the peasants in Om Abdou's village would let me film them. Almost dropping the pan, she said, "Now look, Laila, I don't want any trouble in the village. The peasants are perfectly content the way they are. Don't go around making trouble there. There's nothing you can do to change things. They've lived this way for thousands of years and they're perfectly happy. Believe me. Much happier than you and me." "All right, calm down," I said. "I'm just going to interview some village women. I promise you I won't make any trouble." My mother glared at me distrustfully and returned to her cooking.

Thoughts of Om Abdou flickered through my mind as I headed south along the acacia-dotted corniche. What would she think of me if I abandoned Egypt and left for the United States? She would disapprove, of course. She had been so attached to the land, so rooted to it. To me, she was the land. Why was I going on this pilgrimage? To seek comfort? To reestablish my roots before it was too late?

With such thoughts swirling around in my mind, I made my way over the bumpy, rural road. I had only been driving for an hour, but Cairo seemed very remote. A solitary old woman emerged from nowhere. She carried a mountain of sunbaked fertilizer cakes on her head. Yet she walked swiftly and lightly with her burden. I drove on past vast stretches of green until I reached a small town. Children in rags were playing in the road. A few listless dogs sniffed at the refuse in the street. Again stretches of green satin fields, interspersed with tall, swaying palm trees, and mud huts. I turned onto a massive steel and concrete bridge which spanned the widening river. Soldiers guarding the bridge at both ends, their bayonets in readiness, waved to me as I drove past. I waved back and smiled.

As soon as I got off the bridge, I was greeted with an explosion of green: thick clusters of palms with mellow, red dates erupting from golden branches. A fellah walked serenely by, pulling his water buffalo on a rope. As the palm forest came to an abrupt end I found myself driving along a much narrower road, past more lush, green fields. A little girl of about ten, riding a donkey, emerged from the fields and looked absently in my direction. Farther on, women were busily filling water jugs from the irrigation canals in the fields. Still farther, women sat by the roadside selling eggs and produce. Om Abdou would not have looked very different from these women.

"You'll recognize your grandmother's village by the fence around her house," my mother had told me as I set out. I had been driving for a long time now and began to watch for the fence.

I continued to drive along the green fields, past tiny *kafrs* or clusters of mud huts linked to the outside world by primitive bridges spanning the irrigation canals. Then I saw it—a long gray fence in the midst of the fields. I pulled off the road, the car heaving and bumping on the dusty tracks.

The village was made up of a row of mud-baked hovels. A dirt path ran parallel to these huts which were surrounded on all sides by green fields. There were no electric or telephone cables in sight, even though electricity was introduced to most Egyptian villages after the revolution. A tiny mosque with whitewashed walls stood beyond the huts. As I walked past the peasants' homes, I peered into them: dark, cavelike rooms where crying babies lay on the ground side by side with cows, geese, and chickens. This was the real Egypt. Cairo now seemed like an illusion. As I cut across the fields toward the house with the fence, scores of children, shouting and whistling at the sight of a stranger, joined me. We reached a wrought-iron gate which screeched as it was opened by an old peasant. I told him who I was. He gave me a toothless grin. He used to work for Om Abdou and now he was working for her son, my mother's brother, who owned the land surrounding the house.

We walked through a citrus fruit garden, overgrown with weeds. At the end of the path stood a two-story Mediterranean house with peeling, gray walls. I was almost afraid of getting closer to it, but the peasant beckoned me on. He unlocked the door on the ground level and ushered me inside. Tentatively, I followed him into a dark, empty room which smelled of death. The other rooms were also bare, their walls peeling, the air dank, chilling. I pushed open a door. A rust-scarred bathtub grimaced at me. I rushed out into the warmth of the garden, the villager following me with two broken straw chairs.

I asked the man to let the children into the garden. They rushed in shouting triumphantly, as if they had been let out of prison. A boy of about twelve, his torn striped-calico galabiya barely concealing his emaciated flesh, asked if he could hold my camera. He told me that he was not allowed to go to school be- cause he had to work in the fields. I told him that I would hire him as my assistant director. He smiled happily through broken teeth.

"Your grandmother cared for those poorer than herself. She used to sew clothes for the villagers and their children and she had more respect for the poorest peasant woman who toiled in the fields than for any of the elegant ladies in Cairo," my mother had said.

A gentle wind rustled through the trees and a dog barked. The sounds of the village calmed me. My grandmother seemed closer than ever before.

When I returned to the village again a week later, a young girl of about fourteen approached me. "My name is Enaba. I am Hassan's daughter," she said, offering her hand. She had large, round honey-colored eyes and her hair was concealed beneath a tightly knotted green scarf. Her printed galabiya concealed a slender figure. "My mother, Soraya, would like you to come and visit us," she said.

We made our way down a narrow path that ran parallel to the clustered mud-hovels until we reached a somewhat larger house partially occupied by a grocery store where soap, oil, and sacks of sugar and rice were displayed on unpainted shelves. We walked through the entrance next to the store. Enaba ushered me up a stone stairway into a small room with a window overlooking the fields. A mastaba encircled the room and an old-fashioned radio sat on a small wooden table. Enaba pointed to an adjoining room. "That's the family bedroom," she said.

As we sat down, Soraya entered carrying a tray of tiny glasses. She was in her thirties with beautiful dark eyes and even features. She wore black from head to foot and her tarha covered her hair completely, but her body was vibrant and feminine. As we sipped our tea, she told me how her husband had been killed the year before in a motorcycle accident. They had been married since she was fifteen and she had borne him six children. The youngest was still at her breast. Now her husband's brothers were trying to take the store away from her in order to run it themselves. "But why are they trying to do this?" I asked. "They say a widow isn't fit to run a business," she replied. The old story, I thought wearily.

Enaba broke into my thoughts. "Try to convince my mother to let us listen to the radio," she said. "Why doesn't she like it?" I asked. "Because tradition says we have to mourn our father for a whole year."

In fact, Soraya allowed Enaba's brothers to go anywhere they wished, but Enaba was restricted to school, home, and the fields. The young girl was not even allowed to go to the local coffeehouse to watch the battery-operated TV. But the fact that she was studying for a high-school diploma was a sign of change. Her father had supported the idea of her education, but, as Enaba confided, she feared that she might not be allowed to go on to the university now that her father's support was no longer there. I asked Enaba if she would mind being filmed. She said no.

In the following months, I returned to the village many times. On one of these visits, I found Soraya in particularly low spirits. "Village life is such a heartache," she said, her face revealing utter despair. "There is never any rest. A woman wakes up in the morning, milks the cows, returns home to bake for the family and to wash the clothes and sweep the floors and cook the meals until she is ready to drop off her feet. In the evening, she gets her brood together, scrubs them, sees to this one or that one—just trying to keep them quiet is a chore. It's all a heartache."

Enaba introduced me to Aziza, a peasant woman in her thirties. She was a slender woman with auburn hair and light, smiling eyes. Whenever she saw my car in the distance she would welcome me. She had three children and was pregnant with a fourth. Her home consisted of a ground-floor room for the chickens and other animals, and an upper room that the whole family shared. The only space she had for herself was a hole in the wall where she did her baking.

To talk alone with Aziza, I would have to follow her as she went about her chores. One day I went out to the fields with her as she took her cow to graze. We took a footpath cut through the water-drenched rice fields. "Aziza," I said as we walked along, "what would you like your children to be like if you had a choice?" She did not hesitate. "I would like them to be educated. Like the schoolteacher in the nearby village." "What is she like?" I asked. "She's young, she's lovely, she teaches, she has a university education, and she has two children. What better life for a woman?" she declared with sparkling eyes.

We had reached an open expanse. She released the cow she had been trailing behind her. We watched as the cow began to nibble at the grass. "You know there is no difference between me and the cow," she said. "The cow doesn't know how to read. Neither do I. The cow is not allowed to leave the village and neither am I. I want more for my daughters," she said.

A soft breeze rustled in the grass and only the sound of the cow munching its grass interrupted the stillness. I looked at the woman next to me, feeling very close to her. I wanted to hug her and say, "Aziza, you are not like a cow. You feel anger. You feel rebellious. And that is the beginning of change."

Gradually, I was being accepted in the village. As soon as I arrived, I would go to the homes of the village women and watch them work or listen to them chat. At times, I was allowed to film, but the reality I observed often defied the filmmaking process, and I would all too often find myself setting down the camera in frustration. How could I capture the tragic helplessness, the incredible drudgery, the misery, the disease, the superstitions, ignorance, and fatalism that dictated these peasants' lives? I was also ridden with guilt, for I belonged on my mother's side to a bourgeois, landed family, which must also be held responsible for their exploitation. My brother, like thousands of Cairene doctors, had turned his back on the compulsory heath-care service which Nasser had launched. Even Sadat had failed to motivate educated Egyptians to help in the rural areas. The revolution had not reached the countryside. And nobody seemed to care. Abdel Halim was right: the peasants had been exploited for thousands of years by feudal landlords and foreign occupiers who grew rich off their backs. And now, here I was, with a jolting Super-8 camera, trying to capture it all. I felt obscene.

So I would set the camera down and talk with them. Maybe in this way I could be of some help. I asked them about childbirth. They told me that they had their babies in the fields—all alone. They were lucky if a midwife came to help. We talked about contraception. Some of them did not know what it was. "Is the man or the woman supposed to take these pills?" One woman confided that if she didn't have many children her husband would take another wife. "I have eleven children," she boasted, "and I would have another eleven if I could." "Why don't you?" I asked, trying to conceal my smile. "Because my husband can't jump on me anymore," she declared, prompting a great outburst of laughter. "Are you excised?" I asked in the midst of this merriment. "Yes, of course," she said. "Are you?" asked another woman. "No," I replied. "That's why you can't have any children," she asserted. "What has excision got to do with children?" I asked. "If you don't cut the clitoris, it will grow and obstruct the woman's . . ." Laughter. ". . . and the man won't be able to enter." Laughter.

As I sat among the women, I remembered that this belief was shared by the ancient Egyptians, who also practiced excision. Ancient practices are always accompanied by ancient beliefs: in this case, that a woman who retains her clitoris will be like a man, rebellious and wild.

The subject of excision was taboo in the city, but was spoken of with utter naturalness by the village women. They all tried to tell me about it at once, giggling and laughing all the while. "She lops it off with a razor," said Aziza. "Who does?" I asked. "The midwife. Usually during the feast after Ramadan, and she does it to all the little girls," she said. "The only time I ever got to eat a whole chicken, all by myself, was at my excision," said Badriya, a friend of Aziza's. "Is it painful?" I asked. "Of course, it hurts and burns terribly," she said. "Would you let me see an excision?" I asked. Their faces turned serious. I was curious to see this ritual which Western feminists had made such a fuss about. I wanted to know if it was as bad as they claimed it to be.

On my next visit, Badriya told me she could arrange it. I was pleased that the women would allow me this trust, but at the same time the prospect of witnessing this mutilating ceremony filled me with dread. I knew, though, that I must bear witness to this reality—that only by seeing it could I really understand the condition of women in my country.

A few days later, Badriya instructed me to come to the village at dawn the following morning. I arrived at the appointed time, but found no one there. I went to Badriya's house. "Aren't we going to meet the midwife?" I asked. "Some other time," she replied nervously.

Next, I went to see Soraya. We talked about the operation. She recalled that when it happened to Enaba she couldn't take the screaming and crying. Did she know that Nasser had banned the operation in the fifties? No, she hadn't heard it. This didn't surprise me, though, because Nasser's decree existed only on paper. The authorities had never enforced it.

The following day I spoke to Badriya again. She wasn't as edgy this time. "What happens if you don't excise your girls?" I asked. "They won't find a man to marry them," she replied. "They will say she's impure, *negsa,* unclean." I was silent. I knew I couldn't ask her about sexual pleasure. That certainly was a taboo subject. And even if she did speak about it, I was sure she would be careful to protect her husband's honor. "What if the government banned it, said it was a bad practice?" I asked her. "But these are our traditions," she said.

"It can only be stopped if they say it on the radio," Enaba told me later. "The women listen to their radios all the time. And they believe everything that is said there." Asma was right. The media could play a role in changing women's lives. But they didn't care to. And Asma was dead. "Will you help me see an excision?" I asked Enaba. "Yes, I will. The other women are afraid. But I know the house of the midwife in the neighboring village. I'll take you there tomorrow," she said.

Enaba was waiting at dawn the next day. We drove to the neighboring village and stopped before a mud hut. The hut had a single, dusty room, with a bed on one side, the floors covered with a discolored cotton rug. We were greeted by the midwife. She had a tattooed forehead and a few gold teeth. She was obviously a gypsy, an outsider, and this was the only way she could earn her living.

We sat on the ground while she prepared tea. Sharing the room with her was her sister, her husband, and three children. After a little polite conversation, I asked her about the operation. "There's nothing to it," she replied, taking a piece of paper to demonstrate—she sliced an inch off with a razor. "How old must the girl be?" I asked. "Old enough so that I can hold the clitoris with two fingers. Then I rub it to make it swell and I lop it off," she answered nonchalantly. Enaba told her I was there to see an operation. She said no: "Impossible." I offered her money. She accepted. An appointment was set. A week later, at dawn.

In a week's time, I stood before the midwife's hut again. She asked me to wait for a few minutes while she got her bag. I looked at the water canal, the incredibly green fields, and the cluster of date palms rising above them. The sky was red with the sunrise and a few peasants were already making their way to the fields; they appeared as silhouettes against the vibrant sky. It was very still. Only the songs of the birds could be heard. An eternal landscape. Egypt. Egypt. For a few blessed moments, I felt at one with my country and the earth of my ancestors.

The midwife interrupted my reverie. She wore a black tarha and held a small cloth bag in her hand. Walking in front of me she seemed like a black stain against the red sky. At the edge of the village, we reached a small hut isolated from the others. Three women waited for us inside. No words were exchanged. They spoke, like conspirators, with their eyes. The midwife sat down on the ground. I sat down next to her. "Mabrouk," I murmured to the other women, congratulations; the ritual I was about to witness was considered a happy event, an initiation to womanhood.

The midwife asked for a cloth. A rag was handed to her and she proceeded to shred it skillfully. Meanwhile we all sat in anxious silence. Suddenly there was a cry from one of the children outside: "The midwife is here." Things began to happen fast. A screaming girl was brought in and forced down onto the moist earth by the other women. A smell of cow dung and chicken feed rose from the soil. "Let me go, let me go!" screamed the girl. One of the women, holding the girl's arms over her head, spread her thighs apart by placing her own between them. The girl struggled like an animal who had been

277

trapped. She was completely powerless. "Let me go, rabina ye khallikum, let me go," she kept repeating. Meanwhile the midwife had placed the rag bandages underneath the girl's buttocks. Outside the cows mooed. Implacable nature. Implacable way of life. The midwife began to rub the tiny clitoris. The girl howled in terror. The razor came down, ready for the ritual slicing away of the female core. Blood gushed forth as a piece of flesh was discarded in the dirt. I stifled a scream and dropped my camera, shattered by the pain I was witnessing. The midwife again delved between the thighs for flesh, the razor slicing gently and slowly at the nerves. The little girl screamed as if the screams could drown out the agony. Seven thousand years passed with each slash of the razor. The midwife was now pouring white alcohol onto the wound. She then thrust her blood-stained palm in my face. "Look, she's as clean as the palm of my hand now," she said.

I wished with all my heart that I could stop the girl's screams and all those like it. I wished I had brought along a painkiller. But what can kill eternal pain?

The wooden door screeched as it was opened to let in the breeze. But the stale smell inside the hut was overpowering. Outside the sun was shining, dispelling the morning mist.

When I reached Cairo, I went immediately to see my mother. She was seated on a couch, sewing. She wore black, like all the mothers in Egypt who mourn husbands and children. Did my grandmother suffer this pain? I wanted to ask. But I knew the answer. In those days, as well as in my mother's, women, regardless of their religion, went through this ritual.

I sat down next to her on the couch. My mother, who embodies all the traditions of our society, did not smile at me. She still does not understand my rebellion and she never will. In her presence, I am always confronted with my society's disapproval. Yet at that moment I had an overwhelming sense of gratitude and love for her. At least, she spared me this butchery—this primordial pain which millions of girls in Egypt, in the world, must endure.

Weeks and months later, I still labored on my film: bits and pieces of incoherent, disconnected shots, from which I tried to make some sense. But how could I make sense of the brutality and fragmentation of the lives of my village women? I spent hours before the Movieola, trying to edit with fingers which had grown numb from cutting and recutting. My frustration grew with each passing day. But I persisted. Finally, I managed to complete it. For forty minutes, images of Aziza, Enaba, and Soraya flashed across the screen. The excision was also there. The little girl's face screaming with agony would haunt me for a very long time to come.

I approached the Ministry of Health, which was in charge of dealing with the problem of excision. I was met by a senior official who had known my father. He received me cordially. Yes, the ministry was trying to do something about it. Yes, it was widespread. He would be happy to see the film, he said. He even promised to arrange a screening. For weeks, I waited for him to call. But he never did.

Then I went to see a woman who had a program on TV. We cannot show such material on TV, she informed me. Even the word *tahara*, excision, is taboo.

Shortly afterward I left for England, where I was told a British TV station would be interested in obtaining the film. They grabbed it eagerly and even created a program around it. When it was shown, it created a stir in London. But for Egyptian women it did nothing.

Back in Cairo, I went to see some contacts at the UN regional office. We cannot do anything about female excision, they told me; it will look as if we are interfering in the internal affairs of Egypt. "But it's a human rights issue," I argued. "The international community has to be involved; after all, seventy-five million girls in more than twenty countries are subjected to this." The smartly dressed woman looked at me pityingly. "I'm sorry," she said. "Besides, the film is in rough shape." I looked back at her and said, "The intention was not to make a Cecil B. De

279

Mille production, but simply to record a reality." As she ushered me to the door, I noticed that she heaved a sigh of relief.

I tried to get money from the Agency for International Development in Cario in order to remake the film. They turned me down by informing me that AID gave money only to government institutions, not to individuals. "But the government will never allow me to make such a film. It's a taboo subject," I protested. But they shrugged their shoulders in indifference.

The academic year at the institute has come to an end. I have requested a leave of absence. Everything in my apartment is covered with white sheets. Only my typewriter is visible. I return to it. I am not disheartened as I finish these pages. One cannot lose heart in the middle of the fight. I am tired, but I am filled with hope that somehow these pages will bring Western women closer to their sisters in the Middle East and the Third World. I also hope that they will help Arab women understand the importance of fighting and continuing to fight for their rights. Egyptian women have achieved so much in the past fifty years, and if social change and revolution are to happen, and it must, it will be at the hands of women. Returning to the veil will not bring about the revolution we so badly need. We cannot face our enemies by hiding from them.

There is no hope for Egypt unless the role of women is radicalized. The population problem threatens to devour our country. A new baby is born every twelve seconds, and in 1984 we had a budget deficit of millions of dollars. By the year 2000, there will be one hundred million people in Egypt—living within the same boundaries and resources of the past thirty years. Even though the sheikh of Al-Azhar declared in 1983 that Allah will provide—and that the population of Egypt can easily grow to a hundred thousand million—the infrastructure, even with Allah's help, cannot survive this dizzying baby boom.

There is so much women in Egypt can do, as, for instance, the formation of networks of thousands of small cells capable of mobilizing urban poor and peasant women. It would require great energy and purpose on the part of women—especially from urban women who would work in the rural countryside—and it can be done only within a secular framework. Islam, like Christianity, urges men to proliferate and multiply.

Maybe Third World women should not turn down the help they may get from Western women. Maybe we can help one another by holding hands across the barriers of men's ideologies, religions, and political systems in order to find solutions to our common struggles. The Equal Rights Amendment has not yet been ratified, and Jihan Sadat's law exists only on paper, but the difference between these amendments is a difference in degree, not in kind. In both our worlds, men have little concern for the rights of women. In Egypt, power was transferred from the British to the nationalist, from left wing to right wing, from secular to religious, without concerning itself with the human condition of women. And even in America, women are still the poorest of the poor, and victimized by rape, violence, and pornography. Among the blacks, Hispanics, and other oppressed women in the United States as in Egypt, there are many Sorayas, for whom life is nothing but a heartache.

We share so much pain as women that we must no longer disregard one another. Surely we have at least one crucial goal in common: to liberate ourselves from the injustices and indignities we are forced to endure.

Therefore, I will continue.

I know I would not be here to continue without the inspiration of my grandmother, Om Obdou, without the memory of the love and support of my sister, Asma, without the faith my father placed in me, and without the example and friendship of all the women I have met along the way: Cessa, the feminist pioneer; Ingy, the painter who fought for her beliefs; Mufida, the lawyer who battled every day in Family Law courts; Jihan Sadat, who changed the Family Law; Enayat, who stood by me and gave me back my theater; the Iranian feminists, those unsung heroines of a women's movement aborted by Khomeini; Simone de Beauvoir, who interceded on my behalf in a moment of crisis; Aziza, Enaba, Soraya, Badriya, and all the village women who taught me endurance by their example; and all those named and unnamed women who struggle with me. Like Gloria, they showed me how the gap between worlds and women can be bridged by a simple concept: Sisterhood.

The doorbell rings. It is the cabbie who will drive me to the airport for my plane to New York. There are still a few more seconds to finish these lines. I know I have not yet come to the end of a long corridor; there is still so much to struggle for. I am seized with panic at that thought. But I am not alone. Together with other women, I have imagined freedom—the freedom to be a human being, the freedom to work, the freedom to choose.

And now freedom beckons again, like an enchanting rainbow.